HOUSE of NAILS

A Memoir of Life on the Edge

LENNY DYKSTRA

WILLIAM MORROW
An Imprint of HarperCollinsPublishers

HOUSE OF NAILS. Copyright © 2016 by The Third Chapter, LLC. All rights reserved.
Printed in the United States of America. No part of this book may be used or
reproduced in any manner whatsoever without written permission except in the case
of brief quotations embodied in critical articles and reviews. For information address
HarperCollins Publishers, 195 Broadway, New York, NY 10007.

HarperCollins books may be purchased for educational, business, or sales
promotional use. For information please e-mail the Special Markets Department at
SPsales@harpercollins.com.

A hardcover edition of this book was published in 2016 by William Morrow, an
imprint of HarperCollins Publishers.

FIRST WILLIAM MORROW PAPERBACK EDITION PUBLISHED 2017.

Library of Congress Cataloging-in-Publication Data has been applied for.

ISBN 978-0-06-240737-5

17 18 19 20 21   LSC   10 9 8 7 6 5 4 3 2 1

For Dorothy Van Kalsbeek, you define the words *loyalty* and *trust* and you mean more to me than all the stars in the sky that you love so much . . .

TO AYN AND SAMUEL W. GAILEY,

Thank you for sharing your passion for the power of
words and helping me find the true heart of my story.
Your talent, inspiration, and dedication are appreciated.

TO DR. JIM BERMAN,

When we first met, you were Dr. Berman. Quickly,
you became Jim. Soon thereafter, you became a trusted
friend. Then you became much more. You represent
everything that is right in the world (and you know a
hell of a lot about baseball). Without you, my true voice
would not be heard in this book.

CONTENTS

HOUSE of NAILS

The professional sporting landscape has forever been littered with the carcasses of punctured heroes. Yet . . . no jock in modern lore has traveled a rise-and-fall path quite as jarring—and oddly riveting—as Lenny Dykstra.

—JEFF PEARLMAN, *MAXIM*

PROLOGUE

Growing up, my biggest fear was being average. I wanted to be rich; I wanted to be a millionaire. I get what I want, one way or another. So I became a millionaire—many times over, I might add.

How? *Hard fucking work!*

I knew at an early age I was different from the other kids. I knew I was going to play in the major leagues. In fact, I never doubted it.

As a kid, I loved playing baseball, but I loved winning more. I went to school for one reason: *because I had to in order to play baseball*. I lived and breathed baseball. In high school, I never went to a dance, I never went to a party, I never even had a beer.

I had one friend growing up. *Why?* Because I needed somebody to play catch with. Period.

I made a decision my first year of high school to dedicate my life to baseball because I knew it was my one-way ticket out of the middle.

The simple truth is that I was born in the middle. I had middle-class parents. We lived in a middle-class neighborhood. I had a brother ahead of me and another behind me. I *hated* being in the middle.

I still hate the middle.

Losing was not an option for me then and still isn't today. When I made it to the big show, I loved pissing off the opposing team. Do you think it was a coincidence I was voted the most hated player in the league by opposing teams five years in a row? They hated me because I made their job hard. On the other hand, my teammates loved me. They wanted me in their foxhole.

To be a star you have to have the ability to not give a fuck what others—especially your opponents—think about you. You have to be willing to take risks. You need brass balls, and you cannot be afraid to put it all on the line.

Unfortunately for me, that attitude in life became a double-edged sword. It gave me a huge advantage on the field, but it was a serious liability *off* the field. Going all in can be a great quality if you use it the right way, in the appropriate situation, and, most important, if you know how to control it.

This mentality took me from flying around the world in my own private jet to ending up in prison.

I had it all—fame, fortune, family—and yet I risked it all and lost it all. *Why?* What really led me to lose everything?

What was it that drove me to succeed and kept me wanting more and more, at the expense of everything of true value in my life?

Leading a life of no regrets doesn't mean living without making mistakes. I have made plenty of mistakes, and for the first time I will share them with you, the reader, and let you up close to my world, where no one has been before.

I have been an outspoken, controversial figure wherever I have gone. My highs have been very high and my lows have been very low. I will take ownership of my shortcomings and bad decisions, but I'll also be frank about the corruption by others that led to my imprisonment. The fact is, there are books, articles, and writers out there who have made me look like a hero or a criminal, but *none of them* know what really happened.

The Bottom Line:

- If you want my sports stats, you can look them up.
- If you want to read bullshit about me, you can google it.
- But if you want the truth, the real truth, then come to the source.

I am Lenny Dykstra, and this is my story.

Our greatest glory is not in never falling, but in rising every time we fall.

—NELSON MANDELA

1

FREEDOM

June 21, 2013, Federal Correctional Institution, Victorville, California

Rise and shine, Dykstra. Get the fuck up."

It's three-thirty in the morning, and I'm lying on my cot asleep—or at least what passes for sleep in prison—when two hulking uniformed corrections officers the size of NFL linemen, and just as charming, come crashing into my cell, all attitude and nightsticks. Evidently, this pair skipped courtesy class during their training because they're shouting my name (Who else would be in here? I'm in solitary confinement) and banging their batons against the metal bars in the door of my cage.

"You're leaving," the uglier of the two yelled.

I know. Did they think I'd actually forget the day I'm finally getting sprung from Shawshank?

"I'm going to be picked up at ten A.M.," I mumbled.

"No," he said. "There's been a change. You're leaving now. Grab your shit."

I was groggy, but I got up and dressed quickly. Even with only a few hours left in custody, I knew better than to mess with these dudes. They don't need much of a reason to make things painfully tough for you.

I didn't have much shit to grab—a couple of books and some personal items. I was going to take more, but I looked around and realized I didn't want to remember anything from this joint. No personal mementos or souvenirs from the prison gift shop for me.

"What's going on?" I kept asking them.

They wouldn't tell me. Withholding this information gave them power over me. And that's what these boys loved. Power.

"Don't worry about it. Let's go, man. We have to get these papers signed. And your ride will be here."

"My ride?" I said, still confused about why I was being driven somewhere away from the prison on the day I was supposed to get released from this hellhole. "What do you mean?"

"We'll tell you when we get there."

In exchange for filling out my release paperwork correctly, I was presented with some parting gifts: a prepaid debit card with five dollars on it and a ticket on a Greyhound bus back home to Los Angeles.

Outside the prison gates, a no-nonsense-looking Federal Marshal motioned for me to get in his car. This had gone far enough. Keeping my mouth shut is not the way I'm wired.

"What the fuck, man?" I shouted. "I already have someone picking me up. It's all organized. It's four in the fucking morning. What the hell is going on?"

The Federal Marshal shrugged. He has one job: to drive released convicts from the prison to the local bus station and make sure said prisoners actually get on the bus.

I was going off on this poor guy as he drove, screaming at him in the middle of the night over riding a damn Greyhound bus down to LA, when he finally pulled over and turned to me.

"You want to know something?" he asked. "I've been doing this for over twenty years, and this is a first. I've never heard someone bitch and complain so much about getting out of prison. Do you understand? You are free! You're out! You're now a free man!"

That's when it hit me.

Holy shit! I thought to myself. *He's right. I am out. It's over. I've finally been released. No handcuffs, no shackles. Freedom!*

"You're right, man. I am a free man," I replied, and we both started laughing—the first time I could remember laughing since this living nightmare started four years earlier when I was arrested. Somehow I had lived through it all, and it was finally over.

The feeling I had upon realizing I was free is hard to describe. It was surreal. Mainly because I knew I wasn't a criminal and never once considered myself one, even when locked up.

Don't get me wrong, I was definitely relieved. I mean, who wouldn't be happy to be free after spending the past two years of his life in a fucking cage? I was locked up twenty-four hours a day, every day, in a prison cell six by eight feet in size with steel walls and one solid door that locked from the outside. My cell was equipped with a steel bed that held what passed for a mattress (in actuality it was more like a gymnasium floor mat). I had a one-piece sink/toilet constructed of what appeared to be welded stainless steel. Let's just say it was a long way from the robes and room service I was used to at the Ritz-Carlton.

If you're reading this, the question you must be asking yourself, and one I certainly asked myself, is "How did I get here?"

Trust me, I had a lot of time to figure that out when I was locked up. For now, I'll just say I made some mistakes. Some I am not proud of, and others I had no control over. But did I ever commit a crime that justified the United States of America taking away my freedom and locking me up with murderers for two years? Did I deserve to spend three years on probation? Was it fair that I had to pay $200,000 in restitution to the *same people* who I believe stole millions and millions of dollars from me? After you read all the facts in the chapters ahead, I will let you determine what you believe was fair and just.

◆

When I arrived in prison, the cold, hard reality set in. I realized that bitching about what I deserved was irrelevant. I quickly understood I had two choices: I could sit around and pout and blame everyone else for what happened, or I could learn from it so it would never happen again.

With that said, I was determined not to be crippled by negativity. I had to take on a whole different mind-set—it was almost like I needed to check out of the lifestyle I had grown accustomed to and do what was necessary to survive.

I always have had the ability to not dwell on the past, to live my life going forward. That's why some say I was a good baseball player—meaning, in baseball, even if you are one of the best players in the league, you will still fail seven out of ten times as a hitter. If a player in the major leagues can hit .300, a team will pay him $20 million a year.

Playing baseball at the highest level is all about damage control. As a player, you already know you're going to fail 70 percent of the time, *and that's if you are one of the elite players.* The reality is, at the end of the day, a player who has the ability to stay positive and not let the game get to him has a much better chance of making it to the big leagues, and then staying in the big leagues.

Billy Beane, the celebrated general manager of the Oakland A's who was my roommate and good friend while we were both in the minor leagues, explained it best in Michael Lewis's best-selling book *Moneyball.* He realized that what made me successful at playing the game of baseball was my ability to instantly forget any failure and draw strength from every success. After playing and watching me day in and day out, Billy came to believe that I had no concept of failure.

It was this mind-set that helped me make it to the major leagues, and I knew that if I was going to make it out of prison, I would need to apply the same thinking to get me through two years of living inside the gates of hell.

◆

Later, I would learn that the reason why the feds let me out in the middle of the night was because the warden didn't want a media circus filming me—the famous former Major League Baseball All-Star and now felon—leaving prison. The press knew I was getting out on this day and so did the two filmmakers, Gil Netter and John Lee Hancock, who had signed on to make a movie about my life. Gil and John had arranged for a film crew to wait outside the prison to film me as I was being released at ten in the morning. But this wasn't the warden's first rodeo, and by making me leave unscheduled in the middle of the night, he ensured no media types of any kind would have any reason to hang out in front of his prison.

The warden got his way. It was just me and the wind.

◆

I had no intention of taking the bus from the prison any longer than was necessary. Victorville Federal Prison is ninety miles northeast of Los Angeles at the edge of the Mojave Desert. At the bus station, at around five A.M., I was standing with the Federal Marshal whose job was to make sure I got on the bus. There was one other dude waiting at the bus stop; he was holding a cheap cell phone.

"Hey, man," I called out. "Can I use your phone? I'll give you five bucks for one call."

He figured I was an ex-con and he was naturally wary of me.

"I don't know, man. You have to ask him," he said, pointing to the Federal Marshal standing next to me.

"He's free," the marshal said. "If he wants to give you five bucks for a phone call, and if you want to take it, then take it. I have no say."

I gave the dude my five-dollar gift card to use his phone and called my longtime assistant, Dorothy Van Kalsbeek, easily the most reliable person in my life, and explained the situation to her. She immediately switched gears and met me at the first stop. When I arrived at the San Bernardino Greyhound Station at six A.M. and got off the bus, she was there.

◆

As I sat on that Greyhound bus on the way to San Bernardino, I thought about how wonderful it was not to be locked up anymore. How fantastic it was to see beyond the walls of my cell. Although prison robbed me of precious time and dignity, the one thing it gifted me was clarity. Being forced out of the spotlight and the high-flying lifestyle I had placed myself in, I had plenty of time to do some serious soul-searching.

As that bus rumbled down the empty desert highway, I found my mind wandering to where it all started, well before everything went south, back to when baseball was all I ever wanted and everything I thought I needed.

Impossible is just a big word thrown around by small men who find it easier to live in the world they've been given than to explore the power they have to change it. *Impossible* is not a fact. It's an opinion. *Impossible* is not a declaration. It's a dare. *Impossible*

2

IN THE SHADOW OF ANGELS

Some people are born winners, while others aren't so lucky. I truly believe that.

I was born with the name Lenny Kyle Leswick. My grandfather, "Pistol Pete" Leswick, was a professional hockey player, born and raised in Canada. He was an All-Star in the 1930s in the American Hockey League, and my uncle Tony Leswick, my biological dad's brother, starred in the NHL. He had another brother, Jack, the stud of the family, but he drowned saving a kid's life, an accident that was very hard on the family. Still to this day, I have a fear of the ocean.

My uncle Tony was known as "Tough Tony" and "Mighty Mouse," because, like me, he was small but aggressive. "He's tough as nails," they said of old Tony about sixty years before I earned my famous nickname. Tony played for the New York Rangers, and he and the great Maurice "the Rocket" Richard of the Montreal Canadiens had one of the most intense feuds in hockey history. Tony also had a macho thing going with Detroit's Gordie Howe, who was supposed to be the toughest player in the league at the time. After years of watching Uncle Tony beat the living crap out of their precious Howe, the Red Wings finally decided the best solution to the problem was to bring Tony to play for them. After they traded for him, Uncle Tony helped the Red Wings win three Stanley Cups in the three years he played in Detroit. He scored the winning goal in overtime in Game 7 against the Canadiens to win the Cup in 1954. Now there's someone I'm proud to call family.

My French-Canadian ancestry might explain why all throughout my MLB career, people told me I played baseball like a hockey player. If there had been a penalty box along the right field line, I have no doubt I would have spent my fair share of time in the sin bin.

As for my biological father, the man they called Jerry Leswick, he left when I was about three years old. My only memory of the man is the time my mom threw a shoe across the room at him. I never heard from the man again until *after* I became a millionaire. He called and tried to get us to reunite, but I couldn't get off the phone fast enough.

"Sorry, but I already have a dad," I told him.

◆

I was adopted when I was four by my mom's new husband, Dennis Dykstra. To me, he was everything a father was supposed to be—supportive, tough, and loving. In addition to all those qualities, my dad was equally important in developing my passion for baseball. He coached me all through Little League and never missed a single game. He treated me like his own flesh and blood even though I wasn't his biological son. He was the only man I've ever called Dad.

It was a sad day when he died unexpectedly on October 4, 2000, from a brain aneurysm. It didn't make sense to me. Growing up, I never saw my dad sick once, and then out of nowhere, he died. When things like that happen, it reminds me how precious our time really is. For the most part, we just plow through life, marking days off the calendar, taking time for granted. After all, we live in a world where if one has enough money, he can pretty much buy anything. The exception is time. It doesn't matter how much money one has, or how much money one is willing to spend, time is not for sale.

Our family was just like the Brady Bunch. My mom had three boys: Brian, Kevin, and me. And my dad had three daughters: Danna, Brenda, and Johna. Despite being thrown together by marriage and living on top of one another in the same little house in Garden Grove, California, about an hour south of LA in Orange County, we all got along really well.

When I was growing up, my mom was the most important person in my life. She did everything for her three boys. What was even more amazing is that she did it all on her own. She worked full-time for the telephone company to support us. It wasn't until I was older that I realized how fortunate I was to have her as my mom.

When my mom was working for the telephone company, she met and married my dad, Dennis Dykstra. They both worked full-time for the company. Supporting six kids took every dime they earned. I remember our highlight of the week was on Friday night, when we would go out to eat at Bob's Big Boy, on Garden Grove Boulevard.

I realized at a young age that if I didn't have money, I didn't have options. I hated that feeling. So I went to work. I did anything and everything from cutting grass, delivering newspapers, and sweeping the alleys at a hotel to painting houses, cleaning swimming pools, and even working at the batting cages. Although I never really considered working at the batting cages a job: I got to hit for free! The funny thing is that hitting a baseball really did become my job.

I remember my mom and dad would work forty hours every week for basically nothing; barely enough money to raise our family. That's when I made a promise to myself that I was going to do everything in my power to never have to worry about money when I got older.

My solution? I decided I would take the gift that God gave me, which was playing baseball, to go after everything I wanted. Simply put, from a very young age, I knew I could not live my life in "the middle." I had to be extraordinary! I was determined not to be one of those guys who works his ass off and receives almost nothing in return.

Some of my best memories as a kid were my dad throwing me batting practice. He would throw to me for hours until his arm became sore. When I was eight years old, my dad signed me up to play in the ten-, eleven-, and twelve-year-olds division. The managers in the league thought my dad had lost his mind. That changed quickly once I proved to them what I could do on the field. In fact, I was an All-Star in a league of ten, eleven, and twelve year olds.

Because I was a left-handed fielder and was always the fastest kid on the team, my dad put me in center field. I was mad at the time, because at that age all of the action was in the infield. My dad would always say, "One day you are going to thank me." When I was a kid, there were so many times my dad would tell me things and I would say to myself, *He's crazy.* I'm sure a lot of you thought the same way, only to come to the same conclusion as me, that your dad was right most of the time.

◆

I loved the game of baseball at every level; it started when I was a kid dominating Little League baseball. When I was on the baseball field it was like I had a sixth sense—a knack for being in the right place at the right time. It's something that can't be taught, no matter how many hours you spend running drills.

My first year of Little League, our team was sponsored by Dottie's Beauty Salon. Obviously, the kids on the other teams enjoyed making fun of us because of our name. That lasted about eight games into the season, when we had kicked every team's ass. We ended up going undefeated, with twenty wins and no losses. I can say with certainty they weren't making fun of Dottie's Beauty Salon anymore.

◆

By the time I was in high school, baseball was my life. When I would have to make a decision on something, I would always ask myself, *Is this going to help me become a better baseball player?*

If the answer was no, even if it sounded like something fun to do, I would have the discipline to stick with my game plan.

I had a 3.4 grade point average in high school. Do you think it was because I wanted to get into some Ivy League school and impress the prom queen? *Hell no.* I hit that GPA because I knew it was needed in order to play baseball in college, just in case I didn't turn pro.

At Garden Grove High School, I became the first freshman ever to play on the varsity baseball team. And do you think I just rode the pine while the seniors had all the fun? No, I dominated every time I stepped out onto the field. We had a great coach, Dan Drake, and I can still remember how mad the other players were when he called me up to varsity. The upperclassmen on the squad didn't exactly welcome me with open arms. Instead they would make me pick up their dirty socks and jocks from the floor of the locker room. Although it was humiliating, it only drove me harder toward my goals, and I swore right then and there that I would show them all.

Before a game, while the other kids were talking to girls and fucking around, I pulled out Ping-Pong balls and would throw them at a wall and watch them come back at me, pretending they were baseballs. Then, when it was time for the game to start, the baseball looked so big coming out of the pitcher's hand; it was amazing how much that drill helped me. I did that drill my whole career.

♦

When I was fifteen years old, my favorite place to go was Anaheim Stadium. I would just ride my bike there; it wasn't too far, about a fifty-minute ride. During the summer, I went to almost every game. I'd get to the stadium early to watch batting practice. I loved to watch all the players hit. I would study how they each had a different approach to hitting.

At the time, Joe Rudi was the Angels' left fielder. With a lanky body that could have come only from the 1970s, Joe was one of the most unexciting baseball players who ever put on spikes. It seemed like he had taken a Xanax before every game. Even as a kid, I knew this guy was ripe for a good ribbing, so I stood down the left field line, just hammering away at him.

"Joe!" I yelled. "Throw me the ball." I kept yelling, "You're so old you probably can't even throw it this far." I continued lighting him up; the fans around me were staring at me like I'd lost my mind.

Rudi was at the tail end of his career and really struggling at the plate. He didn't look at me the whole time I was screaming at him. Then, when he got done playing catch, he strolled over to me and handed me a ball.

"Here you go, son," he said.

He made me feel about as big as a raisin.

I have to believe that inside he was probably thinking, *Just shut the fuck up, kid, you little smartass,* but he still treated me with the utmost respect.

Now fast-forward to when I made it to the major leagues. I became known for generously handing out baseballs to the fans. Without a doubt, this was inspired by my humbling experience with Joe Rudi. In fact, when I was playing for the Phillies, I gave away so many baseballs to fans that the team called me up to the front office and said, "Lenny, we think it's great that you love the fans so much, but at the rate you're giving away baseballs, we're going to have to order twice as many balls as we did last year. Just slow it down a little." I walked away with a smile on my face.

On another memorable Anaheim Stadium adventure, I was determined to meet my idol, Rod Carew, who defined what a big-league baseball player was supposed to look and act like. Rod Carew was the reason why I folded my baseball hat and put it in my back pocket throughout my entire professional career. Rod Carew was also the reason I started chewing tobacco—even though I hated the taste of it. I remember I would get sick and throw up when I first started using it. But I was determined to make the big wad of chewing tobacco in my mouth part of my identity as a baseball player. Even at that time, it wasn't hard to figure out that baseball was entertainment. People pay a lot of money to watch a Major League Baseball game, especially in this day and age.

Back to my plan, which was to meet my idol, Rod Carew, face-to-face. When the game ended, after all the fans had left (I was hiding out in the men's bathroom), I walked really fast to the Angels dugout, jumped over the fence, and thought I was home free, but when I started to walk up the runway toward the clubhouse, there were two security guards waiting for me. They got me!

I was only fifteen, but they still put me in stadium jail (it wasn't really jail, it was just an office I had to wait in), my first experience in lockup but, unfortunately, not my last. Security called my mom and dad, and they had to drive to the stadium and pick me up.

The week after the incident, and unbeknownst to me, my aunt took it upon herself to write a letter to Rod Carew, informing him of what had happened at Anaheim Stadium. A few days later, I was at home with my family when the phone rang. I was swinging my bat in front of a mirror and doing push-ups, like I did every night, when my mom said, "It's for you, son. It sounds like a man."

After I got on the phone and said hello, a deep voice greeted me. "Hello, Lenny. This is Rod Carew."

I thought my heart was going to explode in my chest. I was in complete and utter shock. I couldn't believe I was actually talking to my idol on the phone. I tried to figure out what I should say to him. Should I ask him for advice about hitting? Then he told me that he wanted to apologize for what had happened at the stadium. I was so overwhelmed by the fact that Rod Carew had taken the time to call me at home, I never forgot that feeling and did whatever I could to help a person out when I became a major league player.

The first time I met Rod Carew in person was in 1998. I invited him to sign autographs at the grand opening of my second Lenny Dykstra's Car Wash, in Simi Valley. He was so nice and respectful; a class act all the way. I asked him if he remembered calling me at my house, and he quickly answered by saying, "Of course." He went on to say, "I remember receiving a letter from your aunt—it was your aunt, wasn't it?" I answered, "Yes, it was." I went on to tell him that he'd been my idol growing up—I wasn't embarrassed—and that I wanted to be just like him.

◆

I also played football in high school, and I was damn good at it. Like in baseball, my instincts were superb and I excelled at the sport. I played free safety, and Arizona State, who already knew I had a full ride to play baseball for their university, offered me the opportunity to play football as well. But I knew that baseball was my only option and the only way I could realize my dreams. Besides, I was a small kid and not really big enough to play football. Football was fun, but I knew that baseball would be the profession that would make me a millionaire.

◆

Being a star athlete in high school had its social advantages, especially when it came to the girls. My first sexual encounter came out of left field (no pun intended).

I was a freshman, and one morning before school I was invited by a senior to her house. She was very popular and extremely pretty. When I knocked on her door—I'm not going to deny it—I was nervous but excited at the same time. I didn't know what to expect.

"Follow me," she said.

The next thing I knew, I was lying on her bed and she put on the song "All My Love" by Led Zeppelin. Before I realized what was going on, she took off my clothes, climbed on top of me, and had sex with me. She took me to a place I had never been before. So I kept showing up at her house before school, knocking on her door, hoping we could do it again, but she never answered after that day.

I was different from most of the other kids in high school. I didn't need a girlfriend, and I didn't want one either. Don't get me wrong, I definitely needed to clean my pipes, if you know what I mean, but my number one priority was baseball, and having a girlfriend would have only set me back from completing my mission.

As a senior in high school, I was five foot nine and I weighed all of 150 pounds. At that time, it was extremely rare for a major league club to invite a high school player out to their major league stadium to take batting practice, especially with the big leaguers before a game. It just never happened, unless you were related to one of the players or to one of the powers that be.

The Angels invited me to Anaheim Stadium to take batting practice with them before a game against the Texas Rangers. They gave me an Angels uniform, and the next thing I knew, I was walking down the runway from the clubhouse to the dugout, and eventually out onto the field. And what a field. Wow! It was so perfect. I remember saying to myself, *All this for a baseball game.* It was the most beautiful thing I had ever seen. I remember dropping down on a knee and pulling out a piece of the grass, just so I knew it was real.

Then one of the scouts yelled, "Dykstra, get in there. Let's see what you got." So I walked into the cage and up to the plate with my aluminum bat. It was all I had.

Several of the big leaguers stared at me—it was a very uncomfortable feeling—and yelled, "What the fuck do you think this is, Little League? Get the fuck out of there with that metal shit."

What the hell did I know? It wasn't like it is now, with kids already using wood bats in junior high school. A wood bat was foreign to me—it might as well have come from Mars instead of Louisville, Kentucky.

All the scouts and front office people were there; players call them "the brass." I could feel them staring at me; when they looked at my size, it was obvious they didn't take me seriously. Even though I had hit .550 and was the best player in the history of Garden Grove High School—one of the best players in the state of California. To be truthful, when I got in the batting cage to hit, it didn't matter what I did, because I would be judged on my size, not on my hitting. Before I even took my first swing, I knew what they were thinking: *We're going to draft this little runt?*

Only one scout, Myron Pines, believed in me. He recognized I had the "it factor" and could do things on the baseball field that can't be taught. Pines never doubted my ability to play baseball at the major league level. He didn't listen to his fellow scouts when they said I looked like a batboy. In all honesty, it didn't bother me—it just pissed me off and only made me work harder.

After I finished hitting with the big-league players, I saw Fred Lynn, the Angels' star outfielder at the time and one of the premier players of the 1970s, standing near the batting cage.

"Mr. Lynn," I said, approaching him in awe, "I have a full-ride scholarship to Arizona State, but the scouts told me that I am going to get drafted. What do you think I should do?"

I genuinely wanted to know his opinion on what I should do with my future. At that particular time, Arizona State University had the best college baseball program in the country. In 1981, they won their fifth national championship, and they had sent a string of players to the big leagues, including the megastar Reggie Jackson, soon to be an Angel himself.

I waited with bated breath for Fred Lynn to issue a pearl of wisdom that would help decide my future. Instead he turned out to be not only arrogant but a complete asshole as well. He looked me up and down like I was wasting his time and sneered, "This is a strong man's game, son." And he just walked away.

I was crushed. It made me work even harder, and added more fuel to the fire to accomplish my dream. I was not going to let Fred Lynn, or anyone for that matter, tell me I wasn't going to make it to the big leagues.

Funny story: when Fred Lynn was at the end of his career, playing for the San Diego Padres, I was playing for the Phillies, in my prime, and firing on all cylinders both at the plate and in center field. It was a Saturday-night game and Lynn hit three bullets in the gap; I robbed him all three times. He easily could have had three extra-base hits. The next day at the yard, as the Padres were finishing up batting practice, I went out of my way to find him and said, "Hey, Freddie, man"—I couldn't wait to bury his ass—"looks like I got a little stronger, didn't I?"

"Fuck you" was all Freddie said.

Karma is a bitch.

During my eighteen years I came to bat almost

10,000 times. I struck out about 1,700 times

and walked maybe 1,800 times. You figure

a ballplayer will average about 500 at-bats a

season. That means I played seven years without

ever hitting the ball.

—MICKEY MANTLE

3

CLIMBING THE LADDER

In June 1981, I was waiting for my name to be called in the Major League Baseball draft. I was sitting at home. It wasn't like it is today, with players outfitted in Giorgio Armani suits waiting in the greenroom for their first moment in the spotlight.

I wasn't nervous, as I had already prepared myself to be drafted much lower than I should have been. The fact that I wasn't six foot two made me a nonfactor to 99 percent of the typical pro baseball scouts.

My name was finally called when the New York Mets drafted me in the thirteenth round. I was the 315th overall pick in the 1981 MLB draft. That same year, the Mets drafted three outfielders ahead of me: Terry Blocker, John Christensen, and Mark Carreon.

I was disappointed but not mad. The majority of the scouts were former minor league baseball players, or players who got a cup of coffee in the big leagues. Most of the scouts are afraid to hang their balls out there on a player who doesn't fit the so-called pro baseball mold. The majority of the scouts, not all of them, focus on the wrong things when it comes to evaluating a player. Meaning, in today's world, teams must pay players millions and millions of dollars before they even put a uniform on. For example, the first player chosen in the 2015 MLB draft was slotted to be paid a signing bonus of approximately $8.6 million. That's some serious cheddar to pay a player who has yet to set foot on the baseball field.

When I was in high school, I played on a Mets scout team that consisted of all the top baseball prospects in Southern California. A player had to be invited to join this team. I remember being told that the Mets' big boss, Joe McIlvaine, then their scouting director, was coming into town and wanted to watch all the prospects run, throw, and hit.

I was all pumped up; I couldn't wait to put on a show. I later read an article in which Joe McIlvaine talked about my performance in that workout. "I remember one of the scouts at the check-in table looking over Dykstra's small build and mistaking him for a batboy," McIlvaine said. "Dykstra responded by staring down the scouts and sternly telling them, 'I'm Lenny Dykstra, and I'm the best player you're going to see here today!' So we put him out there to run, and he outran and outthrew every kid on the field that day."

McIlvaine went on to say, "I was impressed by Dykstra's bravado—and even more by his skills. I wanted to take Dykstra as high as the third round of the draft, but my scouts assured me there wasn't much interest in him in the early rounds because of his size. So we waited and still got him."

◆

The day after I was drafted by the New York Mets in the thirteenth round, three scouts—Roger and Dean Jongewaard and Myron Pines—showed up at my house in Garden Grove to try to get me to sign a contract and turn pro.

The Jongewaard brothers, especially Roger, were highly respected, as they had earned a solid reputation for drafting players who made it to the big leagues. But it was the third scout, Myron Pines, who had pushed the Mets so hard to draft me. Myron was a very quiet, studious-looking man with glasses. He was a high school teacher and baseball coach. But his passion was running the Mets' scout team. Myron had coached and watched me play in a lot of games. Over time, he knew that I was a special player; he knew that I wasn't going to be denied. But most important, he understood that I loved playing baseball. Myron once told a reporter, "We used to kid Lenny if he ever drove by a baseball field he would stop and play no matter who was playing."

◆

In 2014, my youngest son, Luke, was a senior at Westlake High School. Luke was considered one of the top high school baseball prospects in the country. Luke is the perfect height, six foot one, and weight, 195 pounds, for a professional baseball player. There were always a bunch of scouts at the games to watch him play. At one of the games I looked up and saw Myron Pines. It had been about twenty years since I'd last seen him. I couldn't believe how great he looked. He had on the same bad costume he always wore when I played for him, as well as the goofy goggles he used to wear when he coached me. We gave each other a hug, exchanged some happy rap, and then sat down in the bleachers.

With the June MLB draft just a few weeks away for Luke, it reminded me of something very important that Myron said to me before the 1981 MLB draft in which I was selected. We were working out on the field and he pulled me off to the side with a very serious look on his face and said, "Lenny, I know you're excited about the upcoming draft in June, and you should be— you worked harder than anyone else and proved to everyone that you were the best player on the field. But I want you to know, the draft isn't always fair and it definitely isn't always right."

I remember asking, "What does that mean, Coach Pines?" I have never forgotten the answer he gave me. He looked me in the eyes and said to me, "It's the old story. The little guy has to prove he can play, while the bigger guy has to prove that he can't. If a guy can play, he can play anywhere. It doesn't matter where you get drafted, Lenny, because you can play. Everything will take care of itself; all you have to do is play."

◆

The Mets were stocking up on young outfield prospects. The year before, in the 1980 MLB draft, the Mets were in the rare position of having three first-round picks. Two of those picks were used on the most sought-after outfield prospects in the country. They were both from Southern California and both had story-book names.

Darryl Strawberry was the first overall pick in the country;

Billy Beane was the twenty-third overall pick that the New York Mets also had the luxury of drafting in the first round. The Mets had visions of both Strawberry and Beane manning the outfield for the next World Series championship team to come out of Flushing.

In total, there were five other outfielders drafted ahead of me by the Mets in 1981. I was offered several full-ride scholarships from the best baseball schools in the country. One was USC, with their legendary coach Rod Dedeaux. Even though it was an honor to be offered a full ride to USC, at that time Arizona State was the college baseball powerhouse—they were the big swinging dicks of NCAA baseball. When they offered me a full ride, I accepted. I wanted to play on the best team, with the best players. And that's exactly what Arizona State had. The outfield that next season would have been Barry Bonds, the best baseball player of all time; Oddibe McDowell, who went on to star for the Texas Rangers; and me.

Talk about a college pitcher's nightmare? Ouch!

◆

The Mets offered me $7,000 to sign and told me I would be sent to play rookie ball, which was pretty standard, especially if a player was drafted out of high school. The organizations wanted to let a young player adjust and not feel overwhelmed, as this would be the first time a player drafted out of high school would be away from home.

I responded by saying, *What the hell kind of offer is that?*

"No thank you," I said. "I have a full ride to Arizona State, and I'm going."

◆

After I turned down the offer from the Mets, I called Ben Hines, who at the time was the ASU hitting coach and the person who recruited me. I told him I wanted to play in one of the top summer college-baseball leagues everybody talked about. There were three leagues at that time where the country's best college baseball players would get invited to play. One was the Cape Cod League. There was another in Alaska, and the third was called the Jayhawk League, in Kansas.

Coach Hines told me, "Those leagues aren't for high school players; they are for the best college players in the country." I would not take no for an answer. I pushed and pushed until I finally got what I wanted and was sent to the Jayhawk League. I was assigned to play for a team in Rapid City, South Dakota.

The day after I graduated high school, I boarded a plane destined for a city I'd never heard of and a state I had never visited before. I didn't know what to expect. When I arrived in Rapid City it felt like I'd gone back in time. It's sandwiched between the Black Hills and the Badlands; the Wild West town of Deadwood is nearby. And yes, people really do live there, I promise.

The team set up the players' living arrangements with host families, who would feed us and were very nice people. The only problem was that my host family lived on a working farm. So if I needed to go into town, as they called it, to pick something up,

I was always stuck. It was much too far to walk, and they didn't have an extra car. So one day I asked them, "Would you mind if I used your tractor to drive into town to pick up a few things?"

They said, "Sure, son, no problem. Are you sure you know how to drive it?"

I answered, "Of course, thank you."

I have to admit, it was one of the coolest things I had ever experienced in my eighteen years on the planet.

Because I was from Southern California, the closest I'd been to a tractor was when I'd seen construction workers dig up something alongside the road. This SoCal kid was definitely a fish out of water. I remember the wind blowing in my face as I was driving the tractor down the road. For some reason I felt so cool, so free, almost like, *Look at me, everyone, I know how to drive a tractor.*

My roommate at the farmhouse was Mike Pagel, who would later play quarterback for the Cleveland Browns. He was a journeyman in the NFL, bouncing around from team to team, who had tried to make it in baseball. *Tried* was the operative word here.

From day one I was hitting line drives all over the yard. I was tearing up the Jayhawk League. I was batting .380 after the first three weeks. It didn't take long for the Mets to get word about how well I was playing, so they sent a couple of scouts to watch me play. I continued raking, stealing bases, the whole deal, when the Mets called and offered me an additional $5,000, upping their offer to a whopping $12,000.

"Let me think about it," I said.

Even though I knew the Mets' offer was short a few zeroes, at the end of the day, deep down, I didn't want to go to college, even with a full ride. I'd worked my fucking ass off since I was a young boy to get into this position. More important, I was ready to play pro baseball. I'd been ready since the day I was born.

I called up the Mets and told them I was ready to sign. They put me on the phone with one of their bean counters in the front office. I told him, "I want to get something straight before I sign: if you want me, I'm not going to rookie ball like the rest of the players that get drafted out of high school." I went on to say, "For the last four years, I proved that I can dominate high school players. I want to play A ball."

I could tell the front-office guy thought I was crazy when he fired back, "No one goes to Class A ball out of high school."

"Then I'm not signing," I snapped back.

"You have balls, kid, I'll give you that. But I can't make that decision; it's above my pay grade. I'll have the scouting director, Joe McIlvaine, call you."

When McIlvaine called, I told him that I wanted to start at Class A, one level higher than everyone else.

"Some people may call it cockiness, but it was a good kind of cockiness because he one hundred percent believed in his ability . . . Lenny could never fail in his own mind," McIlvaine later said.

And like that, they agreed to send me to the South Atlantic League, where the Mets' Class A team played in Shelby, North Carolina.

◆

When the wheels touched down in Charlotte, North Carolina, the closest airport to Shelby, I was not prepared for what I was about to encounter. Once off the plane, I was looking for a hotshot wearing a suit to pick me up; after all, I was a pro baseball player. What I got instead were two local boosters, a middle-aged lady full of country charm and her daughter, who had been sent to pick up the California boy who'd just made the team.

"Y'er gonna *luv* Shelby," the mother drawled in the way that could only come from the deep down South in the U.S. of A. "Y'er gonna *luv* our ballpark, too. It's beautiful," she added sweetly.

Driving past the historic homes and farmland, I felt like I had been cast in an episode of *Green Acres*—without Eva Gabor. In fact, in later years a fictionalized version of Shelby would spring up as the inspiration for the HBO comedy *Eastbound & Down*.

After a ways she pulled into the parking lot of a local high school. "What are we doing here?" I asked. "I'm with the New York Mets. The pro baseball Mets. Take me to the professional baseball field, please. This is a high school field."

"This here is y'all's field," she replied. "This is the home field of the Shelby Mets."

Oh my fucking God, I said to myself. I might as well have been in the FBI's witness protection program, as nobody was ever going to find me or see me play down here.

I walked into what looked like a temporary clubhouse, way down the right field line of this high school baseball field. It was around noon, and no one seemed to be around. Then I noticed the Shelby manager, Danny Monzon, sitting behind his desk smoking a cigarette and looking miserable. As I would learn soon enough, for many people stuck in the system, the minor leagues is all about misery and drinking. Lots of drinking!

"Who are you?" asked Monzon, barely looking up.

"Hi, sir," I said enthusiastically. "I'm Lenny Dykstra."

He looked me up and down. I could tell he was scrutinizing my size and wondering, *What have they sent me this time?* "Oh yeah," he said. "I heard we were getting a new guy. What are you, a middle infielder?" Monzon didn't even know who I was. I had just given up my whole college career to turn pro, and my first pro manager didn't have a clue who I was.

He didn't give a fuck either. At that moment in time, it hit me: I was entering a whole new world, with a different set of rules.

Monzon, who was from the Bronx, had been a utility player for the Minnesota Twins before becoming a minor league manager for the Mets. A lot of former players who end up coaching in the minor leagues are not always the happiest people on earth, and for good reason: it's much tougher than the public perceives it to be. Basically, if you coach or manage in the minor leagues for an extended period of time, you have two choices: suffer or become a professional drinker.

I have some compassion now that I look back, but to my younger self he was the enemy. Why? Because he wouldn't play me. It was nothing personal, mind you, but the man was keeping me from pursuing my dream, and I wasn't going to stand for that. Finally, after harassing him weekly, then daily, then hourly—he relented and let me play. The biggest challenge for me was making the adjustment to a wood bat. It was also difficult being away from home for the first time. As much as I wanted to play professional baseball, when you're eighteen years old, there's still the human factor that you can't get away from. This was all part of the process, but I battled for the month and a half I was there.

The next year at Shelby, I played my first full season of pro ball. I was very fortunate to have a manager, Rich Miller, who immediately took a liking to me. He was also a very good outfielder coach. Rich saw the potential I had as a player and worked with me to get the absolute most out of my size and skills. Plus it helped that he was a little fucker like me, and left-handed to boot.

"We're the same, except for the fact that I don't have your talent," he told me one day. Somehow I think this made him even more determined to make sure I succeeded.

To describe Shelby as a small town is an insult to small towns everywhere. "Hellby" is what we called it. We were playing on a high school baseball field, for God's sake. It was pretty damn depressing. I knew there was only one real solution to get out of Dodge: play well, put the numbers up, and move on. That's exactly what I did.

In Shelby, playing under Miller, I led off and had the benefit of a great number two hitter behind me, Mark Carreon. He could flat-out hit. We played together for three years, batting first and second in the lineup that whole time, and we really worked well together.

The next two years, we dominated and won it all twice. When Mark made it to the big leagues, he changed his whole hitting approach and tried to be a home run hitter. It was very confusing to me, because I can say with 100 percent certainty that he was the best two-hole hitter I ever played with—that includes all players from both the minor and major leagues.

John Gibbons, another teammate, was a great guy who would become the manager of the Toronto Blue Jays. John and I rented a place with three other teammates in a big old country house. Gibby, as we called him, was the kind of person you wanted your kid to grow up to be like. But don't let the fact that he was a gentleman fool you: he was one tough dude, a good old boy from Texas. I liked Gibby a lot. He kind of took me under his wing and told me what to do in certain situations so I was prepared. Thinking back to how Gibby respected the game, and how he always played hard, it makes sense that he turned out to be a big-league manager.

Roger McDowell also lived with us. He was not only a talented pitcher, he was a great all-around athlete. I knew Roger was going to make it to the big leagues. He was like me; he wasn't going to be denied. I could see it in his eyes, and it turned out that I was correct. He had an outstanding career before becoming the pitching coach for the Atlanta Braves.

◆

In 1983, my third season as a pro, I broke camp with the Lynchburg Mets; this was the high Single A ball team for the Mets. I knew that it was time to make a move, to bust out of the middle. I remember saying to myself, *Lenny, the time is now. You need to do something this year that will put you on the map, open up everyone's eyes.* It was time to be extraordinary. I needed to make the general manager and the director of the minor leagues say to each other, "Where did this little motherfucker come from?"

This was also my protection year. At that time, all twenty-six teams had to declare which forty players they wanted to protect and put on their forty-man roster. Players who had played three years and were left off the forty-man would be unprotected and would be exposed to the Rule 5 draft by the twenty-five other teams. The forty players the team can protect include the twenty-five players on the big-league club as well, so if you think about it, there are only fifteen open spots on a forty-man roster left, and every November, teams have to decide which of their minor league prospects deserve one of those coveted slots.

To be put on the forty-man roster was and still is a huge deal for a player. Not only does it tell you what your organization thinks of you, it also means you will be invited to major league spring training. It's hard to explain how far away the big leagues feel when you're down in the minors. It almost seems as though the big leagues don't exist. Worse for me, the Mets were loaded with a long list of outfielders who were drafted in the first and second rounds. They were referred to by other players as "bonus babies," because the team had invested so much money in them. This meant they were going to be in the lineup every night no matter what. It's business 101.

My manager in Lynchburg was Sam Perlozzo. He wasn't even on the map as far as the Mets were concerned. That is, until I led off for him two years in a row, and both years we won it all. Talk about perfect timing? Sammy only cared about himself—he defined what players cannot stand, a front-runner. He was one of the typical backstabbers that baseball is full of. Perlozzo knew how to work the front office and even convinced a couple of big-league teams to let him manage. How do you think that went? *Do I even need to answer?* It went bad, real bad. Every player who played for him could not stand him. Players know who the front-runners are; they know which coaches are talking about them behind their backs when things aren't going well.

Perlozzo had me and Dwight "Doc" Gooden on the same team. In 1983, I was the Carolina League MVP, where I led the league in batting (.358), runs scored (132), and walks and had a record-setting 105 stolen bases, shattering all the Carolina League records. Doc was an eighteen-year-old phenom pitcher, and he dominated hitters unlike anything I've ever seen in my life. Doc struck out 300 batters in 191 innings. Nobody in the minors was close to him. The opposing team wanted no part of him. They were scared to even get in the batter's box.

After the 1983 season I said to Doc, "You're going to the show next year."

"What's the show?" he asked.

"You're going to the big leagues, dude. You're going to be pitching in the big leagues next year."

◆

When you're playing in the minors, you have to take an entirely different approach to the game than when you play in the big leagues. At the major league level, the most important thing is winning. That means you have to play the game off the scoreboard, as the scoreboard dictates what a player should and shouldn't do. For example, if your team is losing by two runs in the bottom of the ninth inning, the hitter must take a strike *no matter what*. Why? It's real simple: a player can't hit a two-run home run with nobody on base. Furthermore, as I mentioned earlier, even if you are one of the best players in the league, you are still about a 70 percent underdog if you put the ball in play. The majority of players today fail miserably at this, as they are too selfish. Just to be clear, there are some players who still play the game right, but they are few and far between. The little things turn into big things if you play the game right over the course of a 162-game season.

I will give you another example. If you are playing blackjack at a casino for real money, there are certain rules a player should follow if he wants to put himself in the best possible position to succeed, or win, over the long run. As with baseball, the odds are still against you even if you play right. With that said, if a player uses the probability theory each and every at-bat—which means he understands that over a 162-game schedule, the percentages prove what the outcome will most likely be based on all the possible counts—that player would put himself in the best possible position to succeed.

How do you think I led the National League in hits two separate seasons? It wasn't because I was the best hitter, not even close. It was because I finally figured out the approach, or game plan, that would give me the best results. This way of thinking actually made the game much simpler for me. The less you have to think about, the better.

In order to make this work, a player has to believe and trust that what he is doing is right, and not deviate from it. Much easier said than done, trust me.

In the minor leagues you play to put up numbers, period. The general managers don't give a fuck whether a minor league team wins or loses. It's all about your numbers.

There has never been a meeting where the GM says, "We're going to call this guy up to the big leagues—forget that he's only hitting .220, because he has constantly moved the runner over from second." Sorry, wrong answer.

◆

I n 1984 I was promoted to Jackson, Mississippi, which was the Double A team for the Mets. I had never experienced heat and humidity like I did when I arrived in Mississippi.

If you're a minor league player showing up in a new city, the first thing you do is find a place to live. So I went into the local bank to cash my whopping $300 paycheck. When I walked into this little bank, I saw Terri. Besides having the look I was attracted to, when she started talking, I literally got blood flow. I wanted to fuck her in the safe. I swear to God I did. I was trying to be cool, flirting with her, but all she did was give me some courtesy laughs and basically blew me off.

I said to my roommate, Mark Carreon, as we were walking out of the bank, "Dude, that chick was fucking hot!"

He responded by saying, "Come on, man, they're a dime a dozen."

I immediately fired back, "No, dude, you're wrong. There is something special about that one, and I am not stopping until she goes out with me."

I went back to the bank the next day, cut in front of the people waiting in line, and said, "Would you like to go out with me?"

She replied, "I'm working, I can't talk to you right now, plus I don't even know you."

Blown off for the second time.

I finally had to play on my strength. I told her that I played for the Jackson Mets and asked her if she wanted tickets to the game. She answered, "Sure, that sounds fun." As I was walking out the door, I told her the tickets would be waiting for her at will call.

But she didn't show up. Later I found out that she'd been warned about us ballplayers and she even doubted that I played for the Jackson Mets. Finally, one day she asked her bank manager, a big baseball fan, if he'd ever heard of me. Her boss went on to gush about the last game he'd seen me play. Apparently he was a big fan. He was the one who told her she should go out with me.

After that, Terri and I started seeing each other frequently; there was something about her that set her apart from the rest. I had been with plenty of girls, but I'd never let them get close to me. The last thing I needed was to deal with a girl and all the drama that usually goes along with one, especially when the only thing that mattered to me was making it to the big leagues.

The fact that I had never been in a real relationship that was important to me put me in an awkward situation: I didn't really know how to act or what to expect. It was all new to me.

I can honestly say, before Terri, I was strictly in the "pipe-cleaning business."

We were getting closer and closer as the season was winding down. She was very supportive and had a real clue about how baseball worked. Terri grew up around sports. She'd been a track star in high school and had watched her older brother, Keith, play baseball since she was a young girl.

I saw a lot of players' careers go straight downhill after picking the wrong partner. It takes a special woman to put her partner first and support him through all the ups and downs that define baseball.

Needless to say, Terri was my first and only real keeper. I knew she was wired differently. At the end of the season, I promised her that if I ever made it to the big leagues, I would marry her.

Lenny was so perfectly designed, emotionally,

to play the game of baseball. He was able

to instantly forget any failure and draw

strength from every success. He had no concept

of failure.

—BILLY BEANE, FROM *MONEYBALL*

4

BREAKING INTO THE BIGS

In 1985, my life was about to change in a big way. The man who would help make that happen was Bob Schaefer. He was my manager when I broke camp with the Mets' Triple A team, the Tidewater Tides. Schaef, as everyone called him, loved the way I played. He quickly recognized that I was a winning player. If you looked up the definition of what a true professional baseball coach is, there would be a picture of Bob Schaefer right next to it. He has been in professional baseball for thirty-seven years and is still sharp as a tack. Simply put, baseball is his business.

On May 2, we were playing a game in Tidewater and I hit a triple. As I came into third base, Schaef asked, "Why did you dog it? You should have had an inside-the-park homer."

I responded by saying, "I ran hard all the way."

Schaef just turned around and walked back to the third base coach's box. After the game, as we were shaking hands on the field, Schaef told me, "I need to see you in my office." I was hitting around .300, playing great defense; I didn't know what I did wrong.

I knocked on Schaef's office door, and with his sharp New England accent, he said, "Sit down," his expression serious. "I've got to talk to you about something."

What's going on? I thought.

"See that sport coat over there?"

"What about it?" was all I could say.

Schaef then told me to put it on and asked, "Does it fit?"

I was confused. "I guess, why?"

Grinning now, Schaef responded, "Good, because you're going to need it. The shit you wear around here isn't going to work in the big leagues, which is where you are going tomorrow."

I turned white as a sheet. "Really?"

"Yes, really. Tomorrow night, in Cincinnati, you'll be playing center field and leading off for the New York Mets against the Reds' Mario Soto."

After I started breathing again, Schaef went on to tell me that I would only be in the big leagues for two weeks, because that's when Mookie Wilson was scheduled to come off the disabled list.

When Mookie got hurt again, Davey Johnson, the manager, wanted to call up Terry Blocker, one of the high draft picks, but Schaefer told them, "You're calling up the wrong guy. If you want a guy to lead off and play center field, there's nobody better than Dykstra. You have to call up Dykstra. He catches all the balls out there, and he hits. Trust me. You have to take Dykstra. He's the guy."

Schaef would tell me later that Davey still wanted Blocker, so he called the GM, Frank Cashen, and the assistant GM, Joe McIlvaine, and told them, "I know Davey disagrees with me, but if my job is to help him win up there, then Lenny is the guy, trust me."

They told Schaef to stay by the phone, that they would call

him right back. They called Schaef back fifteen minutes later and said, "Send Lenny."

Schaef then called me into his office and told me that I was going to the big leagues.

"Just play your ass off," he said. "Get on base and play the same way you have your whole life: balls out."

I did.

The rest is history.

♦

Wearing the sport coat Schaef gave me, I arrived in Cincinnati around eleven A.M. I got in a cab and told the driver to take me to the stadium. Even though the game wasn't until 7:35 P.M., I wanted to see the field.

To get to the visiting team's clubhouse at a major league stadium, you have to get through stadium security. I arrived about noon, and I told the guard, "My name is Lenny Dykstra, and I just got called up to play center field for the New York Mets." To say he was skeptical was an understatement. *How could he not be?* I was a twenty-two-year-old kid who looked like I was still in high school.

After I showed him my driver's license, he made me wait in the cab for what seemed like an eternity. After several phone calls, he finally let me in. I was minutes away from walking into a major league clubhouse where I was going to lead off and play center field for the New York Mets. Everything I had worked my whole life for was about to become a reality.

It was only 12:15 P.M., so I was the first player to arrive at the clubhouse. I walked right through and ran straight down the runway and walked onto the field. It stopped me in my tracks. I was completely awestruck at the sheer size of the ballpark. *All this just for a baseball game?*

I kept saying to myself, *I finally made it to the big leagues.* I felt almost light-headed as I soaked it all in—Cincinnati's stadium was all AstroTurf. I had never seen so much green. Sixty thousand empty seats gleamed in the sunlight. It was like being a gladiator entering your first battle inside the Colosseum of Rome.

I didn't know any of the Mets players or coaching staff. Davey Johnson was my manager, but he didn't say anything more to me than "Good luck." I didn't take it personally. Davey didn't have more than two words to say to most people—until he started drinking, which was a nightly event.

I walked back up the runway and entered the clubhouse. I will never forget seeing my nameplate on my locker. It read: DYKSTRA #4.

I was officially a New York Met. I took the field along with my new teammates, without any advice or instruction. I was on my own. But I didn't care, because if I knew anything, it was that I could play the game of baseball. God had put me on this earth to be there. Every time I stepped on the field to play, it was as if I owned it. I'm serious. When I was out there, I felt like I had a fifteen-inch cock. I was home.

As thousands of fans began flooding into the park, I thought to myself, *Watch me. Just sit back and enjoy the show.*

I had been called up to be the Mets' center fielder because Mookie Wilson was injured. *Mookie* is one of the greatest names ever. He was a great guy, by the way, though he had terrible breath. I'm talking death fumes. But Mookie was a good dude. We got along really well even though the Mets platooned the hell out of us and we were essentially competing with each other.

As it was getting closer to game time, I had a feeling of nervous excitement that is hard to explain.

Then it happened: the PA announcer said over the loudspeaker, "Leading off for the New York Mets, number four, center fielder Lenny Dykstra." The fans in Cincinnati didn't have a clue who I was. How could they? I stepped into the batter's box, heard the umpire yell, "Play ball," and Mario Soto threw what would be my first pitch. I didn't know it at the time, but this would be the first of thousands and thousands of pitches I would see over my career.

What I was feeling and thinking during my first at-bat in the major leagues was unusual, especially considering that, on a baseball field, I wasn't afraid of anyone or anything. But this was baffling. It was almost like I mind-fucked myself into thinking that the big-league players were going to be so different, so much more advanced, so much better, I vapor-locked and struck out.

I trudged back to the dugout and attempted to calm myself down. *Relax, Lenny. It's still baseball, man. Just because the stadium is bigger and there are more people in the stands doesn't change the fact that it's the same fucking game you have dominated your whole fucking life. Wake the fuck up and play the game.*

It was just like in *Hoosiers* when Gene Hackman shows the Hickory boys that the court in the state championship is the same size as their court back home.

You either know how to play or you don't. The pitcher still has to throw it over the plate, and you still have to get to first, then to second, then to third, and then home, which is what leads to this thing called a run. Then, after nine innings, the team with the most runs wins!

In my next at-bat, Soto threw me a mediocre fastball. He didn't have shit and I knew it. The only thing he had on the ball was his fucking hand, as he was at the end of his career. The next pitch was a hanging changeup that I fucking smoked! I wrapped it around the right field foul pole. My first big-league hit—a home run. Game on!

I was twenty-two years old playing in the show for the New York Mets, living the dream.

◆

When the 1985 season ended, we finished in second place behind the Cardinals.

There were other big changes happening in my life around the same time. When the Mets called me up to the big leagues, I told Terri that I wanted her and Gavin, her two-year-old son, to move to New York and live with me, but she was reluctant. Crying, she confessed she was afraid that if we were not married and she uprooted Gavin and gave up her job that I might change my mind, leaving their lives completely disrupted. So I called her mom. Afterward, she told Terri, "I think you should go with Lenny. He said he loves you and he fully intends to marry you." That sealed the deal for us. Of course, New York was a long way from Mississippi, if you know what I mean. But I have to give Terri credit: she made the transition without any problems at all.

I was pretty consumed with baseball, but as time passed, she made sure to remind me that I made a promise and she wanted to be married. She was from the South, she said, and marriage was important to her.

Finally, on a morning I was scheduled to play golf with my good friend Bert Brodsky, a very wealthy businessman from Port Washington, Long Island, where we were living, she asked me again, "When are we going to get married?"

I lost my patience.

"Hold on," I said.

I then called Bert. He was the smartest person I had ever met, and is now worth close to a billion dollars.

"Bert," I said, "before we play golf, I have to get married. Can you be my best man? Can you set up a marriage?"

"Give me thirty minutes," he said.

A half hour later Terri, Bert Brodsky, and I headed to city hall and the official who married us said all the right words, Terri and I answered, "I do," and we kissed. After the ceremony was over I hugged her and said, "I'll see you later tonight. I'm going to play golf with Bert."

And, like that, I was officially married.

That's what every young kid thinks about when

they first put on a uniform—is to play in the

Major Leagues and then, ultimately, play in

a World Series. To me, that was the ultimate,

winning in '86.

—GARY CARTER

5

CHASING THE PENNANT, 1986 NLCS: NEW YORK METS VS. HOUSTON ASTROS

In 1986 the pieces of our team fit together like a perfect puzzle.

We had two transcendent talents hitting their prime in Doc Gooden and Darryl Strawberry. Guys with that much physical talent and potential rarely come around—and we had a pair of them on the same team.

In the clubhouse we had the leadership of Keith Hernandez and Gary Carter. Keith played the most important role on the '86 team. He was smart and was the best first baseman I ever played with, or against, in my entire career. I would describe his style of play as "smooth." It was actually fun to watch him play, and anyone who knows me understands I don't say that about many players. Plus he was the best clutch hitter I ever shared the field with. He wasn't overly strong or powerful, but he could leave the yard when he had to. Whenever we needed a hit, he seemed to be able to get it.

Keith also knew how to utilize the rules of the game to his advantage. He wore one of those old batting helmets without the earflaps. This type of helmet allowed him to peek back at the catcher just enough to see where he was setting up, so Keith would know if the pitcher was going to try to pitch him inside or outside. This gave him a leg up, and technically he was not breaking any rule. Truth was that in 1983, MLB made it mandatory for a player to wear a helmet with at least one earflap. Only a player who was active in the major leagues before the earflap era began could use a flapless helmet if he wanted. Keith was one of those players. Keith stayed with the no-flap helmet—and who could blame him! He did anything he could to succeed and defined what a big-league player was to me.

Behind the plate, we had Gary Carter. The thing that Kid doesn't get remembered for enough is how tough he really was. Everyone knows Carter never met a camera he didn't like, and knows he enjoyed being in the spotlight, but behind that he was really a winning player, a guy you wanted to go to war with. He's been remembered as the final piece of the puzzle when he was traded to the Mets before '85. But he was different from a lot of the other wild personalities in the locker room, and he added a special dynamic. By the time he became a Met, the wear and tear of playing catcher every day for a decade was getting the better of him. And yet he was a clutch hitter and still hit cleanup for us despite playing through pain every day. What I'll say about Kid is that he was a different kind of leader on the team than Hernandez, who was more vocal. Carter led by example and really strapped it on every day. What he had to do to prepare himself for games went unnoticed a lot, because he never complained. I'd say he played injured most of the time, and, maybe most remarkably, he did it clean and wouldn't ever take anything. Even I tried to give him some amphetamines to give him a jolt, and he refused without hesitation. He was just that kind of guy, clean-cut all the way around. He didn't really party with the guys, didn't cheat on his wife, didn't lose focus on the game over the season. He was a man on and off the field, and I think maybe in '86 he knew he was running out of chances to play for a championship.

At third base we had Ray Knight, a real veteran player, and Howard Johnson, a truly great guy. Wally Backman, our second baseman, was a smart player; it's unbelievable he is not managing in the major leagues again. I see some of these bozos managing in the big leagues and think, *Why doesn't someone give Wally Backman a second chance to manage?*

◆

On the mound, we would go as far as the foursome of Doc, Ron, El Sid, and Bob would take us.

Doc was clearly the ace of the staff, and his talent was one of a kind. I don't even know how to accurately describe how good he was, since it's really hard to categorize or compare him to anyone else I had seen before.

Ron Darling was the number two starter. He was living proof that you could have a successful career without much stuff. What he lacked in talent he made up for with his preparation and knowledge of the opposing hitters. He wasn't overpowering, but he could throw three pitches for strikes. And that's what matters when you're in a pennant race. I wasn't close to Darling—but I wasn't alone in that respect; he wasn't close with many people. He has always treated me with respect, and I am happy to see him flourish in the booth as a baseball announcer.

◆

Overall, our pitching staff had lacked depth the season before—so our GM, Frank Cashen, remedied that big-time in '86. He made a trade with the Dodgers to bring in Sid Fernandez—a larger-than-life left-hander from Hawaii. He had weapons on the mound and threw gas. He loved to use his rising heater but kept batters guessing, since he wouldn't hesitate to throw the big hook.

I can remember one day at the start of spring training all the brass came down to watch Sid throw his first session of BP to the hitters. Guess who they threw in the fire first? Me, of course. Fuck, did you really think Keith Hernandez was going to volunteer?

So I have all the brass watching and I said to myself, *I'm gonna hang in there against him. I'm not bailing, man. No fear.* So I get in the box, and the first pitch Sid threw came right at me. Fast. I turned to get out of the way, but the ball hit me right in the chest at ninety-five miles an hour. Thump. I went down like a Navy SEAL sniper had shot me.

That was my first experience with El Sid, as we called him. He was a good guy; a gentle, kind, and quiet man when he wasn't beaning batters. And don't let his body fool you; he was a really good athlete. His "overweight" appearance was just the way his body was distributed. He wasn't fat at all. It wasn't fun to hit against him, so I was happy he was now on our side.

Another of Cashen's important off-season acquisitions was left-hander Bobby Ojeda. A veteran pitcher and a leader, Bob was one of the guys who showed us all how important teamwork was. He didn't throw hard, but he had location and a great changeup. He kept hitters off balance and he threw strikes. He would become a key part of our championship formula.

Rarely do you see a team make the playoffs that isn't in the top two or three statistically in pitching. Winning starts with the arms, but the truth is when a pitcher knows he's going to get some run support, he'll relax and pitch better. One has an impact on the other, in my experience.

From a chemistry standpoint, it didn't take long for things to get exciting. In spring training a much-publicized fight between Keith and Darryl broke out during our team photo. They were just fucking around initially, but it escalated into a good little scrap. The media loved it, but it wasn't really anything besides the fact that it was too early in the morning. If you ask any player, they will tell you that adding "early morning" to "spring training" doesn't equal "good manners," by the way. Spring training sucks.

But the fighting wasn't contained to just spring training. We had another classic fight in August while playing the Cincinnati Reds. Eric Davis came sliding into third, and Ray Knight tagged him hard. Eric was dumb enough to mouth something offensive to Ray, so Ray belted him right on the chin. Davis went down, and every player from both teams—except our left fielder George Foster—came running out to join the battle.

For most of '86 I played center field between Foster in left and

Darryl in right. Foster was a strange guy. Talk about a human Xanax. I am falling asleep just thinking about him. Between innings in the dugout or during pitching changes in the outfield, I tried to get him to open up out of sheer boredom. No dice. Talking to George Foster was like attempting to hold a conversation with a piece of furniture.

After the Cincinnati game, Foster told reporters he didn't come out to fight because he didn't want to set a bad example for children. But in my opinion, the real reason was that he was at the end of his career and was pouting because Davey wasn't playing him as much as he hoped. After that game Davey stopped playing him altogether. When Davey announced that Kevin Mitchell was going to be our new left fielder, Foster charged that the Mets were being racist.

The only problem with that story? Kevin Mitchell was black, too.

Kevin Mitchell, by the way, was a beast. People ask me all the time: "Who was the best pure athlete on the team?" It's an easy answer. Hands down it was Kevin. He was the most impressive physical specimen I ever played with. This guy never took drugs, didn't drink alcohol, and never took anything. He was all natural, a born athlete.

In spite of the drama, all the puzzle pieces fit. At the end of the day, we knew how to play together and Davey somehow got the most out of everyone. Each day we had fun winning together on the field and then even more fun drinking together every night. There was just this feeling or attitude that surrounded our team during the season that when opponents would come play us at Shea Stadium, you could sense that they didn't want any part of us. They just wanted to get out of there alive.

♦

The blend of tremendous talent and great team chemistry translated to 108 wins in 1986. We ran away with the division, winning by an astounding $21^1/_2$ games. In essence, we knew we would be playing for the National League pennant by Labor Day. Nonetheless, we would be facing a formidable foe in the Houston Astros.

Remember, '86 was pre-wild-card rounds, so the two division winners squared off for a best-of-seven series to determine the World Series representative. The Astros had home-field advantage for the series, with Games 1, 2, 6, and 7 scheduled for the Astrodome. We were supposed to have home-field advantage in the series, as they alternated every year between Eastern and Western division winners, regardless of regular-season records, from 1969 to 1993. However, as luck would have it, the Houston Oilers had a game scheduled against the Chicago Bears that week, which caused a scheduling conflict. Therefore, the Astros gained home-field advantage.

Moreover, they were led by eventual National League Cy Young Award winner Mike Scott, who was nearly unhittable that year. Scott featured a split-fingered fastball that literally dropped off the table. No doubt his effectiveness was enhanced by the fact that he scuffed the ball, which makes it drop dramatically. Regardless, the dude was flat-out filthy. We realized that getting a W against Scott would be difficult at best, so that put pressure on us to beat their other pitchers.

Game 1 featured a battle of the aces, with Doc facing Scott. Doc did not disappoint in his seven innings of work, yielding only a solo home run to Glenn Davis in the second. Unfortunately, that would be enough for the Astros, as Scott was his usual nasty self, tossing a five-hit, complete-game shutout, punctuated with 14 Ks.

In Game 2 we faced the legendary Nolan Ryan, who had been 12-8 with an ERA of 3.34 and 194 Ks that year, a mediocre season by his standards. An RBI double by Carter and a sacrifice fly by Straw put us up 2–0 in the fourth. Then Wally and Keith combined for 3 RBI in the fifth to give us a comfortable 5–0 lead. Bobby Ojeda scattered 10 hits in a complete-game 5–1 victory, which evened the series at one game apiece. Now we were going back home for Games 3, 4, and 5. Game 3 was a pivotal game in that there was a possibility that Scott could go in Game 4, on three days' rest.

The importance of Game 3 was evident to our fans. The atmosphere at Shea Stadium was electric, with 55,052 fans providing an energy that I had never experienced before. Even though it was only Game 3, it felt more like Game 7. The Astros did their best to take the crowd out of it by scoring two runs in each of the first two innings off Ron Darling. They entered the bottom of the sixth with a 4–0 lead behind Bob Knepper. The energy level in the stadium had decreased substantially. We needed to do something, and soon. Finally we got to Knepper, scoring four runs in the bottom of the sixth, capped off by Straw's three-run blast, which provided the crowd with a supersonic infusion of energy.

Unfazed, the Astros scratched out an unearned run off Rick Aguilera in the seventh, set up by a Ray Knight throwing error. It would be our only error of the series. They took that 5–4 lead into the bottom of the ninth.

With the Astros' closer, Dave Smith, on the mound, the inning started with a controversial play. Wally Backman laid down a bunt and avoided the tag of Astros first baseman Glenn Davis for a single. Houston's manager, Hal Lanier, argued that Backman had run out of the baseline, but first base umpire Dutch Rennert called him safe. He took second on a passed ball and remained there when Danny Heep flew out to center. What happened next would change my life forever.

I was twenty-three years old, playing in my first major league playoff series. I had maintained a high level of confidence throughout the season, always telling myself that all I needed was an opportunity, and I would deliver. This was the opportunity I had been waiting for, and it was time to deliver.

I stepped up to the plate, looking to hit a single to drive Wally in and tie the game. That's what the situation dictated; my job was to drive the run home and swing the momentum back in our direction. I was 0 for 1 with a strikeout on the day, but I felt good in the box. I had a good cut on Smith's first pitch but fouled it back. Smith was a righty, and I was able to see the ball come out of his hand pretty well.

The second pitch was a hanging forkball. As soon as it left his hand, I knew I could drive it for more than a single. And drive it I did. Everything happened in a split second, but I can still remember how surreal it felt as I was running to first, watching the ball slowly drift toward the right field wall. With a helping hand from the baseball gods, the ball landed in the bullpen for a two-run game-winning homer.

In a matter of seconds, I went from running, to jumping, to screaming, to losing my mind. As I circled the bases, I was so caught up in the moment that I could actually feel the adrenaline surging through my body. The noise was deafening, but I couldn't hear it. Upon touching home plate, I was mobbed by my teammates, who all poured out of the dugout. To this day I can't tell you exactly what I saw, what I heard, or what I felt. I *can* tell you that the high I experienced that day has never been duplicated, even with drugs.

The last time I had hit a walk-off home run was playing Strat-O-Matic baseball. From the time I was a little kid, I'd always dreamed of hitting a homer to win the game. Now that I had done it, the feeling was better than I'd ever imagined. With one swing of the bat, we escaped a devastating loss and took a 2-1 lead in the series. A hanging forkball, and I nailed it!

Later that night I went out to dinner with Terri. We went to the legendary Brooklyn steak house Peter Luger's. I was still on a high, even though it had been a few hours since the game, but I needed to just sit down and get something to eat.

The moment we entered the restaurant, everyone gave me a standing ovation. I was totally caught off guard. It was an incredible scene.

As special as this game and moment were for me at the time, I never imagined that Mets fans would talk about my home run for so many years to come. Whenever fans have come up to tell me about their memories of that game, I'm brought back to that moment and reminded how locked in I was.

◆

Great game. Incredible moment. But the series was far from over. We still needed two more wins to get to the World

Series. As we suspected, Scott came back on three days' rest to pitch Game 4 at Shea.

Sid gave up two homers in six innings, which accounted for the Astros' three runs. Scott pitched a complete-game three-hitter, with the only blemish being a solo shot by Straw. So we went to Game 5, the last game at home, tied 2-2 in the series. Needless to say, Game 5 was a must-win for us.

Game 5 was originally scheduled for Monday, October 13, 1986. It was postponed because of rain. The game was rescheduled for a one-thirty start on Tuesday, October 14, 1986. This allowed the Astros to start Nolan Ryan again on normal rest. We had Doc on the mound, and neither pitcher disappointed. The Astros nicked Doc for a run in the top of the fifth, but Straw hit a bomb, our first hit, in the bottom of the fifth to tie it at 1–1. The game remained 1–1 until the bottom of the twelfth, when Backman got an infield single off Charlie Kerfeld with one out. He advanced to second on an errant pickoff throw by Kerfeld. Understandably, Kerfeld walked Hernandez intentionally to get to Gary Carter, who was mired in a 1-for-21 slump in the series. The move backfired, as Carter stroked a single to center to drive home Backman with the winning run. Despite getting only four hits in twelve innings, we were going back to Houston, up 3-2 in the series. Carter delivered in the clutch, and our closer, Jesse Orosco, earned his second victory of the series.

Even though we had a 3-2 series lead, we approached Game 6 as though it was Game 7, because we knew Scott would be on the hill for Game 7. Arguably, Game 6 would become one of the most exciting games in postseason baseball history.

The Astros staked starter Bob Knepper to a 3–0 lead in the first inning with RBIs from Phil Garner, Glenn Davis, and Jose Cruz. Our starter, Bobby Ojeda, did not surrender any runs after that, but we were unable to dent Knepper. Aguilera gave us three innings of shutout relief, but we entered the ninth still down 3–0. We were not exactly brimming with confidence in the dugout, with the reality of having to face Scott in Game 7. Moreover, I was pissed, because even though Knepper was a lefty, I thought I should have started. After all, I had hit the walk-off homer to win Game 3. Knepper was throwing his typical pus, but we couldn't do anything with it. Obviously, Davey didn't share my thoughts. Nonetheless, prior to the start of the ninth, Davey walked down to where I was sitting on the bench.

"Lenny, get ready. You're leading off the ninth," was all he said.

"You want to win, huh?" I replied. "It's about time you put me in the fucking game."

I got in the box and something amazing happened—again. Sometimes it's impossible to predict what is going to happen in sports.

And this was about to become another example of that.

Knepper had me down 1-2. I hit the fourth pitch decently to right center, but the Astrodome was a big yard that gobbled up fly balls. I could see Billy Hatcher and Kevin Bass converging on it. They both looked at each other hesitantly, and then . . . they didn't get to it. It was almost like they thought it was a grenade. Neither of them got any leather on the ball. It took a bounce off the wall, and I raced around to third base.

And that started everything.

Mookie hit a weird humpback liner to Billy Doran, the kind the Houston second baseman caught ninety-nine times out of a hundred. But on this ball he mistimed his jump, and I scored to make it 3–1. With Mookie on first, Keith then doubled to send him home to make the score 3–2. Houston's closer, Dave

Smith, was ordered to walk Gary and Straw intentionally, and Ray Knight hit a sacrifice fly to tie the game. We had come back from the dead. Those mystical baseball gods were smiling at us.

I stayed in the game on a double switch and played center. Six innings passed until finally we ended up scoring three runs in the sixteenth and taking a 7–4 lead after I drove in Wally, who had walked. It turned out we needed all three of those runs, because the Astros stormed back to score two in the bottom of the sixteenth. With two outs and the tying run in scoring position, Jesse Orosco struck out Kevin Bass to end the game and send us to the World Series against Boston.

For that Houston series, the Mets as a team hit .189 with three home runs. My personal stats: I hit .304 with a double, triple, and a home run. I led the team in batting average, on-base percentage, slugging percentage, and OPS.

Some might argue I did enough to be the MVP of that series, but the award went to Scott. It is extremely unusual to give the MVP to a member of the losing team. Although he only pitched two games in the series, Scott was incredibly impressive: two complete-game victories, 8 hits, and an ERA of 0.50, yielding only 1 run in 18 innings. Regardless, I was in the zone. I can only imagine what I may have done had Davey played me more. Most important, we were going to the World Series.

In 2011, MLB Network ranked Game 6 of the 1986 NLCS as the fifth-greatest game in the previous fifty years of postseason baseball.

As memorable as that series was against the Astros, the best was yet to come. Our performance in the 1986 World Series against the Boston Red Sox would become even more legendary. We were about to participate in a Fall Classic for the ages.

You don't win a World Series drinking milk.

—KEITH HERNANDEZ

6

1986 WORLD SERIES: NEW YORK METS VS. BOSTON RED SOX

After winning one of the most famous games in baseball history, we were on our way to the World Series.

Our opponent, the Boston Red Sox, had just defeated the California Angels, 4-3, in a tense seven-game struggle to win the ALCS. The BoSox had been literally one pitch away from elimination. Coupled with the fact that we would have home-field advantage in the World Series, we truly felt as though nobody could beat us. I was hoping Davey would play me more based on my performance in the NLCS.

Saturday, October 18, 1986, in the best sports city in the world, New York, would be the beginning of the greatest World Series in baseball history. In Game 1, we had Ron Darling on the mound with Boston countering with Bruce Hurst. A classic pitchers' duel ensued, with Darling yielding only an unearned run in the seventh inning, after an error by our second baseman, Tim Teufel. Hurst was even better, as he kept us at bay with his combination of gas, a nasty hook, and a forkball. He pitched eight shutout innings, allowing only four hits. Sox closer Calvin Schiraldi came on in the ninth to seal the victory and earn a save. Although we were down 1-0 in the series, we still felt good knowing that Doc was starting Game 2.

On the mound for Boston was a young Roger Clemens, who was filthy and mean. Trust me, that guy was one bad motherfucker. He was an ultra-competitor. Forget the bullshit about Clemens and steroids. This was 1986, and he was already a gas-throwing stud. How is this dude not in the Hall of Fame?

Well, the anticipated pitchers' classic did not occur, as the Sox put up three runs in the third, and we came back with two in the bottom of the third. With the aid of dingers by Dave Henderson and Dwight Evans, the Sox took a 6–2 lead in the fifth, and Doc was gone. Despite the nice cushion, Clemens left in the bottom of the fifth with runners on the corners and one out. We had Kid and Straw coming up, but we were only able to plate one run. Boston scored three more times, and we lost 9–3.

Suddenly we were staring at a 2-0 series deficit, and to make matters worse we were going to Fenway for Games 3, 4, and 5. Not many teams climb out of that kind of hole. Needless to say, the odds were stacked against us.

Most pundits and all the other "experts" out there would have expected a closed-door players' meeting or an inspirational "pep talk" by Davey at that point. However, even though we were staring at an 0-2 hole, there was no Knute Rockne, no Rudy, not even the famous Belushi line, "What did we do when the Germans bombed Pearl Harbor?" No, we did nothing. We were the fucking New York Mets, the same crew who dominated the NL that year with 108 wins. We knew what we had to do, and we were surprisingly calm. We also weren't stupid. If we lost Game 3, it was *over*. As we traveled to Boston, I started to think that I needed to do something different to start Game 3 in order to swing the momentum back to our side.

Dennis "Oil Can" Boyd was on the hill for the Red Sox. We had pretty much been dominated by their pitchers in the first two games, so I thought it was important to put a crooked number on the board early. I actually told my wife before the game that I was going to try to go yard with one of Oil Can's garbage batting-practice fastballs in my first at-bat. While I would rarely look to hit a homer leading off the game—because it is very difficult—I knew a leadoff homer in Game 3 would silence the crowd and give us some much-needed momentum.

It was a Tuesday night in Boston, and the Red Sox fans were pumped, anticipating the end of their horrific, decades-long history of bad luck. I got into the box to start the game, and I just kept thinking to myself, *I am going to take this motherfucker deep.* I got the pitch I wanted and turned on it beautifully, lofting a fly ball deep to right. The fucker wrapped around the foul pole at Fenway for a homer that gave us the spark we needed to turn the series around. We dented Oil Can for three more runs in the first to put up that crooked number I knew would change things. Bobby Ojeda pitched seven innings, surrendering only one run, and Roger McDowell pitched the last two innings to earn the save. We claimed a 7–1 victory, and we were back in business.

I truly recognized the significance of my home run when I got back to the dugout and was greeted by Lee Mazzilli, who flat-out said, "That's going to win us the series." Maz was a key player for us, a wily veteran with a keen understanding of game situations and moments that only comes with years of experience. It meant a lot to me for a guy like Maz to say that in the moment. Remember, despite my cockiness, I was still just a twenty-three-year-old kid in my first big rodeo. Over the years, many others have told me that my leadoff homer in Game 3 was the turning point of the 1986 World Series. Who am I to disagree?

Nonetheless, we were still down 2-1 in the series. Game 4 featured Ron Darling versus Al Nipper for the Red Sox. The game was scoreless until the fourth, when Gary Carter deposited a two-run blast over the Green Monster in left, the first of his two dingers that day. Ray Knight drove in Straw, and we were up 3–0 in the fourth. The score remained 3–0 until the seventh, when I hit a two-run shot off Steve Crawford to give us a 5–0 lead. Ron Darling had a great outing, and we went on to win 6–2, evening the series at 2-2.

We felt good going into Game 5 with our ace, Doc Gooden, on the mound. Unfortunately, Doc struggled again, giving up four runs on nine hits in just four innings of work. Despite a terrific relief effort from El Sid, we were unable to get to Hurst, who was masterful again. Hurst scattered ten hits and gave up two runs in a complete-game performance. So we were down 3-2 in the series, but we were going back home to Shea for Game 6, and hopefully Game 7.

In the face of elimination, we still felt confident about our position: win two games at home, and we would be World Series champs. We knew we could do it. No one could have predicted that Game 6 would become one of the greatest games in the history of the World Series. While everyone remembers what happened at the end of the tenth inning, most people forget the series of events that sent the game into extra innings. I always talk about "winning baseball," doing things that only true students of the game understand and appreciate. This game was the epitome of a team truly working together, sacrificing personal stats in order to achieve victory.

Game 6 matched Clemens versus Ojeda. Boston got single runs in the first and second to take an early 2–0 lead. We tied it up with two runs in the bottom of the fifth. An error by Ray Knight led to an unearned run for the Sox in the seventh. In the top of the eighth, Boston manager John McNamara pinch-hit for Clemens with rookie Mike Greenwell, a move that was later questioned by some. Regardless, the Sox failed to score, and Boston's closer, Calvin Schiraldi, was summoned to try to nail down a two-inning save that would give the Red Sox the World Series championship.

Maz, who was pinch-hitting for Jesse Orosco, greeted Schiraldi with a single to start the eighth. I bunted to sacrifice Maz to second, but I was able to reach first on the play as well. Wally laid down a sacrifice bunt, advancing Maz and me to second and third with one out. Schiraldi walked Keith intentionally to set up a force at any base and a potential double play. Carter came up and worked a 3-0 count. Given the green light, Kid lifted the next offering to left for a sacrifice fly, which tied the game at 3–3. The only hit in this sequence was the leadoff single by Maz. We manufactured the run, and it was a beautiful thing.

In the bottom of the ninth, Knight worked a walk off Schiraldi to lead off the inning. Mookie bunted, and catcher Rich Gedman threw to second in an attempt to cut down the lead runner. The throw sailed wide, and we had first and second with nobody out. HoJo struck out as a pinch hitter, and Maz, and then I, flied out to end the inning, leaving Ray stranded in scoring position. We had blown a golden opportunity to put up a W.

In the tenth, Boston stormed back and went up 5–3 on a blast by Dave Henderson and an RBI single by Marty Barrett. Mc-Namara allowed Schiraldi to hit for himself in the top of the tenth, so he was on the mound for his third inning, in the bottom of the tenth. While it is almost unheard of today for a closer to go two innings, let alone three, this was not unusual for Schiraldi. In fact, in 1986 he averaged more than two innings in his 51 appearances.

In the bottom of the tenth inning, Wally and Keith both flied out. Keith went straight to the clubhouse without saying a word after his long fly ball was caught for the second out of the inning. I was sitting on the bench, next to Howard Johnson. We both were dumbfounded and pissed. "I can't believe we're going to lose the World Series," I said to Howard. "I just can't fucking believe it." I slouched farther down on the bench, fuming. The entire bench was silent and in a state of disbelief.

I looked across the field into the Red Sox dugout. I swear on everything I love that I could see some guys down the steps and in the tunnel drinking champagne, and for a pretty good reason. There were two outs and nobody on. And they were up by two runs. What were the odds of our coming back from that? I don't even know if there are odds for that. Adding insult to injury, the Diamond Vision scoreboard at Shea actually posted the message CONGRATULATIONS BOSTON RED SOX. They were a strike away, but they hadn't won yet! (Truthfully, I wish I was that optimistic at the time, but I was like everyone else and thought it was too big a hole to get out of at that point.)

Gary Carter stepped into the box to face Schiraldi. Then, suddenly, a series of events unfolded that is now etched in the minds of baseball fans everywhere. Gary singled to center. Davey wanted Kevin Mitchell to pinch-hit for the pitcher's spot, but Kevin was on the phone booking his flight home when he got the call to get in the game. He scrambled and put the phone down, went up to the plate, and singled. Ray Knight had two strikes on him when he singled to drive in Gary and move Kevin to third.

It was 5–4 now. One run down and two outs in the bottom of the tenth inning. Mookie Wilson was up next.

Red Sox manager John McNamara responded by bringing in Bob "Steamer" Stanley to pitch. Mookie kept fouling off pitches until Stanley threw a wild pitch that got past the catcher. Kevin scored as Ray raced to second. Tie game. Toilet paper came streaming down from the delirious Shea stands.

Three pitches later, on the tenth pitch of his brilliant at-bat, Mookie hit his famous ground ball toward Billy Buckner at first. I noticed that Buckner seemed to have trouble bending over as the ball hopped over first base and went bouncing through his legs—*through his fucking legs.* Before we knew it, the ball was rolling onto the outfield grass, and we were celebrating at home plate.

Pandemonium! The entire stadium went crazy.

"What was it like when you saw the ball roll through Buckner's legs?" people ask me.

Freaky? Crazy?

Look up the word *unbelievable.* It's a simple, common word. I don't know any other description for it. Unbelievable.

◆

There are a few things that people don't realize about that Game 6. John McNamara, the Red Sox manager, may have let his feelings get involved, leaving Buckner out on the field even though he had gimpy ankles. He had subbed defensive replacement Dave Stapleton for him during the late innings in games all year, including Games 1, 2, and 5 of the World Series—every game that Boston had won. Buckner was an offensive player, and this play is just another example of how a manager not making the right decision or pushing the wrong button can affect the outcome of a game. McNamara wanted to give Buckner the chance to be on the field when they won, and he used his heart instead of his brain. That said, the game was already tied when this happened—and frankly you could argue that Bob Stanley's wild pitch was just as big a blunder as Buckner's error. If Buckner had fielded the ball cleanly and beat Mookie to the bag in a foot race (Stanley didn't leave the mound to cover first base), then we would have gone on to the eleventh inning. We were home, and we had the momentum, and truthfully I don't think we were losing that game no matter what. Long-suffering Boston fans treated Buckner as if that play could have ended the World Series and that he was solely responsible for that breakdown.

Let's not forget that Billy Buckner had an outstanding twenty-two-year major league run, batting .289 for his career. Unequivocally, certain moments, particularly when they occur on a national stage, are indelibly etched in the minds of those who view them. Hence, for many, Buckner will be remembered only for his blunder in the World Series.

Unfortunately, that is the world in which we live. Fair or not, Buckner is infamous, for his name will forever be synonymous with all-time blunders.

After our unbelievable victory in Game 6, it was a foregone conclusion that we were going to win Game 7 and the World

Series. Honestly, there wasn't a single thought that we were going to lose that game. As far as we were concerned, after the ball went through Buckner's legs, giving us Game 6, the World Series was over. Obviously, the reality was the series was not over; it was tied at three with one more game to play.

Looking back, I barely remember anything that played out in Game 7. It's all a blur. We didn't play Game 7 the next night on October 26, as it rained all night. Pretty early they announced Game 7 would be played Monday night, on the 27th. This was big for Boston, as they had been planning on sending Oil Can Boyd at us on Sunday night, but with the extra day, McNamara decided to throw Bruce Hurst back at us again. Hurst was 2-0 after throwing eight shutout innings in Game 1 and a complete game against us in Game 5. He was the front-runner to win the series MVP. It also meant that with the lefty throwing against us, Davey would decide not to start me in Game 7 in favor of switch-hitting Mookie Wilson.

I understand the lefty-righty philosophy. But the thing is, in baseball sometimes you are better off just playing your best players. I loved that team and my teammates, but anytime I sat that year I was pissed off. But this one stung a little more. I loved playing when the stakes were high—in fact I got off on it! And if you look back now, ask anyone to dispute the fact that not too many players have played at the level that I rose to, or accomplished the things I did in the postseason over my career. Davey should have been able to realize it in the moment—that was his fucking job. But as I have mentioned before, he was a lucky manager. He was drunk every night and frequently hungover just enough the next day to not always know what was going on. That, and he was probably the worst communicator I've ever been associated with in baseball, and that includes a lot of fucking people! Other than all that, Davey was great. Ha!

Boston jumped on an ineffective Darling in the second when Dwight Evans and Rich Gedman went yard, back to back. Wade Boggs drove in Dave Henderson, and the Sox had an early 3–0 lead. Darling was pulled after three and two-thirds innings. Enter El Sid to stabilize the ship.

Hurst was cruising along, continuing his mastery over us, hurling a one-hitter, as we came to bat in the bottom of the sixth. With one out, Maz pinch-hit and stroked a single. Mookie followed with a hit, and Tim Teufel walked to load the bases. Finally, Hurst was showing signs of being human. Hernandez singled in Maz and Mookie, bringing Gary Carter to the plate. Carter hit a line drive to right that Dwight Evans, a superb right fielder, was unable to come up with despite diving. Wally, who was pinch-running for Teufel, scored the tying run easily, but Keith, who got a late jump because he had to wait to see if Evans made the catch, was gunned. Hurst then retired Straw to end the threat.

Meanwhile, El Sid had come on in the fourth with two outs and held the Sox scoreless for three and one-third innings. Most people have no clue how difficult it is for a starter to come in and provide quality middle relief in the cauldron of the postseason. El Sid's contribution cannot be overemphasized!

Hurst was scheduled to lead off the seventh against Roger Mc-Dowell, who was called upon to replace El Sid. McNamara sent up Tony Armas to pinch-hit, thereby ending Hurst's night. On the surface, this seems like a relatively innocuous move. However, there is a backstory that complicates the move. Oil Can Boyd, who was bypassed in favor of Hurst as the Game 7 starter after the postponement due to rain, was not happy with McNamara's decision not to hand him the ball for Game 7. Oil Can disappeared into the club-house, where he medicated his bruised psyche with alcohol. Pitching coach Bill Fischer eventually found Oil Can in a highly intoxicated state, rendering him unavailable to pitch in relief that night.

With a short bullpen and Oil Can unavailable, McNamara opted for Schiraldi, his closer, who was coming off his Game 6 outing, where he pitched two and two-thirds innings. Ray Knight welcomed Schiraldi to the mound by going yard to lead off the seventh, giving us a 4–3 lead. I pinch-hit for Kevin Mitchell and got on with a single. I went to second on a wild pitch and scored the fifth run when Rafael Santana poked an RBI single to right. Joe Sambito came in and walked Wilson and Wally to load the bases for Keith, who had a sacrifice to center, plating the sixth run. Armed with a 6–3 lead, we could actually start to taste the championship.

However, the Red Sox were not dead yet. They entered the eighth having only a lone base runner since the third. Nonethe-less, Buckner and Rice had back-to-back singles, followed by a two-run double from Evans that made it 6–5. Davey summoned Orosco from the pen to squelch the rally. Jesse got Gedman on a lineout and struck out the dangerous Dave Henderson. He then got pinch hitter Don Baylor to ground out, thereby ending the inning with Evans stranded in scoring position.

Al Nipper, the Game 4 starter and loser, came on in the bottom of the eighth for the Sox. Straw went yard to lead off, giving us a 7–5 lead. Knight followed with a single and advanced to second on my groundout. Nipper walked Santana intentionally, knowing Davey was not going to pull Orosco. The strategy backfired when Jesse got a base hit and drove in Ray Knight.

Jesse was facing the top of the order in the ninth. Unlike virtu-ally every other aspect of the postseason, the ninth was completely uneventful. Foul popout. Routine groundout to second, and we were one out away. Marty Barrett was the batter; Jesse worked the count to 2-2. Jesse delivers. Barrett swings and misses. Strike three. Jesse throws his glove high into the air and drops to his knees as Gary Carter races to the mound to hug our closer, with the rest of the team in hot pursuit. Cue Queen: *We Are the Champions!* The New York Mets, 1986 World Series champions.

After the series was over, the city threw a parade for us. The celebration was insane even by New York standards. It felt like every single person in the city, including Yankees fans, came out to cheer our achievement. It's an awesome feeling when you have an entire city—and not just any city, but the greatest city in the world—behind you. Being so young, I felt tremendously privileged to be part of this team and this victory. I know this will come as a shock to most, but I was not into wild celebrations at this point in my life. Other than a little drinking here and there, I didn't even know what drugs looked like then. Steroids were not on the radar yet. I know it's hard to believe, but I would more than make up for my innocence when I played for the Phillies.

Although I would experience the World Series stage again in 1993, 1986 was the only time in my career that I was part of a team that won it. I am truly blessed to have experienced that, as many players are deprived of that incredible feeling. In the 1986 World Series, I batted .296 with 8 hits, 4 runs scored, 2 homers, and 3 RBI. Undeniably, I would have liked to have played more, but I feel as though I made a valuable contribution that had a direct impact on helping the Mets win the 1986 World Series.

Most important, I was a contributing member of the World Series championship team. That was the best feeling in the world, and undoubtedly the high point of my playing career.

A conversation with Dykstra, especially one that stretches for more than two hours, is a rare and peculiar experience. He is foul-mouthed and funny, juvenile and intelligent, intense and prone to mumbling.

—RICHARD SANDOMIR, *NEW YORK TIMES*

7

REDNECKS & RIFLES

I feel like I have spent half my life—shit, *all* my life—hunting for something. Hunting to succeed as a professional ballplayer, hunting for pussy, hunting for a new kind of high, you name it. But the one thing I never found myself hunting for was *animals.* The kind of hunting one does with a gun, running around in the woods and shooting bullets at things with an actual heartbeat.

That all changed in 1987, when the Mets obtained outfielder Kevin McReynolds in a deal with the San Diego Padres. Kevin and I quickly became very tight. Kevin was an honest-to-God redneck from Arkansas—and also happened to be one of the most talented players I'd ever seen on the field. The only problem with Kevin was that he hated baseball. Fucking hated it. All he wanted to do was be on his duck farm and in that hunting lodge of his in Arkansas. So, during the off-season, he talked me into going down to the Deep South to experience what he considered *real living.*

I met him and some other guys there, and the second I arrived, I realized that Kevin had big plans for us to go deer hunting together. Remember, I grew up in Southern California, and I'd never shot a gun before in my entire life, let alone shot a living, breathing animal.

But Kevin wouldn't take no for an answer.

The morning of the hunt, Kevin and his hillbilly buddies woke me when it was still dark outside and the sun was nowhere to be seen. I'm talking about four fucking A.M. The redneck crew were all wearing camouflage costumes to blend into the trees and leaves and shit. Against my better judgment—yeah, I *do* have better judgment on occasion—I found myself walking into the pitch-black woods, clutching a rifle and freezing my balls off. I felt like I was in a scene from *Deliverance,* but everyone else seemed to be loving every second of it.

"How exactly does this work?" I asked.

"You see a deer, you shoot it," Kevin said, like it was as easy as buttering a slice of toast.

"Let me ask you something, Kevin," I said. "There are five other gun-carrying motherfuckers with us. I'm not too smart, but I know that bullets travel and they travel fast. So how do I know one of those other motherfuckers isn't going to shoot and miss, and kill me instead?"

McReynolds ignored my question and stopped under a tall tree that had a wooden ladder going up the side of it.

"Climb up the ladder and stay good and quiet," he said.

"Why do you want me to climb a goddamn tree?" I asked.

"Because that's where you wait for the deer to come along. It's a deer stand."

"You want me to sit in a fucking tree by myself with a gun that I have no idea how to use? And then what? How long do I wait there? Do we set our clocks? Is there a time limit? I'm not going to sit in this fucking tree freezing my ass off for very long, I'm telling you that."

The joke was on me because I sat up in that stupid tree for hours, and when my patience finally ran out, I decided to climb down and find my way back to the hunting lodge. As soon as I got back to the ground, I heard a rustling sound coming from the woods, and I turned to fucking rail into Kevin, but it wasn't Kevin. Not even close. It was a goddamn black bear. That fucker could have weighed eight hundred pounds for all I knew, but I didn't waste any time hauling my ass right back up that ladder, where I stayed put for a few more hours.

In the end, McReynolds and his redneck friends had to come and get me back down out of that tree. A couple of them had shot a few deer, and they dragged those poor dead animals back to the lodge. You should have seen all the work it took to gut them out. It was goddamn disgusting.

I thought, *This is backwards as shit*. Maybe it's me, but I like to work smarter instead of harder. See, in civilization, we have a fucking place called a *grocery store*. And it has a section called the meat department. Choose what type of meat, and what cut of meat, you like. Buy it. Cook it. Eat it. Simple.

That was the beginning and end of my hunting career—for animals. Of course, the true hunt never ends. It's always been about the thrill of the kill. Different kind of market. Same selection process.

There are three types of baseball players: those who make it happen, those who watch it happen, and those who wonder what happened.

—TOMMY LASORDA

8

1988 NLCS: NEW YORK METS VS. LOS ANGELES DODGERS

In 1988 we steamrolled over the rest of the National League East, finishing with a 100-60 record and beating the second-place Pirates by fifteen games. We should have won our second World Series in three years.

On the contrary, 1988 would mark the beginning of what turned out to be a long, miserable eleven-year drought, before the great fans of the New York Metropolitans would watch their team play in October again.

In the end, one could make a strong argument that Davey Johnson was an overrated and underachieving manager. He built his reputation by winning only one World Series, which in reality ought to have been two or three.

Just in case any of you don't remember, because I sure as fuck do, let me take you back in time. We were three outs away from winning Game 4 of the National League Championship Series and taking a commanding 3-1 lead over the Dodgers, which would have all but eliminated them, as we were too good of a team in 1988. The reality of the situation is that a 3-1 lead would have simply been too much for the Dodgers to overcome.

Doc battled his ass off in Game 4; he was solid but not masterful. Still, it was good enough to give us a 4–2 lead heading into the ninth. He had already thrown 117 pitches after 8 innings of work. For the season, Doc had 255⅓ innings of wear and tear on his arm. It was obvious that Doc was tired. After all, he is human.

Instead of having our closer, Randy Myers, who was fucking lights out that year, not to mention available, fresh, and cock-strong, close out the ninth, Davey, for whatever reason, decided to let Doc start the ninth. That was fuckup number one. Fuckup number two was too much for the baseball gods to take, so they made us *all* pay, and pay we did, in a big fucking way.

After Doc walked John Shelby, a player who owned a career .281 on-base percentage, to lead off the ninth, with the left-hand-hitting catcher Mike Scioscia up next, we were all looking in the dugout, waiting for Davey to make the change. It was Baseball 101. Instead, Davey failed us as players; he failed you, the fans; he failed the people who put their faith in him—the New York Mets organization—and ultimately, he failed himself.

We aren't talking about just another baseball game. Far from it. The stakes were extremely high. The company paid Davey a lot of money to make the right decisions when it mattered most. Millions of fans lived and died with the team. The players worked their asses off for months—years, really—to get to this stage. Unfortunately, on Sunday, October 9, 1988, in front of 54,014 fans, Davey failed miserably at his job.

Here are the four basic steps that Davey should have followed if he was doing his job in the ninth inning of Game 4 of the 1988 NLCS:

Step 1: Davey walks to the mound, tells Doc, "great job." Doc hands Davey the ball. Doc walks back to the dugout and the fans greet him with a standing ovation.

Step 2: Davey signals to the umpire that he wants the lefty, our closer, Randy Myers.

Step 3: Davey hands Randy the ball, then Randy performs his job like he did all season long, closing out the ninth to preserve the win. The Dodgers would never have experienced their Hollywood fairy-tale ending.

Step 4: We win, shake each other's hands, and head back into the clubhouse to enjoy cold ones, knowing we are now one game away from returning to the World Series.

◆

Back to reality. We were all wondering what the fuck Davey was doing. Our closer, Randy Myers, one of the most dominant closers in baseball at that time, was waiting by the bullpen door to come in and close out the ninth, which would have all but buried the Dodgers and left them for dead. But that door never opened—until it was too late.

We ended up losing in the twelfth, when Kirk Gibson hit a home run off Roger McDowell. Instead of going up 3-1, the series was now at 2-2.

◆

It would come down to Game 7 to determine which team would represent the National League in the 1988 World Series. Unfortunately, our skipper made another monumental mistake in Game 7 at Dodger Stadium.

Davey's decision to not start Doc Gooden—clearly our best pitcher that year—was another clusterfuck move. To make matters worse, Davey announced that Doc would be available out of the bullpen. *WTF?* If he was available out of the bullpen, he should have gotten the ball to start Game 7. For the record, Doc pitched three innings in Game 7, and gave up one hit.

Davey wasn't done yet. To add more fuel to the fire, he gave some good pregame locker room bulletin board material to the Dodgers, when he actually went on the record and suggested to the media that starting Orel Hershiser on short rest was a mistake: "There's no telling what kind of condition The Bionic Man will be in. I was amazed he was throwing [in the bullpen in Game 5]. He's going to have to be Superman. I don't expect him to have much stuff."

Davey must have been "oiled up" to tell the press something that stupid; but that wouldn't have been anything new; he and Jack (as in Daniel's) had become close personal friends.

Hershiser was told of these comments and responded, "Tell him to grab a bat."

Darling would start Game 7 and got knocked out early after giving up six runs in the first two innings. After the game was out of reach, Davey brought in Doc Gooden, who should have started the game. It didn't matter, though; the damage had already been done. We were down 6–0 after two innings, and that's how it would end up. Hershiser was lights out, and would go on to lead the Dodgers to the World Series title, while we were sent home dazed and confused. You have to remember, we dominated the Dodgers during the regular season, winning ten out of eleven times and outscoring them 49–18. But there were just too many wrong buttons pushed by the manager in the short series, which we were unable to overcome this time around. The National League pennant should have been ours, but the man in charge, Davey Johnson, failed us again.

It's hard for the public to grasp the long-term effect that Davey's failure to do his job on October 9, 1988, would have on millions of people in years to come.

It turns out the baseball gods weren't going to let Davey off the hook so easy.

This wasn't just another game, far from it. This was one of the most important games in Mets history. Think about it. Since our inception in 1962, we, the New York Mets, had made it to the World Series just three times. This was a game that could have made that *four* times.

Davey lost the game before it started. When the Dodgers learned that Doc wasn't going to start Game 7, it was like a shot of adrenaline for them. This is nothing against Ron Darling. Ron had a great year for us, but Doc Gooden was one of the best pitchers in baseball. There was no logical reason for Davey's decision, especially in a business where confidence plays such a huge role. Anyone who understands baseball knows Davey made another disastrous decision that ultimately led to the Dodgers winning the National League pennant. Moreover, Davey single-handedly set off a time bomb that would dismantle the organization for years to come.

Unfortunately for the great fans of New York, and for the Mets organization, Davey continued to make one bad decision after another. It was almost like he was trying to sabotage the team.

For some odd reason, at that time Davey Johnson was enamored with Gregg Jefferies, a rookie who had come up late in 1988. It didn't take the players long to figure out Gregg Jefferies was a losing player, not to mention a whiny little bitch. I am quite certain he set a record for being the most disliked player in the clubhouse—*after two days!* I'm serious. This guy had no concept of what being a "team player" meant. He was so clueless that he didn't even try to hide it. The only person who didn't figure him out from jump street was Davey. He had to be "deep in the sauce" to miss it. It was so bad you would have thought that Jefferies had naked pictures of Davey in a compromising act.

Jefferies didn't bring a whole lot to the party. Yes, Jefferies was a switch-hitter, but he didn't have any real home-run power and was only an average runner, not to mention he was definitely allergic to leather. He even made a key error in the '88 playoffs against the Dodgers. But for some reason, Davey kept trying to accommodate this little crybaby. Jefferies failed miserably at second; then they moved him to third base, with the same results, all bad.

Gregg Jefferies was a real bizarre guy. He would spend hours rubbing his bats with some special concoction and specifically requested that they be stored separately from the rest of the team's bats so they didn't chip. When things went bad for the Mets in '91, some of the players sounded off to the media about Jefferies, and he responded by writing a letter to WFAN, the New York local sports radio station. He actually wrote an open letter to the public, asking that it be read on the air, whining like a little pussy about his teammates. He asked them to stop complaining about him to the media and pleaded with the fans for love and support as well. The savvy Mets fans saw right through this fucking guy. Essentially, Jefferies was the poster child for those disastrous years, when the Mets began sliding downhill. After establishing himself as a joke on and off the field, he ensured that 1991 would be his last season with the Mets. Ownership couldn't take it anymore and traded him to Kansas City along with Kevin McReynolds, in a deal that brought back the aging Bret Saberhagen, whose most memorable moment as a Met might have been when he sprayed bleach on members of the media in the locker room when they were interviewing Gooden after a game.

After 1989, the Mets fans saw what was happening, and they were pissed. The Mets had just two position players in their starting lineup in 1990 (Straw and HoJo) who had been there in '86. The bad personnel decisions, spearheaded by Davey, piled up, and unfortunately the team would continue to spiral downward into irrelevance, where they would remain until they traded for Mike Piazza late in 1998.

The bottom line: if you take the time to evaluate Davey Johnson's career as a manager, the only conclusion one can come to is that he was an overrated and underachieving manager. That's just the cold hard truth.

Don't be afraid to give up the good to go for

the great.

—JOHN D. ROCKEFELLER

9

PLAY ME OR TRADE ME

When the 1989 season began, it was obvious that Davey was going to continue to platoon Mookie and me, so I decided it was time to move on. In order to get paid real money, you have to be an everyday player. Platoon players, utility players, and bench players, while essential components of a winning team, don't get paid the real money. I realized that the window of opportunity for me to make some serious cash would not stay open much longer.

I had no doubt that I was an everyday player; however, I was never given the opportunity to prove it with the Mets. In fact, I told anyone who would listen to me that I could hit lefties better than righties. My base knock that saved us from losing the World Series to the Red Sox in Game 6 was against a lefty. Unfortunately for me, Davey was committed to platooning, and he was not about to change.

So I began to let Davey know how dissatisfied I was, gently at first, but more and more forcefully as the days and weeks went by.

On days I was not in the lineup, I would say to Davey, "Fuck this. Trade me." In time, I was hammering Davey and the organization on a daily basis to trade me.

◆

The Mets were playing the Phillies in Veterans Stadium on June 18, 1989, a park in which I loved to hit. I was three for three in the sixth inning when Davey came over to me in the dugout and declared, "Lenny, that's enough."

"What the fuck are you talking about?" I said. "I'm going to get five hits today."

"No, that's enough," he said.

Davey and I got into it, but he didn't back down, and he took me out of the game. I stormed off to the clubhouse.

After the game ended, I felt a tap on my shoulder.

"Davey wants to see you in his office."

I walked over to his office, where I saw Davey sitting at his desk accompanied by Joe McIlvaine. I was not exactly sure what to expect.

"We want to thank you for your services," said Joe. "You helped us win a World Series, and you've been great, but we just traded you to the Philadelphia Phillies. Thank you, and good luck."

"Wait a second," I said. "You just said the Phillies. That's the other dugout. That's the team I just finished beating the shit out of today. Do I walk over there? Do I meet them at home plate? What do I do?"

"Their general manager is coming to get you," Joe said.

And that was it. I was no longer a New York Met.

Pain is temporary. It may last a minute, or an hour, or a day, or a year, but eventually it will subside and something else will take its place. If I quit, however, it lasts forever.

—LANCE ARMSTRONG

10

A SHOT IN THE BUTT

U pon my trade from the Mets to the Phillies in mid-June 1989, I got exactly what I had asked for: an opportunity to play every day. As the season moved into August, I came to the stark realization that while my heart and head were ready for everyday status, my body was an unwilling participant. The daily physical grind was taking a toll on me. Davey platooned me in part because he didn't think I could hold up for an entire season, and as much as I hated to admit it, I was beginning to think maybe he was right. Once August rolled around, my bat started to feel like a telephone pole, and my numbers started to decline.

Obviously, I didn't forget how to hit. I just wasn't physically capable of performing at the same level for a full season. I needed to get stronger; my weight had dropped from 160 to 150 pounds. I took more amphetamines, hoping they would give me the jolt I needed to finish the year. On the contrary, they caused me to lose more weight that I couldn't afford to lose, which only served to sap my strength even further. By the end of the season, I was physically spent, and it was evident in my performance.

Despite my abysmal performance at the end of the '89 season, the Phillies' GM, Lee Thomas, assured me that I was still going to be his everyday guy the following season. "You have all of 1990 to prove to us that you can be the guy," he said.

What he was actually saying was, 1990 will determine whether you are a millionaire or taking orders from some Bozo.

I had the opportunity I coveted, but I didn't have all the tools I needed to cash in. Physically, I knew I was not built to withstand the rigors of playing every day for a full 162-game season. Moreover, I was certain the Phillies were now thinking maybe the Mets were right. *Maybe he can't play every day.* I knew I had to do something fast.

At season's end, Terri and I returned to our home in Jackson, Mississippi, where her parents lived. Soon thereafter, I found myself in the Jackson Public Library one afternoon. Unfortunately for me, Google hadn't been conceived then, so I had to grind through the ancient card catalogs and microfiche. Nonetheless, I came upon some great, insightful research on how to get bigger, faster, and stronger. I read with great interest about Ben Johnson, the Canadian sprinter, who had won the 100-meter dash in the Olympics due to steroids increasing his speed and making him stronger.

A lightbulb went on in my head. This was the solution I was seeking. This would allow me to gain weight, maintain it, and stay strong so I could perform at the level I was capable of performing at throughout the torturous grind of a full season.

I realize that players have taken a lot of heat for hitting the juice over the past couple of decades. I get it. And players like Barry Bonds and Roger Clemens, two of the greatest players of all time, are still waiting to get inducted into Cooperstown because of steroid use. The critics—mostly in the media—have no clue about what it's like to be a professional athlete, and all the pressure you're under to perform. What are you going to do? Are you going to sit back and let the guy next to you do it, and then he takes your job, you get released, and you have to take some shitty job where you take orders from an asshole rather than rake in $10 million a year?

No, not me.

What I did next was call up a doctor—picked him out of the Jackson, Mississippi, Yellow Pages, in fact. I walked into his office and I told him the straight story.

"My life is on the line," I told him. "My . . . life . . . is . . . on . . . the . . . line. This next year is going to determine whether I'm going to be a millionaire, or whether I'll have to get a real job. I need you to give me something that's going to keep me durable and allow me to maintain my strength for six months. I need your help. I have a family to take care of, and I'm going to be one of twenty-six people in the whole world to start on a Major League Baseball team, playing center field."

Is this something I'm proud to say I did? No. But purely and simply, I did it for my family, and to be able to provide for them. The fact of the matter is that I wasn't physically constructed to withstand an entire 162-game season, particularly with the way I play the game. I did it for my livelihood. It was the only way I could physically survive and perform through an entire season.

The doctor wrote me a prescription for Deca Durabolin, one of the cleanest steroids there is. I went to my local Rite-Aid pharmacy and I stood in line like everyone else. Was I worried? Nervous? Paranoid that somebody would see me? Not at all. Because the fact was, steroids weren't illegal in baseball at the time, and the doctor had given me a legal prescription.

"After you get it filled, come back to my office, and I'll show you how to inject it," the doctor said.

I went back to the office a few days later and the doctor pulled out a needle that could have taken out Moby Dick—the thing was a damn harpoon and it hurt like a motherfucker when he shot it in my ass. I was thinking, *This had better be some magical juice to make sticking myself with this pole worth it.* The doc also gave me the lowdown on timing to get the most results out of the steroids: every day for six weeks, and then be off it for two weeks.

Now, I don't want to come off as a bad example for the kids or anything, but I have to share three facts with you. One: I would go on to lead the Phillies to the World Series. Two: I would go on to make millions of dollars and live the dream of every boy and man in America. Three: I could not have done One and Two without using steroids. I would have fallen short, because no matter what anyone says, the baseball season has the toughest, most demanding schedule of any major sport, unless you are a starting pitcher. Don't tell me about how hard football is. Yeah, it's a rough, brutal sport, but they only play once a week.

Now let's get back to the pitchers for a minute. In baseball, they only play in thirty-five games (assuming they don't go on the disabled list) and get to rest for four days after a start. Come on, man. If you're a pitcher and you stay healthy, you have to play in a whopping thirty-five games, and if you're in the American League, you don't have to haul your ass off the bench to hit, which is the hardest part of baseball. Even in the National League you get pinch-hit for—or they put some fucking Windbreaker on you after you reach base.

Furthermore, you can give up four or five runs a game, play only six innings, and make millions and millions of dollars. My feeling about pitchers is the same as the guys who are making $20 million a year at some cushy corporate job. If you can get that gig, who wouldn't want it? And if someone has a problem with that, well, it's a free world. You try doing it. If you don't have the talent, you'll just have to get a real fucking job. Whose fault is that, the players'?

Armed and ready to hit the weight room and take advantage of my *special vitamins,* I hired a personal trainer to push me, and keep pushing me, to put myself in the best position to succeed in what was the most important season of my life. Now let's go back in time to spring training in 1990. I walked into camp—more like strutted into camp—with an ego just as big as my muscles. I weighed 190 pounds, cut up and ripped with not an ounce of fat on me. I looked like a fucking Greek statue. I walked onto the field like I had a fifteen-inch cock, and it was like, "Okay, motherfuckers, there's a new fucking sheriff in town."

I'm a quick learner at everything I do, so I became a virtuoso with the pin; for you amateurs out there *pin* means "needle." I wasn't shy about it either. Sometimes I'd drop trou and load up right in front of the other players. Because the shit was so thick I had to use a big gauge needle. There were times I would show up at the yard the next day, forgetting to take the Band-Aid off my ass. It didn't matter; everyone knew why it was there. But they didn't give a fuck. They wanted results. They wanted to win. And Lenny Dykstra *on* steroids was going to give the Philadelphia Phillies a much better chance to win than Lenny Dykstra *off* steroids.

That's just the way it is. It's all about results!

With the help of my new regimen, I became an All-Star. I was on the cover of *Sports Illustrated*. I was hitting .400 in June. A coincidence? I think not!

All season long, through August and September, because of the steroids, I was able to play at the level I started at, not withering away like some kind of runt. It wasn't like the year before, when I'd walk up to the plate at the end of the season knowing I had no chance because the bat felt like lead. There were times I felt so weak that it seemed like the pitcher was laughing at me. *Look at this pussy.* A year later, I was walking up there with a different attitude: "You really want some of this, motherfucker?" They knew I was on a whole different level than the other players. They knew I was loaded up. And they knew that I was going to find a way to beat them and make their lives miserable. Because on the baseball field, that's what I do.

So that's what I did every fucking night I stepped on the field.

I am not here to make money; I'm here to make history.

—LENNY K. DYKSTRA

11

THE POLITICS OF STEROIDS

The United States Congress passed the Anabolic Steroids Control Act in 1990, making the illicit use of anabolic steroids illegal. Moreover, criminal penalties would be assessed to violators, including athletic trainers who induced players to take anabolic steroids without a legitimate prescription. The following year, MLB commissioner Fay Vincent acknowledged in an official MLB memo that indeed anabolic steroids were a significant problem in baseball.

While the purchase or use of steroids by a player without a prescription was declared illegal, there was no testing program in place at that point. Hence, without any testing program, the pronouncement that steroids were illegal had no teeth. In essence, the MLB memo was saying, "Gentlemen, if you're taking steroids, and we don't want to know, but by all means, please, whatever you do, don't get caught."

The player lockout in 1994 resulted in the cancellation of the remainder of the season, including the World Series. In addition to losing their season, MLB lost a portion of their fan base, who could no longer relate to the greedy millionaires sparring in the headlines. The game was in desperate need of "a shot in the arm," and steroids were more than happy to oblige, although the shot was usually in another part of the anatomy.

Suddenly, in 1996, balls were rocketing out of parks throughout the league on a nightly basis. Moreover, it wasn't just the usual suspects who were launching balls out of the yard; it was players who had a track record of rarely hitting home runs who were joining the party as well.

Brady Anderson, usually a leadoff hitter, parked 50 that year. Ken Caminiti had 40 that year and won the MVP. In 1992, 3,038 home runs were hit during the season. When millions of dollars are at stake, it changes the way people think. It's simply too much money to walk away from. To prove my point, during the 2000 season, a staggering 5,693 balls left the yard, which translates to an 87 percent increase from 1992. As for yours truly, prior to 1993, the most home runs I ever hit in a season was 10. In 1993, with a big boost from steroids, I hit 25, including the postseason.

The sight of more balls landing in the seats put more people in those seats. Fans love majestic home runs more than anything else; the power surge fueled by steroids drove fans to the park to witness the barrage. Unequivocally, there would be a direct correlation between the increasing number of dingers and increased attendance throughout major league parks. Do you honestly believe MLB did not know what was happening? Come on, dude, I'm the one without any degrees. Dingers equals dollars, pure and simple.

◆

A round the year 2000, I received a call from Kevin Hallinan, who was in charge of security for Major League Baseball. Hallinan was one of the most powerful men in the league. Kevin and I would develop a special relationship, which is what led him to ask Terri and me to speak to FBI agents in Washington, DC, about fame—and everything that comes with it.

During spring training, I would speak to many of the teams' players about the perils of drugs, alcohol, and gambling, and how they could ruin your career.

One day, sitting at home, I received a call from Kevin. "The big man wants to meet with you in New York next week," he said.

"Who?"

"Bud."

"What about?"

"He wants to understand where the game is at when it comes to drugs."

Trying to help the game, I agreed to meet with MLB commissioner Bud Selig and his entourage at the presidential suite of the Four Seasons Hotel in New York.

At the meeting, Selig asked me about cocaine, amphetamines, and all of the other shit that can help someone go north, south, and sideways, and every other kind of drug that can help a player check out, even if only for a while.

"That's not your problem," I said. "That's not even close to the problem. Because coke and the other drugs don't help you make any money. The problem is steroids. They help you make money."

Attending the meeting were Bud Selig, his assistant Sandy Alderson, and Hallinan. I told them, "Steroids take you to a place where you can do things you can't do without them. And when you do that, you earn more money. Money changes the way people think, so everyone is going to take steroids. You'd take them, too. Everyone in this room would take them, unless you don't like money."

I asked them, "Who in here doesn't like money? Because you can't compete if the guy next to you is loading up. What are you going to do? Retire graciously? You're going to use them, too, and start pounding the ball out of the park."

We all know what happened next. The big guys who didn't need them, the studs, started loading up on steroids, which resulted in a fucking skyrocket show as balls were flying out of ballparks around the major leagues at an alarming pace. This led to players shattering records. In 1998, Mark McGwire hit 70 home runs and Sammy Sosa hit 66. Barry Bonds, who won two MVP awards for Pittsburgh long before he ever took a steroid, would soon start to hit home runs at a record pace for the Giants. Players hit more home runs than at any time since 1930, when the ball was juiced.

Baseball had returned from the dead.

By this time the job of the Players Association was to make sure nothing happened to the players who were taking the steroids. It dragged its feet as much as it could in light of what everyone saw was happening. In 2001, it allowed testing in the minor leagues, but not in the major leagues.

That year, 2001, Barry Bonds hit 73 home runs. Sosa hit 64, Alex Rodriguez hit 52, and Luis Gonzalez, of all people, hit 57.

Reporters began to write about how steroids had changed the game, and finally in 2003 the Players Association allowed anonymous testing. If a player was caught juicing, there was no penalty. The idea was to survey how many players were taking steroids. If 5 percent of the players were taking them, baseball would act.

No surprise, more than 5 percent of the players were taking steroids. But MLB was still taking baby steps, not wanting to kill the golden goose.

In 2004, the Players Association agreed that if a player tested positive for steroids, he would agree to get medical treatment. Still there was no punishment. The names of the players would not become public. So the players kept right on juicing. In December 2004, the union allowed for some minor penalties: a ten-day ban for the first offense, thirty days for a second, sixty days for a third, and a one-year ban for a fourth. This time the names would be made public.

In March 2005, the federal government got involved. Exactly why it felt the need to do so, I haven't figured out to this day. They said they were doing it because of the children. What a crock. The House Committee on Oversight and Government Reform, which was supposed to clean up the mess in government, decided it could get some cheap publicity by going after the steroid users in baseball rather than fuck with more important, lower-profile issues in Washington. On national TV they interviewed a group of players including Mark McGwire, Sammy Sosa, and Rafael Palmeiro and asked them if they took steroids. McGwire refused to answer, as was his right under the Constitution, and Palmeiro denied any steroid use. It was on TV live, and I had to laugh when Sammy suddenly forgot how to speak English. The guy speaks perfect English. He kept saying, "*No comprendo.*" It was fucking hilarious.

In 2005, a dozen players were caught taking steroids and suspended. After the 2005 season, the punishment was upped to fifty games for a first offense and a hundred games for a second. Amphetamines were added to the list of banned substances. Very few people outside of baseball realized it, but that would hurt the players most of all, even more than banning steroids.

In 2006, Senator George Mitchell published his report with a list of more than a hundred players' names, including mine, supplied to him by my former partner.

I was also named as a steroid user by Kirk Radomski, the Mets' clubhouse boy who wrote a "tell-all" book about the use of steroids by Mets players. Including me in his book was a joke. When I was with the Mets, I never took a single steroid. When I was with the Mets, I didn't even know what a steroid was. But one thing he said was true: the coaches, managers, and owners all knew what was going on with steroids, and everyone chose to look the other way. They were making too much money not to ignore what was happening.

The bottom line is that after the 1994 strike, baseball needed to turn up the volume in a big fucking way, and with so many players taking steroids and hitting home runs, people were starting to come back to the game. Basically, it was a fireworks show every night. Barry Bonds, Sammy Sosa, and Mark McGwire, just to name a few, hit tape-measure shots into the stands on a nightly basis and fans flocked to the ballpark to watch. Today the moralists scream about these players, but have the owners given back any of the ticket money they reaped from the barrage of homers? Did they donate their "ill-gotten" booty to prevent steroid use in the future? Don't hold your breath if you're waiting for that to occur.

Naturally, there was a lot of crying from those same moralists among the powers that be to keep all those who are suspected of having taken steroids out of the Hall of Fame. It's totally ridiculous. Like so many things in life, it's hypocritical, too. Maybe they should have two Halls of Fame, one for the players who performed best and another for the milk drinkers who were the best citizens off the field. By the way, I'm not taking a shot at the more wholesome dudes who have played the game. They were a lot stronger than I was, but I guarantee you they didn't have as much fucking fun as I did.

But the shit we do know about is enough to keep a lot of players out, even though a stumbling-drunk womanizer like Babe Ruth gets in? That's okay? He gets a pass? What about Mickey Mantle, who admitted to showing up to games drunk off his ass? What about the racists like Ty Cobb and Rogers Hornsby? Is it okay for a guy like Hornsby, who was in the Ku Klux Klan, to be in the Hall of Fame? Where do you draw the line? What about all the players who took greenies?

Everyone admits that. Again, I ask, where do you draw the line? It either has to be what you did on the field, or what you did off the field.

My favorite sports quote of all time comes from Lance Armstrong. I could make a strong argument that he is/was the greatest athlete in the world. When the reporters kept asking him, "What are you on?" his answer was "I'm on my bike six hours a day working my ass off. What are you on?"

That motherfucker beat every rider in the world in the Tour de France seven times in the most grueling competition on the planet. He won even after he took cancer head-on!

This guy must have had an amazing constitution. He obviously put the *d* in *discipline*. And he put the *d* in *wouldn't be denied*.

Since its inception in 1997, the LIVESTRONG Foundation (formerly known as the Lance Armstrong Foundation) has raised more than $500 million to support cancer survivors.

With that said, I don't give a fuck what drugs he was on. How could those drugs be helping him that much? It wasn't about strength. He didn't look bigger and stronger. It wasn't until I researched it that I learned that he had this doctor in Italy who performed a procedure to increase the precise amount of oxygen to his brain to optimize his performance for the race. It's called blood doping. He was like a machine—much like the Six Million Dollar Man.

The doctor knew exactly how much to give him. That's fucking unbelievable. That said, you don't think the rest of the riders found out about this and did it themselves? Of course they fucking did! They were all on the same shit.

This is a guy who raised more than $300 million for cancer research. It didn't matter. Why? The federal government came into the picture. As soon as the feds get involved, the party is over! Lance Armstrong learned how powerful our federal government is. They have so much fucking money, with unlimited resources, it's scary. They win before the game starts or they don't play.

And that's true for anyone who goes up against them—including yours truly.

If you're playing a poker game and you look

around the table and can't tell who the sucker is,

it's you.

—PAUL NEWMAN

12

THE BIG BLIND

After the 1989 season, I returned to Jackson for the off-season. I played a ton of golf and eventually got hooked up with Herb Kelso, a cardsharp bookie who wore this god-awful cologne and had a big fucking cigar in his mouth 24/7 with a boiler to match it.

Throughout the entire off-season, which was approximately four months, the schedule never changed. Every Friday we would play golf, at which I would beat the shit out of my boy Kelso, as he was a fucking hack. Normally, when you play a round of golf with someone that horrible, it's four hours of fucking pain. But this guy was so fucking funny, and his rap so smooth, I couldn't wait to tee it up with him. After each round of golf, we would go back to his penthouse, which was used strictly for Friday-night poker games. He would have the best steaks catered in, prime pussy would always be within proximity, and the cocktails were flowing all night.

Over a few months' time, I probably clipped Kelso for about $100,000 on the golf course, but it wasn't Herb Kelso's first rodeo—what I didn't realize was that he *wanted* to lose that money to me, so he could get me to play in the big poker game each Friday night. That's why he said he would just pay me in poker chips, instead of paying me in cash. I was a young kid and didn't realize that those southern boys were pretty smart, too. Even though they played me like a fiddle, I didn't give a fuck because I was having so much fun.

Herb Kelso ran the biggest poker game in the whole Mississippi Delta. We played Texas hold 'em.

In 1990, the feds sent an FBI agent over to my house to pay me a little visit. This was when I learned that I was being robbed.

The agent held in his hand a personal check. "Is this your check?" he asked.

It had been made out to "cash" for $78,000, and there was my John Hancock on the bottom of the check—I couldn't exactly deny it.

"Look," he said, "we have been investigating Herb Kelso for a long time, and now we are going to indict him on money-laundering. Your check was one of the pieces of evidence that proved he was not paying his taxes."

Like I said, I was just a kid and didn't know how those things worked. But what I did learn was that you never write a personal check to a professional gambler.

"We just need you to show up one day in federal court and point him out," the FBI agent said. "That's it. After that, you can leave. We don't want to hurt your baseball career. You did nothing wrong."

When the feds got involved, there was a pretty good chance MLB would find out and want to know what was going on. Remember, this was right after baseball's lead investigator, John Dowd, took out Pete Rose for betting on baseball.

My uncle, "Tough Tony," helped the Red Wings win three Stanley Cups in the three years he played for them. He scored the winning goal in overtime in Game 7 against the Canadiens to win the Cup in 1954. I guess you could say grit and glory were in the blood.

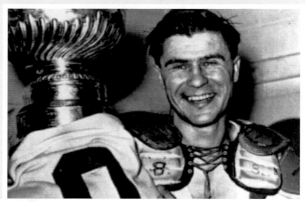

The Dykstra brothers, Garden Grove, California, circa 1968—that's me, on the top right. A few years after this photo was taken, alarmed neiqhbors called my dad at work, begging him to come home and break up a fight that had been waging between my older brother and me for two hours outside our house.

Senior year at Garden Grove High School, 1981. Baseball was my golden ticket out of the middle. When I was drafted by the Mets in June, there was no way I wasn't going to cash it in.

Young guns: me, Doc Gooden, and Darryl Strawberry hanging in the dugout before a game against the Padres in San Diego. (*George Gojkovich/Getty Images*)

With my man Straw (aka Soul Pole).

Never knew I could jump that high. This game-winning home run in the 1986 playoffs against the Houston Astros put me on the map. My do-whatever-it-takes-to-win attitude made me a fan favorite in the Big Apple! What a feeling! (*Manny Millan*/Sports Illustrated/*Getty Images*)

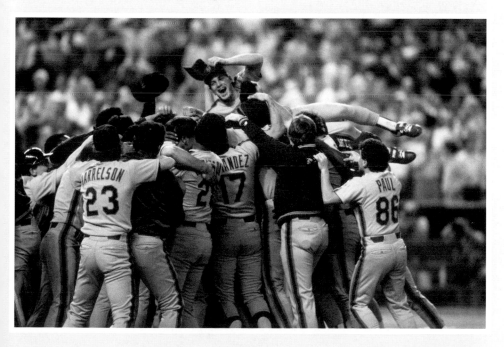

Headed to the series! Celebrating our NLCS victory over the Astros, October 15, 1986. (*Richard Mackson*/Sports Illustrated/*Getty Images*)

Down two games to none in the 1986 World Series, I led off Game 3 at Boston with a home run off Dennis "Oil Can" Boyd. Keith "Mex" Hernandez watches from the on-deck circle. (*Paul Bereswill*)

Sliding headfirst into home to score a run in the 1986 World Series. Notice Rafael Santana signaling me to get down. (*Focus on Sport/Getty Images*)

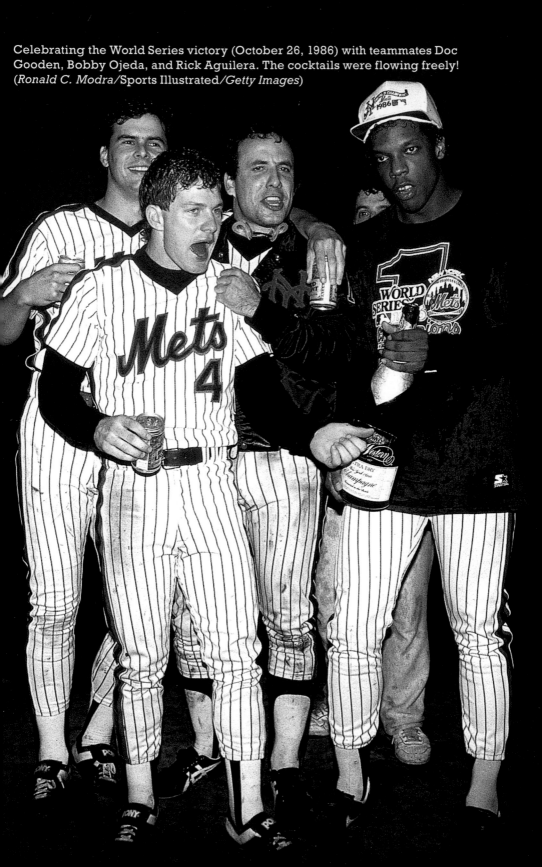

Celebrating the World Series victory (October 26, 1986) with teammates Doc Gooden, Bobby Ojeda, and Rick Aguilera. The cocktails were flowing freely! (*Ronald C. Modra*/Sports Illustrated/*Getty Images*)

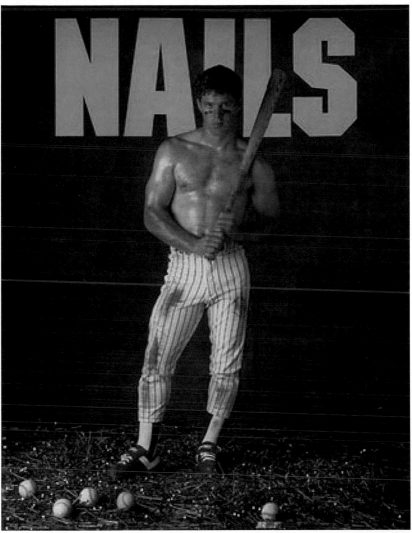

Fresh off the 1986 World Series win, this NAILS poster turned out to be a big hit. By the way, this is me "all-natural." (*Costacos Brothers*)

With my wife, Terri, waving to the crowd at the tickertape parade to honor our World Series championship win over the Boston Red Sox. The date was October 28, 1986, a day I will never forget. The streets of New York were filled with cheering fans. (*D. Ross Cameron*)

It all came together in 1990, during my second season with the Phillies. I was hitting .400 in June, as celebrated by this *Sports Illustrated* cover. With a little help from the "good vitamins" (wink, wink). I finally figured out how to hit over the 162-game schedule. *(John Iacono/*Sports Illustrated*/ Getty Images)*

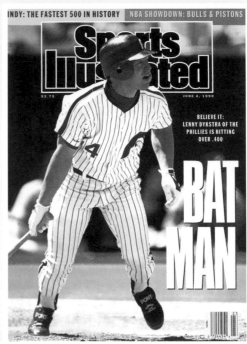

INDY: THE FASTEST 500 IN HISTORY   NBA SHOWDOWN: BULLS & PISTONS

Sports Illustrated

$2.75   JUNE 4, 1990

BELIEVE IT:
LENNY DYKSTRA OF THE
PHILLIES IS HITTING
OVER .400

BAT MAN

A Greek fucking statue! Deca Durabolin at its finest! *(John W. McDonough/*Sports Illustrated*/Getty Images)*

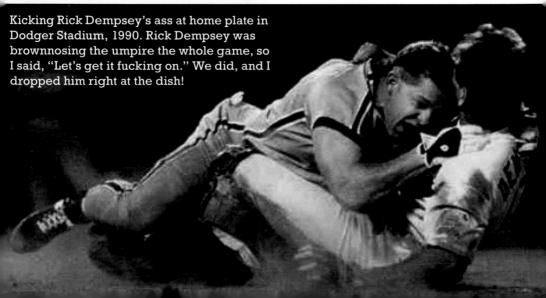

Kicking Rick Dempsey's ass at home plate in Dodger Stadium, 1990. Rick Dempsey was brownnosing the umpire the whole game, so I said, "Let's get it fucking on." We did, and I dropped him right at the dish!

Bulked up, badass, and on a "mission of mercy"! Bring it! (*Peter Power/Getty Images*)

My teammates, Curt Schilling and John Kruk, greeting me after I scored a run to win a game. (*Tom Mihalek/AFP/ Getty Images*)

This was one of the farthest balls I ever hit. It was in the 1993 World Series against the Toronto Blue Jays, in Toronto. Down 5–0 with two men on base, I connected on a Dave Stewart fastball and hit it to the fucking moon! (*Rick Stewart/Getty Images*)

This was the 1993 NLCS in Atlanta, top of the 10th, two outs, nobody on base—I hit the game-winning home run off Mark Wohlers. One of the most satisfying moments of my career. (Check out the smile on third-base coach Larry Bowa.)

I loved silencing the crowd on the road. This home run put an end to the Braves. (*William Glover/ Associated Press*)

At the Hôtel Ritz Paris after the 1993 season. Somebody thought it would be a good idea to send me to Europe as an ambassador for Major League Baseball, so I flew across the pond and fucking loved it. (*Lane Stewart*/Sports Illustrated/*Getty Images*)

Once I got a taste of the good life as a professional athlete, I was hooked when my playing days ended. Here I am living large at a $5,000-a-night presidential suite at the St. Regis, on the corner of Fifty-fifth and Madison in New York City. If you only knew what happened between those walls!

Entrance to my Simi Valley car wash—the Taj Mahal of car washes and the source of my post-baseball wealth. Inside the complex, I built a saltwater shark tank and displayed world-class sports memorabilia. We would wash about one thousand cars on a Saturday!

Luke, Cutter, me, and Terri living the dream at Sherwood Country Club in Thousand Oaks, California, one of the most affluent neighborhoods in the country. If you had to ask how much it cost to join, you weren't invited.

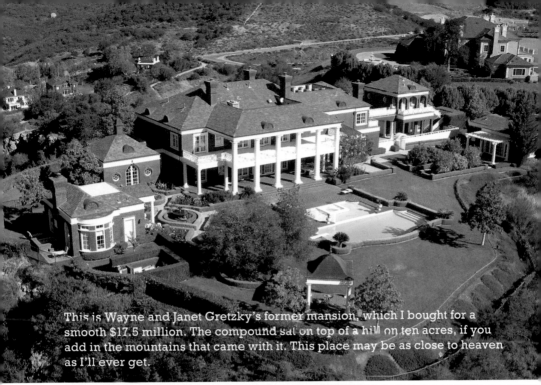

This is Wayne and Janet Gretzky's former mansion, which I bought for a smooth $17.5 million. The compound sat on top of a hill on ten acres, if you add in the mountains that came with it. This place may be as close to heaven as I'll ever get.

My Gulfstream, the biggest swinging dick of private aviation! Tell me that doesn't get you hard?

The interior of my customized Maybach Gulfstream.

With Jim Cramer at the *Players Club* launch party on April 1, 2008. Cramer was the only person who got it right when he went on national TV and said, "Lenny Dykstra is one of the great ones." At the time of that interview with Bernard Goldberg on *Real Sports,* my win-loss record was 110 wins and 0 losses. Since Cramer made that ballsy call about me, my win-loss record has soared! My website NailsInvestments.com has since accumulated 570 wins and 1 loss. The numbers don't lie! Nailsinvestments.com is still going strong today. (*Jamie McCarthy/Getty Images*)

A sample of covers for *Players Club* magazine.

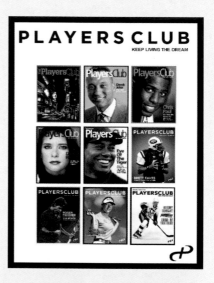

The end of an era: With fellow Mets greats celebrating the team's last season at Shea Stadium, September 28, 2008. Shea would be demolished a few short months later; the wrecking crew came for my life next. (*George Napolitano/Getty Images*)

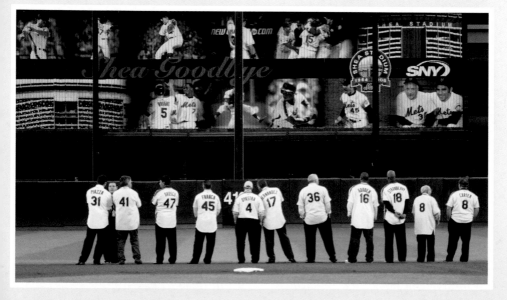

Pearl Harbored! Taken into custody, June 6, 2011. If they want you, they get you, period. The end! (*Michael Robinson Chavez/Getty Images*)

The House of Pain!

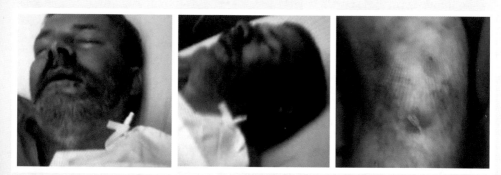

Pictures taken after the beating I took from the deputies at Los Angeles County Men's Central Jail. The inmate abuse was so widely known that, after a five-year investigation, the FBI arrested, prosecuted, and put in prison numerous deputies who abused inmates on a regular basis. Sheriff Lee Baca's guilty plea capped off a string of prosecutions beginning with low-ranking officials and working all the way up the chain of command. Numerous deputies willfully entered my jail cell and proceeded to beat me to the point of unconsciousness. I am lucky to be alive.

Happy to be free, and now ready to be a factor again in this game called life!
(*Carlos Delgado Photography*)

My awesome grandson Beau Kyle Dykstra. A future All-Star!

My son Cutter and his new wife, Jamie-Lynn Sigler, with my grandson Beau Dykstra at their wedding.

A couple of sharp dressed men: My adopted son Gavin and my grandson Marshall at Cutter's wedding.

#4 lives on: My youngest son, Luke Dykstra. He was drafted by the Atlanta Braves in the seventh round out of high school and is on his way to being a star.

I would have to testify in front of a federal grand jury—which was sure to attract the wrong kind of attention from the brass in the league office. And, sure enough, right before Herb's trial in March, I got a call from Kevin Hallinan, the man in charge of MLB security.

"Mr. Vincent wants to see you," Hallinan informed me.

Baseball commissioner Bart Giamatti had died suddenly on September 1, 1989, and his best friend, Fay Vincent, had taken over as the new commissioner. I was very nervous and scared, as I didn't know what to expect. I started worrying they weren't going to let me play anymore.

They flew me to New York, where I discovered that we were *not* meeting at headquarters. Instead we were having a hush-hush meeting in a private conference room at the top of the Helmsley Building. When I got there, Gene Orza, who was the Players Association's second in charge behind Don Fehr, was waiting for me. He was one of those kinds of guys who thought he was smarter than everyone else. He pulled me aside and told me not to say a fucking thing, that I had rights.

Wait a minute, I thought. *All I did was play poker.* When I walked into the intimidating room, I saw Fay Vincent, Kevin Hallinan, and John Dowd. Now I'm really panicking, thinking to myself, *What the hell is Dowd doing here? They brought in the big swinging dick just for me?*

Hallinan, one of the coolest guys on the planet, pulled me aside. "Listen, we looked into everything. We know for a fact that all you did was play poker. You tell Fay the truth, and you'll be fine. If you lie to him, then it'll be a problem."

When the meeting started and Fay Vincent asked me what happened, Gene Orza jumped up and got all bent out of shape.

"Don't say anything. Don't answer one question. You have rights," he barked.

"Listen, man," I said to Orza. "First of all, I don't even know who in the fuck you are. Second, I didn't invite you here, so shut the fuck up or leave. I got nothing to hide. I played poker. That's it."

I ended up only getting probation, just like Hallinan said.

◆

Shortly after the actual grand jury hearing, when we played at Wrigley Field in Chicago, the Bleacher Bums—I used to fuck with these fans all the time—held up five large playing cards: a full house. Even though the joke was at my expense, I thought it was pretty hilarious.

But soon enough, there wasn't much to laugh about. In early May 1991, two months after my grand jury appearance, I attended Phillies first baseman John Kruk's bachelor party. After the party, I was driving my teammate Darren Daulton home in my brand-new Mercedes 500SL. It was pounding rain, and where we lived in suburban Philadelphia, it was dark as hell because there were no streetlights. I had been drinking, but that's not why I crashed. Of course I take full responsibility for what happened, but I was unfamiliar with the roads, it was dark and wet, and there was a sharp left turn. All of a sudden, the car started to hydroplane like it hit a sheet of ice.

I don't remember seeing the tree coming at me. Unfortunately, I didn't have my seat belt on, and the next thing I remember, I was

lying in the middle of the road, busted up and bleeding like hell. I should have been dead.

Then the cops came. You should have seen my car. It was smashed, totaled. The tree, which is a famous landmark now, was fucked up, too.

The police drove us to the station to go over everything. Luckily for us, they were huge Phillies fans, so they decided to let us go with just a slap on the wrist.

Until that point, we'd been holding up on adrenaline alone, but as Darren and I walked out of the police station on unsteady legs, I looked at him and said, "Dude, I don't care whether you call me a pussy or not. I think I'm going to die. I need to go to the fucking hospital."

He didn't argue.

I can't honestly remember how we got to Bryn Mawr Hospital, whether by cab, or if we got a ride, or maybe the cops took us. But it was a good thing we got there. I stayed in the hospital for three weeks, and Darren missed three weeks himself to treat a fractured eye socket. I had broken my collarbone, a bunch of ribs, and my cheekbone. I also punctured my lung, and my heart was bruised—that's what the doctors were worried about the most. One of the doctors later told me, "If this happened to anyone else, they would have been dead."

In a way, steroids saved my life that night. A broken heart can get you down, but a *bruised* heart can be fatal.

I came back to play in less than a month, and I was having another great season. That was, until August, when I ran into the center field wall in Cincinnati chasing down a fly ball and broke my collarbone again. Baseball had passed a rule stipulating that every stadium had to install padding on the walls, but Marge

Schott, the owner of the Reds, was so fucking tight that she hadn't done it yet. Marge Schott was such a cheapskate, I heard that she limited the number of bats the Reds' players could order. She was even a cheap drunk. I was told she only drank Popov, which costs about fourteen cents a bottle.

After I snapped my collarbone, I was out the rest of the '91 season.

When the '92 season began, I was healthy again, and pumped and ready to go. Then on opening day at the Vet, on my very first at-bat of the season, I was facing the Chicago Cubs' Greg Maddux. From the very beginning, Maddux and I hated each other's guts. I had a terrible batting average against him, though I did get some key hits when he was on the mound. That day, I had an 0-2 count, and that *motherfucker* threw a ball right at my neck—he had such good control, I knew this wasn't a mistake. I threw my left arm up to block it from hitting my face, and the ball shattered my wrist. I never left the game, but I knew it was broken.

I was only on the DL for fifteen days, but I really think breaking my wrist had actually helped me, because I had been over-swinging during spring training. When I came back, I had a 92-game stretch where I was hitting .301, scored 52 runs, stole 30 bases, and had 39 RBI. Then I had another nasty break, literally, as I broke my hand diving into first base at Shea Stadium. Being on the DL was always frustrating, and now I had lost the rest of the season to yet another injury. But what was waiting for me the following season would end up changing my life forever.

Because if you're prepared and you know what it takes, it's not a risk. You just have to figure out how to get there. There is always a way to get there.

—MARK CUBAN

13

BRASS BALLS

By 1990, I understood the business of baseball from the inside out. The one thing that I realized influenced my performance more than anything else were the men in blue—the fucking umpires. It didn't matter that I was twenty-seven years old and, with the help of my steroid regimen, in addition to working out intensely every day, I was firing on all cylinders. *All that* and it *still* wasn't enough. The umps were the men who could either destroy me or put me in a position to make my job a hell of a lot easier.

If I wanted a monster year, I would have to eliminate the uncertainty factor controlled by the umpires and get the count in my favor. And I wanted a monster year.

But how does one get the count in one's favor? As Gordon Gekko said in *Wall Street,* "The most valuable commodity I know of is information." Well, it turns out information is a valuable commodity in the world of baseball, too.

In professional baseball, the pitchers are so fucking good that practically every pitch they throw is borderline. A pitcher can put a ball on the paint and hit a gnat's ass on the black, and the ump can call it either way, and no one can really complain.

If they call it a ball, the count is 1-0, and if you look at major league stats, it will show that a hitter with that count will hit somewhere close to .280. Whereas if the umpire calls it a strike, which means the count is 0-1, then the hitter is going to hit .220. In baseball, that is a huge fucking dip in your hitting percentage.

These are the little things that will determine if a player stays in the big leagues and makes millions of dollars a year, or gets fired and has to get a real job, taking orders from some asshole.

Let me break down what the average is for each possible pitch count so that you can better understand how much control an umpire truly has on a hitter. To come up with these results, I took all of the major league hitters with each pitch sequence, and this is what the combined average came out to be:

After 0-1 count: .221 average
After 1-1 count: .234 average
After 2-1 count: .252 average
After 3-1 count: .274 average
After 0-2 count: .166 average
After 1-2 count: .178 average
After 2-2 count: .193 average
On a 3-2 count: .216 average
After 1-0 count: .268 average
After 2-0 count: .281 average
After 3-0 count: .282 average

These numbers don't lie, so how do I get the umpires on my good side and have them call a close pitch a ball rather than a strike?

Brass fucking balls, that's how.

I hired a private detective agency that cost me $500,000—one paycheck from the Phillies—to have their PIs follow umpires around so I could uncover dirt that I could use against them. They shit like the rest of us. Some of them like to gamble. Some of them like to do blow. Some of them like road pussy. Some of them like dudes. I'm telling you, everyone's got something they don't want the world to know, and umpires are certainly no exception.

Take the case of one veteran umpire. I don't want to name him because he's retired and there's no point in dragging his name through the dirt. He umpired for a long time, almost forty years. On the field, he was a miserable son of a bitch. My PI learned the guy was also a degenerate gambler, losing money hand over fist, betting on sports. After I received that juicy nugget of information, the next time I went to bat and he was behind the plate, I gave him a little grin.

"Hey, blue," I said. "How'd you do last night?"

He did a double take. "What?"

"Sports betting is tough, man. Especially for umps," I said. The next thing I knew, my strike zone was as big as—let's put it this way—there *was* no strike zone.

One of the other umpires, my PI discovered, happened to be gay—but in the closet.

"Hey, blue, how was Rick's last night?"

Rick's was a notorious gay bar.

He looked at me like, *What the fuck?*

Yeah, it's all about leverage and fear. Fear does a lot to a man. Fear of losing his job. Fear of being turned in. Fear of being exposed.

◆

One of my favorite hits during this period of my career was when John Smoltz was pitching a no-hitter in Philly—and the only reason he didn't have a perfect game going into the ninth was because he walked me earlier in the game. Smoltz's shit was electric. He sawed right through our lineup like we were a bunch of amateurs. He takes his no-hitter into the ninth, and guess who's up third in the ninth inning? That's right, me. And I was hitting close to a .400 average, making my monster year come true. He starts out the ninth like he did the rest of the game, mowing down the first two hitters like they were toddlers. So he's one out away from what every pitcher dreams of: a no-hitter. Smoltz had a six-run lead, but his ego wouldn't let him pitch around me, so the baseball gods had to make him pay.

The count was 1-0 and I'm thinking, *This guy is feeling so cocky, he's going to try to sneak some gas by me.*

I was sitting dead red, inner half, and I hit a tracer, a frozen fucking rope off the glass in right field. As I stood on second base, Smoltz was stomping around the mound like a spoiled five-year-old, and when he looked over at me, I took my chew out and threw it down. "You dumb motherfucker," I told him, "that's what you fucking deserve."

◆

That was also the year I got into the infamous fight with Rick Dempsey. We were playing at Dodger Stadium, and one of

the regular umpires was on vacation. In other words, the home plate umpire wasn't one of the umps I had my PI investigate. The new ump had been called up from Triple A, and Dempsey, the Dodgers catcher and a longtime veteran who knew how to work the umps, was brown-nosing him. How else could Dempsey stay in the big leagues for as long as he did? He couldn't have hit water if he fell out of a fucking boat.

I was up against pitcher Mike Morgan, and his first pitch hit Dempsey's glove two inches outside and the umpire called it a strike. Then Dempsey said something to the ump, and the two of them started laughing.

I was furious.

"What the hell are you guys laughing at?" I said. "I'm playing for real money here. I have to pay my bills. This is how I feed my family."

I was putting up Ted Williams–style numbers at the time, so I said directly to the replacement umpire, "You see that fucking scoreboard up there? What's it say? Four fucking hundred. Do you know why? Because I know what a strike is, and that was not a strike."

At that point, Dempsey stood up. "Oh, stop whining, Lenny."

"You've been brown-nosing this motherfucker all fucking night, man," I said. Then I called him a cunt, and Dempsey took something that resembled a swing at me. We went at it right there at home plate, and I landed a couple of pretty good punches on the stupid bastard.

They suspended Dempsey, because unlike today, where everyone involved gets punished, back then you got suspended *only* if you threw the first punch.

I only got fined, but I had made my point.

Even the media took notice. Here's how Jim Murray, the esteemed sportswriter for the *Los Angeles Times,* wrote about it:

> When Lenny Dykstra picked a fight with Rick Dempsey recently, no one in baseball was surprised. If he'd been there at the time, Lenny Dykstra would have picked a fight with Jack Dempsey. And expected to win . . . Lenny Dykstra doesn't belong in this point in time anyway. . . . He should be matching spikes with Ty Cobb, trading insults with John McGraw, playing on a team called the Gas House Gang. Lenny is like a lot of us, in the wrong century . . . Lenny plays it as if it were a guerrilla attack on a munitions train. Lenny doesn't take prisoners either. Lenny doesn't make friends. He comes to beat you.

Man, that made me proud as hell, but I was still feeling unfulfilled. I was on a mission to bring the Phillies a pennant and a world championship and we hadn't accomplished it yet. To really help get us there, I needed to remain injury-free.

But the way I played, it wouldn't be easy.

The truth is rarely pure and never simple.

—OSCAR WILDE

14

CHARLIE SHEEN

I first met Charlie Sheen during the 1993 season when the Phillies visited the Dodgers in Los Angeles. A clubhouse guy approached me before we took the field and handed me a piece of paper with a phone number on it; he told me that Charlie Sheen wanted to meet me after the game.

The Phillies were in first place, dominating the National League. We were the most talked-about team in baseball, with me leading the charge. When I would step onto the baseball field, I was arrogant and cocky, combined with a fuck-you attitude. I wanted the other team to hate me; I wanted the opposing team's fans to hate me. When I would lead off the game, I would strut up to home plate like I had a fifteen-inch cock. This was all part of the master plan. I never did anything on the baseball field that wasn't planned out. And it worked: everything went according to plan, with the exception, of course, of the fifteen-inch cock.

After the game I called Charlie, we had a brief conversation about the game that night, and he then invited me over to his compound in Malibu. Of course I accepted.

I admired his work as an actor, especially his portrayal of Bud

Fox in Oliver Stone's *Wall Street*. I genuinely looked forward to meeting him.

When I arrived, Charlie gave me a big hug and took me on a tour of his spread, which was impressive to say the least. Charlie then asked me if I wouldn't mind checking out his swing. I thought to myself, *Another actor who wants to be a baseball player; this is going to be painful*. But I gave him the courtesy. "Sure, Charlie, but it's kind of dark, how are you going to see the ball?"

Charlie then walked me around to the side of his mansion, and the next thing I know he flips on a switch, the lights come on, and I see the best batting cage I have ever seen in my entire life. It was better than any batting cage in the major leagues.

The next thing I know, Charlie tells his longtime friend Tony Todd to get the machine ready. Charlie starts taping up his wrists, stretching, puts on his game face, the whole deal, almost as if he was getting ready for a World Series game. I'm thinking to myself, *This guy has been watching too much baseball on TV.*

Charlie steps into the cage and asks me if I want to see him hit left-handed or right-handed. Now I'm thinking, *This guy is taking himself way too serious*. I said, "Whichever side you want, Charlie. Doesn't matter to me."

Charlie gets in the box from the left side and shouts to Tony, "Turn it up to ninety." Tony hit the power button, and the next thing I see is Charlie fucking raking! He is hitting bullets all over the cage. I was blown away, and I said to Charlie, "Dude, you can fucking hit! Holy shit! That's a real baseball swing."

Charlie showed his baseball skills in three very popular movies about baseball: *Eight Men Out, Major League,* and *Major League II*. In the two *Major League* movies, Charlie played relief

pitcher Rick Vaughn. In the movie, he would walk from the bull-pen to the mound to the tune "Wild Thing." Today, hitters and pitchers all have walk-up music. Charlie Sheen, as Rick Vaughn, was the trendsetter.

One of my favorite baseball stories from Charlie was when he told me, "One time, I bought every seat in the right field stands of an Angel game to make sure I would catch a home run ball. It was like three thousand tickets I had to buy, and I ended up with air. Nobody hit a home run that game. Can you believe that?"

◆

After Charlie finished hitting we sat down at his customized bar that took the cool meter off the chart. Charlie asked me if I liked wine. I said, "Sure, what do you have?"

Charlie comes back by saying, "A better question would be, 'What don't I have?'" He pulled out some $3,000 bottle of red wine; we drank and talked baseball for the next four hours. Charlie knew his shit when it came to baseball. He told me as a kid his dream was to be a Major League Baseball player.

◆

Years later, our paths crossed again. My career was over, so partying became my full-time job for a while. Eventually I landed in a rehab facility, but I was so fucked up that I didn't know where

I was. When I came out of my coma, I realized I was part of a star-studded group at Promises, the famous rehab in Malibu that overlooks the Pacific Ocean.

This place is so exclusive that they always have a waiting list. If you were a big-name celebrity, they magically found a way to move you to the front of the line. Charlie Sheen was there along with several other famous actors and celebrities. Trust me, I was the low man on the totem pole there.

When I arrived, I slept for four days straight. Now that I was finally able to reenter the world, I looked around the place and said to myself, *What in the fuck am I doing here with all these fucking losers? I'm getting the hell out of here.*

Then one of the counselors walked over to me and started barking out orders. I fired back, "Who in the fuck do you think you are talking to, motherfucker?" I didn't know the system yet and how it really worked. Plus, I had been living a life where I wasn't used to taking orders from anybody. *I* gave the fucking orders.

Then one of the bean counters said to me, "You're not getting your money back."

I shot back, "Money? Do you think I give a fuck about the money? Keep it. Keep it all. I don't give a fuck. It's only paper. I can make more of that. But let me tell you what I can't buy back: the fucking time I just wasted listening to your bullshit."

Looking back, I shouldn't have behaved that way. I had all my shit packed, just waiting for my limo to arrive, when Charlie showed up out of nowhere. I didn't know any of the other actors; I wasn't into all of the Hollywood bullshit.

I was completely caught off guard.

Charlie walked up to me and said, "Hey, man, I know what you are feeling, I was just like you. I felt the same way. But you should try to stick it out. It's not so bad. After the third or fourth day, it gets better. It gets easier."

Charlie had a way of talking to you that's hard to describe. When he was sober he was a very humble man, and there was an inexplicable "coolness factor" to him.

"I'm not telling you what to do. But you're here. You might as well stick it out a few more days and see what happens. I'll be here, and we'll go hit and take batting practice. It's not as bad as you think. Trust me, bro. Just stay a little longer until you get sober."

◆

Let's fast-forward to the year 2014. I was out of prison, I was in New York, and I received a call out of the blue from Charlie, telling me that I was right about all the people who were stealing his money, and then he said, "When are you going to be back from New York?"

I said, "Friday night."

Charlie responded by saying, "If you have time, you should stop by when you get home. We have a lot to catch up on."

I responded by saying, "That sounds great. "

When I showed up it was like old times, Charlie and me sitting on his top-notch outdoor furniture, staring out at his picturesque backyard. The first thing Charlie said was "I want to apologize for what happened, for how it ended before you went away." He went

on to say, "When people kept telling me lies about you, I believed them, and for that, I am sorry."

"Charlie, you don't need to apologize, especially when these are supposed to be people you trust, people that supposedly are on your team." I went on to say, "Charlie, I don't live in the past, I live my life going forward. It's all good, bro, all good."

We started talking about everything and anything, like old times. Fifteen minutes later, this chick walked up to Charlie and gave him a kiss, the kind of kiss that told me they were a couple. Charlie introduced her: "Lenny, I want you to meet my fiancée, Scottine."

As soon as I met her, I knew she was bad news. I have always had a talent for reading people, especially when it comes to pussy. My instincts immediately told me that she was a selfish bitch, that she only cared about herself. It wasn't until later that I found out she was a porn star. *Guess how I learned that?* Scottine herself told me.

A few days later, Charlie and I were talking and he brought up his Warner Bros. deal. I only knew what I read—that he'd sold all his syndication rights back to Warner Bros. for something like $100 million.

Charlie asked me if I could recommend an investment expert. One of the things Charlie liked about me was that I did not waste his time. I am a "whale hunter," I would always tell him. "I only bring you the decision makers, Charlie, no fucking middlemen."

While I was talking to Charlie, Scottine showed up out of the blue and asked, "You know I was the world's number one woman-on-woman porn star, don't you?" Talk about being Pearl Harbored. How do you respond to that?

So I said, "Oh, okay, congratulations . . . *I guess.*"

◆

A few weeks later on a Friday afternoon, around five P.M., I received a phone call from a woman who was crying hysterically. I kept saying, "Who is this? Who is this?"

She finally caught her breath and said, "It's Scottine, remember, you met me at Charlie's? I'm his fiancée."

I said, "Okay, why are you crying?"

She said that Charlie was smoking crack and that he had been holed up in his room for nine straight days. She said he told her to leave and to stop ruining his buzz.

I asked, "Why are you calling me?"

"Because everyone told me that you are the only person that Charlie will listen to who has the balls to stop him."

I said, "Where are you?"

She said she was in the bathroom having a nervous breakdown.

I said, "Get in your car right now and meet me at Beverly Glen Center."

"But I look like shit."

I said, "I don't give a fuck what you look like, get in the car and meet me there now."

When I pulled up she was waiting in one of the numerous different Mercedes Charlie owned. She looked like death; she was obviously shaken up. I said, "Get me through the gates, and I will take care of it."

She responded with something that caught me off guard: "You will never find him."

I responded, "What are you talking about? I've been to Charlie's house thousands of times."

She said, "Nobody knows about this room. It's in the master bedroom but it's behind a bookcase and you have to punch in a code to get in."

I said, "Okay, then you'll have to walk up the stairs with me and punch in the code. I'll handle it from there."

She said, "How are you going to get through security at the house?"

I said, "Don't worry about it."

We pulled up to Charlie's house, and as I was walking up to his master bedroom, one of Charlie's security guys said, "You're not allowed up there. Charlie gave us strict orders that nobody is allowed in the house."

I fired back, "Fuck you, the only way you're going to stop me is to shoot me! You fucking people are as bad as the drug dealer— you're just an extension of his drug dealer. So call the cops or shoot me in the back, but I'm going up to save my friend's life."

The room was right out of an Alfred Hitchcock movie, a sliding bookcase and all. It felt like I was a character in a mystery spy thriller.

I walked in and Charlie was standing there with a glass dick, or crack pipe, in one hand and his phone in the other, obviously surprised to see me.

I took one look around and said, "Charlie, I have to admit, if you're going to smoke crack, this has got to be the best crack room on the planet!"

It was unbelievable. A theater, Babe Ruth's ring, Cincinnati Reds jerseys, and some of the coolest paintings I have ever seen. All fucking amazing. After breaking the ice, I got serious with Charlie.

"Is this it? Is this what you've worked your whole life for?

Charlie, do you realize you have been up in this room for nine straight days? What the fuck kind of life is this, holed up in a room, smoking crack by yourself? Come on, Charlie, wake the fuck up!"

I told him, "You remember that show you own, *Anger Management*? Today is Friday and you have to be at work on Monday. Give me all the drugs. I'm flushing them down the toilet." Charlie handed me the poison, and I said, "Are you sure that's all of them?"

"Yes, I'm sure, I'm positive. I was just getting ready to call my drug dealer to order more shit, then you walked in."

"Charlie, you have to go to sleep. Where do you keep your sleeping shit?" He opened up a drawer and pulled out a bottle of Valium, and I said, "Take two and go to sleep. I'll call you tomorrow to check on you."

He quickly responded with desperation in his voice. "Wait, wait, can you do me a favor?"

I said, "Of course, you're my friend. What do you need?"

He said, "I need you to stay here at the house, because if you don't I know I'll order more shit."

I was caught off guard. I said, "Sure, Charlie, of course. But I'll only stay if you call your Israeli hit squad down there and tell them that *every* package that comes to your house must come through me first, and then I'll bring it up to you, and we will open it together."

Charlie immediately picked up his cell phone and called his security and told them, "Listen, all packages, mail, or anything else delivered to my house must immediately be brought to Lenny."

For the next four days, Charlie went dark. I checked on him every few hours and would bring him a pizza when he would get hungry. (He told me that was all he wanted to eat.)

Eventually, Charlie started feeling better, which was good and bad, and I'll tell you why. Obviously the fact that he was off the drugs and moving around was a good thing, but the humiliation factor of having to reenter the world was the hardest part for Charlie.

◆

When Charlie decided to come downstairs, he immediately started drinking anything and everything. He had one goal: to escape reality. But what I witnessed was a guy who seemed like he was on a mission to check out permanently.

"Charlie, what in the fuck are you doing? It's almost like you want to kill yourself."

Charlie quickly responded, "I do."

I said, "What are you talking about?"

Charlie then somewhat pulled himself together and said to me, "I'm fine, bro, I'm fine. Thank you for being here."

◆

The following night, I was in the downstairs guest room, where I had been staying. It was about eight P.M., when Charlie walked in and said, "Do you have a minute? I need to talk to you." I noticed that Charlie was emotional, almost like he was about to break down and cry. He wasn't annihilated either. I could tell he

had been drinking, but he had the kind of buzz that brings out courage, the truth-serum buzz.

I replied, "Sure, what's up, bro, are you all right?" He came over to the couch I was sitting on and sat next to me on the left. "Dude, what's going on, talk to me," I said.

Charlie then leaned forward, turned toward me, and said in a soft tone, "I got the HIV."

I didn't follow what he meant. "What? I don't understand."

As I was getting ready to ask him another question, Charlie sat up, tears dripping down his face, and said, "HIV. I am HIV positive." He went on to say, "Dude, you have no idea what it was like to get that news."

I was stunned. I have never felt so bad for a person, and I became emotional. "Are you sure?" He nodded. I didn't know what to say except "I'm so sorry, Charlie." But I remember thinking to myself, *You need to turn this conversation around, Lenny. Give Charlie hope.* That's when I said, "Charlie, you can live forever with the medicine they have now. Look at Magic Johnson."

Then Charlie did a complete 180 and said, "Yeah, bro, I'm fine. I got it under control."

I asked, "How long have you had it?"

"Five years."

Wow, I said to myself. "How did you get it, needles? One of the women you have been with?"

I could tell he didn't want to talk about it, so he just said, "Something like that."

The next night, Charlie walked in the room and just started talking. He told me how he was being extorted by people for millions and millions of dollars. I got up off the couch and said with authority, "Fuck it, Charlie, go public. You can't live like

this—in fact, this isn't living. You have to take this head-on and get in front of this thing. It all makes sense now," I told him. "No wonder you acted the way you did with Warner Bros." I went on to say, "Charlie, you have been living with impending doom for five years. You do not have to live this way, Charlie. If this is handled right, then you will not only save your own life, you will literally help and give hope to millions and millions of people around the world."

I then asked him, "What do your parents"—Martin and Janet—"say, do they want you to go public?"

Charlie didn't hesitate for one second. "Yes, they both have been trying to get me to go public. They see what it's doing to me."

I fired back, "Charlie, I will hunt down the best person on the planet who handles crisis situations like this. This person will know the best way to do this, the best way for Charlie Sheen—that's what matters. You have to go public so you can be in control of everything, as opposed to having to play defense. You and I both know this will eventually get out; you can't stop it, Charlie. The media is too powerful."

I then asked, "Charlie, do you want to go public? Are you ready to go public?"

He looked me straight in the eyes and said, "Yes. I can't live like this anymore. I'm ready."

I found the perfect person to help Charlie manage this very delicate situation, Larry Winokur, cofounder and co-CEO of BWR Public Relations. Larry is one of the smartest men I have ever met, a well-known public relations crisis manager who has represented presidents and billionaires. There was nobody better. Larry also turned out to be a very special person and friend.

Everything was falling into place. Charlie was eager to get this dark demon off his back and be free again.

What followed was one of the worst days of my life. Literally one hour before the meeting with Winokur, who agreed to help Charlie for free, I received a call from Winokur. "I'm on my way over, but Charlie won't answer his phone. He went dark."

I was so disappointed. We were one fucking hour away! Charlie had been completely on board. I knew his people must have talked him out of it. They knew that once Charlie had clarity, they would all be eliminated. They would no longer be able to steal from him, and they weren't about to let that happen. So they sabotaged the plan.

Unable to contact Charlie, I felt compelled to write him a letter, detailing our conversations. My hope was that he would read the letter and summon the strength and courage to do what needed to be done.

FROM: Lenny K. Dykstra

TO: Charlie Sheen

SENT: Saturday, November 29, 2014 12:55 PM

SUBJECT: Private and Confidential

Charlie:

I am writing this letter to you in an attempt to save your life. In my world, loyalty is everything! And a true friend doesn't give up on someone he cares about, especially when that friend's life is on the line.

Your life is more important than the bullshit drama you

deal with every day. When the people that you think you can trust tell you lies, I am not going to judge you, or blame you.

Charlie, we sat in your house many nights talking about this, and I remain resolute in my belief that your decision to go public and get ahead of this thing is a must, not only for you but also for all of your fans around the world. There is no reason to wait any longer. The time is now.

For that to happen, you must take this "head on" and get in front of this thing. I remember like it was yesterday when I asked you, "Charlie, do you want to go public? Are you ready to go public?" You looked me straight in the eyes and said, "If you think about it, I have everything to gain, and nothing to lose."

As I mentioned earlier, taking responsibility, and having the courage to go public, will not only set you free, you will be in a position to help millions and millions of people around the world. Charlie, you have the power to change lives, to help people, and let them know that they don't have to live in fear or ignorance about HIV anymore. Moreover, you can tell the world, "If it can happen to Charlie Sheen, it can happen to anyone. HIV does not discriminate!"

You have no idea how many people love you. Wait until you take ownership of this, and sit down at the press conference with Martin on your left and Janet on your right. From that day forward, I can say with certainty, your life will immediately change for the better.

Charlie, when we were having those talks at your house, you became so emotional, I almost cried with you. That was when I realized that the "pain and suffering" you have been living with for the last five years must be indescribable.

Nobody truly understands. And it was then that I realized, "Right now, my friend is a broken man." I even asked you, "Charlie, how do you do it? How do you live like this?" I then said, "You do not have to live this way. If this is handled right, then you will not only save your own life, you will literally help and give hope to millions."

You are not like a baseball player, Charlie, in fact, not even close, as you are world famous! The whole world knows who Charlie Sheen is. I told you then and I will tell you now, Charlie, you will be "bigger than life," as your fellow actors and fans will rally around you and respect you for having the courage to go public and take ownership of this.

And, more importantly, you won't have any reason to continue killing yourself with drugs and alcohol.

So, dig in and fight!

You have "shocked the house" your whole career; and as soon as they count you out, you always land on your feet and prove to everyone that you are a winner. The same thing will happen here, as you will be bigger and better than ever . . . for the right reasons!

The Charlie Sheen everyone knows and loves can be that guy again. As people around the world will get to see the humble side of Charlie Sheen. The Charlie Sheen I know is a great person, a gifted person, as your ability to entertain people can't be taught.

Charlie, and I say this with all sincerity, I believe your biggest and best days are still ahead of you. You will finally be able to live your life, and not look over your shoulder worrying about who is coming out of the woodworks next.

The ball is in your court, Charlie. I have done all I can do.

The world is ready for this news, and then you can move forward and live the life you deserve, as opposed to living in impending doom.

In closing, if you are truly being honest with yourself, then you know everything in this letter not only makes sense, it will literally change your life. There is nothing but upside, and anyone that tells you different is a person that doesn't care about you.

In closing, I know the real Charlie Sheen. He is an awesome person. The public needs to know the real Charlie Sheen, too. You grow by giving and helping others; it can change you in ways you never expected.

Respectfully,
Your Friend,
Lenny Dykstra

Charlie distanced himself from me after that letter, and we have maintained that distance ever since. Charlie helped me a great deal by convincing me to stay at Promises. And I did everything in my power to help him when he needed me most, because I owed him that. I acted on his recommendation; he didn't act on mine.

◆

Approximately one year later, Charlie was finally forced to go public about his HIV. The consequences remain to be seen.

How you play the game is for college ball.

When you're playing for money, winning is

the only thing that matters.

—LEO DUROCHER

15

1993 NLCS: PHILADELPHIA PHILLIES VS. ATLANTA BRAVES

As we entered the 1993 season, there were certainly no reasonable expectations by any of the so-called experts that we would achieve greatness that year. You can't really blame them, in that we did finish dead last in the National League East the season before, suffering through a long, miserable season with just 70 wins. On top of that, it's not as if we completed a major overhaul of our roster.

Moreover, 1992 was not an exception. It was the norm, as the Phillies finished last five times in eleven seasons, from 1987 to 1997, exceeding 78 wins only once, in 1993. Therefore, 1993 was a welcome aberration in the Phillies' otherwise putrid display of ineptitude over more than a decade. Needless to say, the starving fans of Philly turned out in droves to propel us, and ride us, to heights that few, if any, thought we could achieve.

Our lineup featured our leader, Darren "Dutch" Daulton, who managed our pitching staff extremely well and had a great year offensively, at catcher. The staff consisted of Curt Schilling,

Danny Jackson, Tommy Greene, Terry Mulholland, and Ben Rivera. Schill, Jackson, Greene, and Mulholland combined for more than 800 innings of work in '93, an average of more than 200 innings per starter. They were complemented by a bullpen that included David West, a lefty setup man; Larry Andersen; Roger Mason, who we acquired during the season; and our closer, the unforgettable Mitch Williams.

West, a very large dude with an undeniable edge, learned how to harness his impressive heater and became an integral part of our pen, leading the team in appearances with 76. LA, as he would come to be known in Philly, is far more acknowledged as a beloved member of the Phillies' broadcasting team. However, he was an excellent right-handed reliever, who had the best ERA on our staff in '93 at the age of forty. Mason provided us with another quality right-handed option in the pen. Which brings us to Mitch, who was decidedly different from Jesse Orosco and Randy Myers, the closers I played with for the Mets.

In a previous life, Mitch could have been the closer for Alfred Hitchcock's suspense thrillers. Hitchcock's philosophy was to "always make the audience suffer as much as possible." Mitch adhered to that philosophy throughout the '93 season. Given that, it is important to remember that in addition to his Hitchcockian style, Mitch must have been a disciple of Harry Houdini, as he had an amazing ability to escape from precarious predicaments that were invariably self-created. That Houdini-like quality allowed him to register 43 saves in 1993.

Our everyday lineup featured yours truly playing center field (no platoon) and leading off. Jim Fregosi, our manager, who pushed all the right buttons that year, employed a platoon at both corner outfield positions. Milt Thompson, a slick-fielding left-

handed hitter, platooned with Pete "Inky" Incaviglia in left field. Inky was perhaps the greatest batting practice hitter I've ever seen. He hit so many bombs in practice that he could've taken out small cities with his power. In right, we had a tandem of Wes Chamberlain (righty) and Jim Eisenreich (lefty).

In the infield, we had John Kruk, who looked like anything but an athlete, at first base. I know most people would have a hard time believing me when I say that John Kruk was a damn good athlete. Krukker was born to hit and was way smarter than his West Virginia, Academy Award persona would lead others to believe. Mickey Morandini, a left-handed hitter, manned second base, and Kevin Stocker, who was called up from the minors during the season, was our shortstop. Despite playing only 70 games for us, Stocker had the greatest season of his career, by far, in '93. At third was Dave Hollins, known as Head, a switch-hitter with a quiet demeanor coupled with a menacing glare that instilled fear in opponents and teammates alike.

Arguably two of the biggest reasons for our success in '93 were the versatility and contributions from our bench, led by super-sub Mariano Duncan, who could be plugged in at any infield position. We also had backup catcher Todd Pratt, backup first baseman Ricky Jordan, and utility infielder Kim Batiste.

We were not necessarily a team that beat you with power, as Dutch and Inky led the team with 24 homers each. I had a career-high 19 homers in '93, with a little help from my "friends," and Head hit 18 homers. What we were extremely adept at was getting on base and hitting balls in the gaps. With the exception of Kim Batiste at .298, all of our position players, including bench players, had an on-base percentage of .300 or greater. Moreover, I had 129 walks, Dutch had 117, Krukker had 111, and Head

had 85. In short, we were grinders, forcing pitchers to throw a lot of pitches. This served to drive up their pitch counts, which led to less innings pitched by our opponents' starters. In turn, this exposed their bullpens and gave us more opportunities to hit against their middle relievers, who invariably are the most vulnerable members of the pen.

As I mentioned previously, we were great gap hitters, with six players hitting 20 or more doubles, and seven of us with at least four triples. I believe this is indicative of how disciplined we were as a team, in our at-bats. We worked pitchers continually and took advantage of their mistakes.

Nonetheless, many people believe that we were just incredibly lucky that year, that seemingly everything fell into place perfectly for us. Granted, some of us, myself included, had career years. Most of us outperformed our career batting averages. But most important, we were healthy. Dutch and I achieved our career highs in games played in a season in 1993. Krukker, Inky, and Milt would never play in more games in a season for the remainder of their careers. Also, many of us were at the ages where careers tend to peak. Regardless of the whys, we came together as a team and maximized our collective talents. Fregosi did a tremendous job that year of utilizing the deep, versatile bench that we had. Furthermore, because of our starters' ability to go deep into games, he was able to deploy the bullpen in the best fashion.

We won the National League East in 1993 with a regular-season record of 97-65. Standing in the way of a National League pennant were the National League West winners, the Atlanta Braves, who sported a regular-season record of 104-58. The Braves were in the playoffs for the third straight year and were the clear favorites to go on to the World Series. With the best

pitching staff in baseball, featuring three future Hall of Famers in Greg Maddux, Tom Glavine, and John Smoltz, as well as Steve Avery, who was a stud in his own right, the Braves presented a formidable challenge. However, our blue-collar band of brothers, with mullets flowing, reveled in our underdog role.

We had energized a city with our scrappy style and *never say die* attitude. With multiple come-from-behind victories that year, we were never out of it. We relished the idea of being underestimated; it merely increased the size of the chips on our shoulders. We had overcome the odds all year, and we were not about to stop now.

We were an extremely confident bunch, especially when Schill was on the hill. Everyone would get on Schilling because he cared so much about his numbers, but I would always tell them, "I wish we could have five of him." I like knowing what to expect, and Schill rarely disappointed. He peppered the strike zone, so he was constantly working ahead of the hitters. He did his homework so that he was thoroughly prepared for every game. Rarely did he ever shake off Dutch.

This translated into a fast-paced game, which helps you defensively because you are always on your toes. With Schill pitching, we knew if we scored a few runs, we were going to put up a W, and we would be off the field in two hours and fifteen minutes. That gave me more time to put up a second W *after* the game.

The first game of the NLCS went our way when Kim Batiste, our backup utility infielder, doubled in Krukker to win the game. This was poetic justice for Batiste, who had earlier committed an error that allowed the Braves to tie the game. Games 2 and 3 went the Braves' way with Maddux and Glavine keeping us at bay.

Down 2 games to 1, Game 4 became, in essence, a must-win

for us. We led 2–1 for most of the game, as Mitch came on in the ninth for the save. As was his usual, Mitch walked the leadoff hitter and the next guy got a hit. Standing in the outfield, I'm saying to myself, *What the fuck? Here we go again!* Thankfully, Mitch got Ron Gant to hit into a game-ending double play, and we were tied at two games apiece, with Schill going next.

Schill was our horse, and we had the utmost confidence that he would plow the way, leading us to victory. Game 5 in Atlanta was vintage Schill, as he pounded the strike zone, dominating the Braves for eight shutout innings. We were up 3–0 in the ninth, when he walked the leadoff hitter and the next hitter reached base on an error. Suddenly, the tying run was at the plate. To add insult to injury, Fregosi decided to bring in Mitch, causing me to have angina in center field. Unquestionably, Mitch wiggled out of plenty of jams, most of which were of his own doing. Nonetheless, he put us through a great deal of unnecessary pain and suffering.

On cue, Mitch gave up a run-scoring single to Fred McGriff, to make it 3–1, followed by a long sacrifice fly to David Justice, to make it 3–2. Then back-to-back singles to tie it up at 3–3. So much for Schill's monster effort. Mark Lemke, the next batter, hit a rope down the line that had game-winner written all over it, but mercifully it landed just foul. Mitch retired Lemke, and then Bill Pecota, ending the inning with the score tied, setting the stage for me.

Mark Wohlers, the Braves closer, came in to pitch the top of the tenth. Wohlers was high-octane, throwing consistently 100 MPH gas. I worked the count to 2-2 and took a pitch that was borderline. The ump called ball three, and with the count full, I knew what was coming. I got ahead of the heater and jacked it to

dead center and out. That proved to be the game-winner as we held them scoreless in the bottom of the tenth. We were heading back to Philly for the potential clincher in Game 6.

Unfortunately, we had our work cut out for us, because the virtually unbeatable Maddux was going for the Braves. Despite that, Game 5 was a turning point for us, which generated tremendous momentum going home. We caught a break in Game 6 when Mickey Morandini hit a liner back through the box, which hit Maddux in the leg in the first inning. Arguably, Maddux should have been removed from the game, but his competitive fire would not allow it. Dutch doubled in two runs, and my boy Head hit a two-run homer. Mitch even came in and pitched a perfect ninth, which was a miracle unto itself.

Game 6 ended. The fans went crazy. We had won the National League pennant. We were going to the World Series!

The victory over the Braves was especially sweet for me, particularly because my homer in Game 5 was a big momentum changer. It also served as a reminder to Atlanta manager Bobby Cox that not selecting me for the All-Star game that year, despite the fact that I was leading the league in four categories, was inexplicable. To this day, I still have no idea why. Moreover, I hated the Braves then because they had an irritating arrogance. Of course, I love them now, because they drafted my kid.

I've missed more than 9,000 shots in my career.

I've lost almost 300 games. Twenty-six times I've

been trusted to take the game-winning shot and

missed. I've failed over and over and over again

in my life. And that is why I succeed.

—MICHAEL JORDAN

16

1993 WORLD SERIES: PHILADELPHIA PHILLIES VS. TORONTO BLUE JAYS

With our total focus on the Braves, I didn't have much time to think about our next opponent, the Toronto Blue Jays. After celebrating our National League championship, we were all about completing our mission—bring home the World Series trophy to the starving fans of Philly. They had gone a decade with no championship in any major sport, since the famous fo', fo', and fo' of Moses Malone and the 1983 76ers.

The Blue Jays' pitching staff, featuring Juan Guzman, Dave Stewart, Pat Hentgen, and Todd Stottlemyre, was certainly a quality staff, but it paled in comparison to the Braves' four Clydesdales. On the other hand, the Blue Jays' everyday lineup was an offensive juggernaut with three future Hall of Famers. They could flat-out hit from one through nine (they have a DH) and put up a lot of crooked numbers. In fact, they had only been shut out once in 1993. They had a veteran lineup with Rickey Henderson,

Roberto Alomar, Devon White, John Olerud, Paul Molitor, Joe Carter, Tony Fernandez, Ed Sprague, and Pat Borders—not an easy out in the bunch.

It was a battle of the aces in Game 1 at the SkyDome in Toronto. Schilling facing Guzman. The expected pitchers' duel never materialized, as a Devon White homer tied the score 4–4 in the fifth. Olerud homered in the sixth to make it 5–4, and the Blue Jays tacked on three runs in the seventh to put the game out of reach, eventually winning 8–5. Robbie Alomar took a double from me when he made an incredible diving catch on a looper I hit over first base in the fifth. Schilling had a rare pedestrian outing, but we knew he would come back with a vengeance.

Game 2 was Mulholland versus Stewart. We put up a five-spot in the third when Krukkie and Head had RBI singles, followed by a three-run jack by Eisey to dead center off Stewart. Eisenreich was probably more well known for his Tourette's syndrome, but that dude was an integral part of our success. He was a good defensive outfielder and a quality major league hitter, especially in the clutch. He handled his Tourette's, a neurological disorder that causes involuntary tics and speech, in a manner that helped us to adjust to better understand his behavior, which, to be honest, was bizarre at times. We went on to win Game 2, 6–4, and we were going back to Philly with the split we desperately needed.

Most people will remember the '93 Phillies as a group of characters who played hard and partied harder. Nobody had more fun than we did, or did as much outrageous shit. But know one thing: when we stepped between those lines, we were all business. Game on, dude, and we would do whatever it took to win. Unlike today, when opposing players are all chummy with each other, back then you didn't even talk to the players on the other team. Everyone

hated us for the way we did things, and that's the way we liked it. It was comforting to know that we had Dave Hollins, my man Head, who was one of the most feared players in the league. It was like having the toughest dude in the schoolyard, who always has your back. Nobody fucked with Head!

Game 3 at the Vet presented an interesting decision for Blue Jays manager Cito Gaston. Since we were in a National League park, there would be no DH. This created a dilemma for Cito, because their DH was future Hall of Famer Paul Molitor, who was a hitting machine. Gaston decided to bench John Olerud, the American League batting champ with a .363 average, and insert Molitor at first base. Gaston was sacrificing defense as well, as Olerud was an excellent left-handed first baseman while Molitor was right-handed and inferior defensively to Olerud.

The pitching matchup was Pat Hentgen versus Danny Jackson. Danny got lit up early, surrendering three runs in the first inning, en route to a 10–3 shellacking. Hentgen had a quality outing, giving up one run in six innings. Molitor made Gaston look like a prophet, as he went three for four with a dinger and three RBI and handled first base without any difficulties.

Game 4 would be pivotal.

It was a rainy day in Philly prior to Game 4, which only served to make the archaic turf even more treacherous than usual. Starting pitchers Todd Stottlemyre and Tommy Greene did not last long. Stottlemyre exited after giving up six runs in two innings, and Greene left after allowing seven runs in less than three innings. Meanwhile, I was in the midst of possibly the greatest day of my career. I led off the first with a walk and hit a two-run blast in the second off Stottlemyre.

Going into the bottom of the fifth, the score was tied and Al

Leiter, a lefty, was on the mound for the Jays. Dutch hit a two-run shot, and Milt Thompson had an RBI single. I then deposited a two-run homer into the right field bleachers, which opened the floodgates. We had broken it open and were leading 12–7 after five.

In my previous at-bat against Leiter, I thought I had my third dinger of the game, but I had to settle for a double when it hit the top of the wall. In total, I had a walk, two homers, a double, four RBI, four runs scored, *and* a stolen base. I had surpassed Joe DiMaggio with my eighth and ninth postseason homers. The great "Where have you gone, Joe DiMaggio?" who was in the pantheon of the greatest center fielders—or baseball players for that matter—who ever lived. That is some rarefied air, dude. This should have been the greatest day of my baseball career.

Entering the eighth inning, we were leading 14–9 when Fregosi summoned Larry Andersen, another one of our short relievers, out of the pen. Larry promptly gave up a single, a walk, and a double to make the score 14–10 with one out. Enter Mitch. Tony Fernandez singled to left to bring in another run. Pat Borders walked, but Mitch struck out Ed Sprague for the second out. This was so fucking familiar. I was desperately hoping that Mitch would somehow wiggle out of this. But no, desperation was about to turn into devastation. One more out to get out of the eighth. Henderson singles to center to drive in two, making it 14–13. Then Devon White hits a triple to the deepest part of the yard, chasing home two more runs, and we go on to lose 15–14.

Yes, our starter, Tommy Greene, had given up seven runs in less than three innings, and the Blue Jays had eighteen hits that day, only a few of which were off Mitch, but he was our closer, and he didn't close the deal.

As devastated as we were, I felt horrible for our fans. These

fans had lived with us through all our ups and downs. They had learned to love us because we had epitomized the blue-collar work ethic of the city of Philadelphia. They identified with our scraggly looks and our scrappy, swashbuckling style. They knew we brought our lunch pails every day. They also understood that you could work hard, grind it out, but let your hair down and enjoy it when you were not working. Philly fans are real fans. They wear their hearts on their sleeves, living and dying with your successes and your failures. They always stayed until the last out because we gave them a reason to stay. We always battled to the end. The Philly fans cared. That was what made the winning there so enjoyable.

The best thing we had going for us was that Schill would be on the mound for Game 5, in a rematch of Game 1 against Guzman. Neither pitcher disappointed; a true pitchers' duel ensued. I walked to lead off the bottom of the first, stole second and went to third on a Borders throwing error, and scored on a groundout by Kruk. True aficionados of the game appreciate the value of manufacturing a run without a hit. In the second, Dutch doubled, went to third on a groundout, and scored on an RBI single by Kevin Stocker. We were playing small ball and led 2–0 after two innings. It would prove to be more than enough, as Schill dominated the Jays with a five-hit, complete-game shutout, only the second shutout the Jays experienced that year. Our Clydesdale pulled the carriage, and the ride was smooth, dude.

Our confidence restored, it was back to Toronto for Game 6. We realized that winning two games there would be difficult, but we felt it could be done. Toronto got on top quickly with three runs in the first on Molitor's RBI triple, a sacrifice fly by Carter, and an Alomar RBI single. In the fifth, with a chorus of "MVP!"

echoing throughout the SkyDome, Molitor went yard, ensuring that he would receive the MVP trophy.

Things were looking bleak as we entered the seventh down 5–1. However, we had fought back all year and we were not about to quit now. I hit a three-run homer off Stewart to get us back in it. Head had an RBI single to tie it, and Inky—Pete Incaviglia—had a sacrifice fly to take the lead. Roger Mason, a big old right-handed country boy, came in from the pen and mowed the Jays down in the seventh and eighth. Suddenly we could taste a W and a Game 7, where anything can happen. Three outs and we were there.

Fregosi summoned Mitch, who promptly walked Rickey Henderson to lead off the ninth. Walking the leadoff batter in any inning is a no-no in baseball. Walking the leadoff batter in the bottom of the ninth in a one-run game is a fucking cardinal sin. Walking Rickey Henderson, the greatest base stealer in the history of baseball, in the bottom of the ninth in a one-run game *in the World Series* is egregious.

Recognizing the distinct threat of Henderson, who stole 53 bases that year, Mitch decided to go to a slide-step delivery to keep him close to the bag. Ordinarily a good idea, except that Mitch had never used a slide-step delivery prior to that moment. Nonetheless, he got Devon White to fly out deep to left. We were only two outs from victory. Just as I started to think, *Maybe, just maybe,* Molitor hit one of the hardest balls I've ever seen hit. It was a rocket into center. The ball was hit so hard that Henderson stopped at second without rounding the bag. There was no thought of going to third. Joe Carter was the next batter.

I'm going to ask you to recall the details of what happened next, since to this day I can barely talk about it. Here are the

basics. Carter went yard, and I stood and watched as the ball flew over the left field wall to end the World Series.

Joe was and remains only the second player in history to hit a walk-off home run in the World Series finale; the other was Bill Mazeroski with a famous shot in 1960, which handed the Pirates the World Series over the mighty Yankees.

I have an interesting perspective on it, because remember, I was on the field during the 1986 World Series when we got the last out and won. So I knew what it was like to be on the winning side celebrating on the field in front of the whole country. And then in Toronto, in '93, I got to experience what it was like to lose a game on the final play.

When it happened, I stood there in center field in complete disbelief. I could see the Blue Jay players celebrating at home plate. It was like, *I have to get out of here now. Do I run off? Do I walk off?* I decided I would jog off, and when I did, I focused on our dugout and stopped paying attention to what the delirious Blue Jays were doing.

Both of my World Series had ended in craziness. One on the winning side, the other on the losing side. That's pretty much par for the course of my life.

All or nothing.

It comes down to that.

After the game everyone on our team handled it pretty well. It wasn't too maudlin in the clubhouse. Fregosi handled it well, too. Even though Mitch found a way to hit the fat part of Carter's bat, it wasn't Mitch's fault that we lost. We were a team, and as much as there were mixed emotions, we fully supported Mitch. That's what you do.

One thing about Mitch: he worked hard, and he gave you

everything he had out there. When you go out there, you succeed or you fail, but he never once lost because he didn't try his best. He was a competitor, and he wasn't a quitter. I liked that he was a competitor, because in spring training he and I played golf, and I would bury him for thousands of dollars. Mitch was a fighter, but things happen, and it was unfortunate. But on the flip side, man, he sure made it a long year. It was as though we played three hundred games. The ups and downs of the ninth inning . . . it seemed like it was never easy. Fuck, it was a torture chamber out there.

That was the character of the club. We were a bunch of brawlers. We had been picked to finish last, but this team had tremendous chemistry. In a way, it was similar to my experience on my '86 Mets team.

I was sorry to see the season come to an end. We had accomplished a lot.

I had given everything I had. In the World Series I hit four home runs, and nearly had a fifth. Had we won, and we should have, I would've had a second World Series trophy and probably a World Series MVP trophy as well. But we didn't. It wasn't meant to be.

Nonetheless, as our 3,137,674 home attendance can attest, 1993 was a magical year. Despite the fact that we didn't achieve our ultimate goal, we invigorated the city of Philadelphia, and it rewarded us with its undying support.

I have come to realize how truly special the relationship was that we had with our fans. They supported us until the bitter end. The Phillies gave me the opportunity I craved, playing every day. I will be forever thankful to them for that. I was privileged to have played in that organization, especially with that unique group of characters that constituted the '93 Phillies. We certainly made baseball fun again in Philly.

If women did not exist, all the money in the

world would have no meaning.

—ARISTOTLE ONASSIS

17

AMBASSADOR LENNY

In November 1993, after dominating the game of baseball like not many players have ever done before, I was invited by Major League Baseball to tour Europe as MLB's ambassador to represent and promote the game of baseball. *An honor? Sure, maybe.* The only problem was that they wanted me to promote baseball in places where the people didn't have a fucking clue about baseball.

Accompanying me were my wife, Terri; my business partner, Lindsay Jones; and his wife, Sheri. These were the days before I discovered Lindsay was stealing me blind, so at that time the four of us were having a blast traveling around Europe together. It was the first time I had ever been to Europe, and it was the beginning of my education in world-class travel.

Ironically, before I landed on French soil, I actually thought Paris was a *country*. In high school, I was a good student, but my real focus had been on what I had to do to become a Major League Baseball player. In other words, subjects like geography and world history tended to take a backseat.

We went to Amsterdam, Holland; Paris, France; and Düsseldorf, Germany. I talked to kids, participated in baseball clinics,

and did whatever the MLB had lined up for me. In Düsseldorf, I signed autographs at the Hard Rock Cafe, and even though there was a mob of people attending, it seemed like most of them didn't know what they were showing up for. I guess the mentality of people in Europe is the same as it is in the United States: when you put a celebrity in front of a crowd of people, whether they know who you are or not, they go nuts.

I was thirty years old and happened to be firing on all cylinders. Not only was I put together like a Greek statue, and felt bulletproof, I was on the verge of signing a new contract that could potentially pay me $30 million over five years. Life couldn't have been any better. Throw in the handful of pain pills and amphetamines I was swallowing at will, and days would turn into nights, and nights would turn into days, with the lines blurring in between.

◆

The city of Amsterdam was a complete trip. One minute you're strolling along a street dotted with nice restaurants and hotels, passing by families, then the next thing you know, you're in the red-light district, with its prostitutes, sex shops, peep shows, and sex museums. But since my wife was with me, it goes without saying that we didn't spend a lot of time browsing the goods and services of the red-light district. We stayed at the Amstel Amsterdam, which had been completely remodeled. They gave me a suite that was off the charts, and after we got settled in our room, I walked down to the concierge to ask him where we should go.

He told me that Amsterdam was known for its diamonds, informing me that the diamond industry went back more than four hundred years and that the city was still the best place in all of Europe to buy diamonds. I asked him to give me the name and address of the best diamond shop in Amsterdam. I told Terri that we needed to go somewhere, but I didn't tell her where, because I wanted to surprise her. When we walked into the best diamond shop in Amsterdam, I said to the man who greeted us, "I want the biggest and best diamond you have for my wife."

Terri was speechless, as I caught her completely off guard. She never was a big spender, and kept saying to me, "Lenny, I don't need anything that expensive."

I shot back, "Terri, here's the deal: you pick out whatever diamond ring you want, or I am going to tell the guy to give me the biggest and most expensive diamond ring in the store."

Terri settled on a three-carat diamond ring that cost me about $50,000 when all was said and done.

◆

Another one of the appearances I did was for a retail chain in Amsterdam. It turned out the owner was cool as shit. (I'll leave his name and company anonymous.)

When I finished signing autographs and shaking hands, along with the courtesy smiles and the fake laughs, the owner said, in his thick Dutch accent, "Let's get the fuck out of here and get a drink."

I rarely turned down a drink and said why not. He had a new

Benz, and even though he was an older dude—I would have guessed he was about sixty—he definitely had a clue. We ended up at a fancy restaurant, and the person who greeted us at the door gave me the impression that he was the owner. The owner introduced me to the man, then waved for me to follow him.

We went up a set of narrow stairs, and the owner pulled out a key and swung open a door. I followed them into what looked like something out of a luxury magazine: a huge room with state-of-the-art everything, very modern and very sleek. I was confused as to why we were there, but then I got unconfused real fast when twenty of the most beautiful girls I had ever seen appeared.

The owner turned to me and said, "This is how we do it in Amsterdam." The next thing I know, he pulls out some blow. I couldn't believe this sixty-year-old dude brought Richards to the party. He then signaled for the girls to come over, and it was on.

If someone would have said to me that I would end up partying with the sixty-year-old owner of a major retailer in Amsterdam, and that we would be swimming in pussy, with enough powder to make Keith Richards proud, I would have said no fucking way. The story of my life—unpredictable.

◆

The next stop was Paris. On advice from my limousine driver, we went to dinner at La Tour d'Argent, where four hundred years ago customers apparently dueled to get a table. It was still one of the most celebrated restaurants in the world. When I walked in, a tall, tuxedo-clad maître d' wanted me to take off my

driving cap. *Thanks but no thanks.* I considered it elegant. It was made by Kangol, a premier brand of hats. When I wouldn't give it to him, he started talking angrily in French to one of the waiters.

I knew that this guy was about to blow a gasket, so I said to my interpreter, Bob Schueller, "Tell him I have a baseball injury that it's covering, and I don't want to alarm the other customers."

The maître d' finally relented, but he was pissed. You can probably guess what this guy thought about Americans in general, and here I was bringing the stereotype to life. But I didn't really give a fuck.

When they brought out a wine list bigger than *The Baseball Encyclopedia,* I turned to Bob and told him to order the best, most expensive bottle of wine in the whole place.

"Their dessert wine, Château d'Yquem," Bob said, "is the finest in the world."

Bob started speaking to the maître d' in French, then looked back at me. "He will offer you a bottle of the 1936 Château d'Yquem for sixteen thousand francs."

"Offer me?" I said. "Sixteen thousand francs? How much is that?"

"Three thousand dollars," Bob said.

"No problem," I replied without blinking.

Up until then, the maître d' had been flashing me dirty looks, but after I ordered the Château d'Yquem, he became much more subservient. And at that point my Kangol hat became an absolute nonfactor.

The maître d' brought out the bottle of wine and explained how difficult it was to produce, requiring a rare summer heat, and an autumn of moist mornings to properly rot the grapes. Each grape is picked individually, only after it has dried and shriveled

on the vine. Picking this particular crop takes care and a lot of luck.

All of that aside, the Château d'Yquem tasted like liquid gold. I'm not kidding you. You have to drink it almost chilled, almost icy, then you sip it slow. It's hard to explain to someone how it tastes, as there is nothing comparable.

The son of André Terrail, the founder of this famed restaurant, stopped by our table and explained that during World War II, his father had bricked off his stash of 1936 Château d'Yquem to hide it from the Nazis. The five bottles in his wine cellar were the last ones left in the world, and I had just ordered one of them.

"Monsieur," said Mr. Terrail, "it has been a pleasure to meet you. You have just bought the best bottle of wine in the world." I adjusted my hat and I said to him, "Let me get another bottle—to go."

I wanted a third one, but Terrail refused to sell it to me. He said that he needed it for his wine cellar, and it didn't matter how much money I offered for it.

I guess sometimes money *doesn't* buy everything.

◆

Our next stop was Düsseldorf, which is one badass city. Germany was fucking cool and right up my alley. I mean, they start drinking beer at ten o'clock in the morning, which to me shows that they understand the good things in life.

We checked into this beautiful hotel, and when Terri and I got up to our suite on the twentieth floor, I was looking down on the

sidewalk below, and I could see a lady walking this magnificent German shepherd. Growing up, we had German shepherds—it was the only breed of dog I ever had.

My dad bought them and taught us all about them, and from then on, it was the only breed of dog I ever wanted to own. They are the most loyal and intelligent dogs on the planet, hands down.

"Terri," I said, "we're in Germany. This is where German shepherds come from. See that lady right there with the dog? I'm going to go down and buy that dog."

"You're out of your mind," she said.

"Watch me."

I ran to the elevator and raced to talk to the concierge, who spoke enough English to help me. I said to him, "You have to come with me and talk to this lady outside. I want to buy her fucking dog." The guy looked at me like I was nuts, but he helped me anyway.

We ran down the street and finally caught up with the woman and her German shepherd. I asked the concierge to tell her that I wanted to buy her dog. They started yakking in German, but she kept shaking her head no.

"What did she say?" I asked.

"She says she thinks you're crazy," he said. "She said she won't sell her dog for any price."

"You want to bet?" I asked, but didn't give him the chance to answer. "Tell her I understand, and that I didn't mean any disrespect. Then ask her if she would be so kind as to bring the dog to the hotel for a few minutes so my wife could at least see how beautiful her shepherd is."

The concierge looked at me funny and started talking to her in German again, but this time the conversation had a much nicer tone. Finally, he looked at me. "She said no problem."

Little did she know what she was walking into. When I want something bad enough, nobody can operate like me. As we made our way back to the hotel, I asked the concierge, "How much money do you want to bet that I get the lady to sell me her dog right in the lobby of your hotel?"

This German dude already thought I was a little bit off, but after making that statement, he had a look on his face like I'd lost my fucking mind. "You are crazy. She already told me that there is no way she is selling her dog to you."

I said it again: "How much do you want to bet I own that dog in less than sixty minutes?"

"I'll bet you one hundred American dollars," he fired back.

"You got it. It's on."

The next thing you know, we were standing in the lobby of the nicest hotel in Düsseldorf with this beautiful German shepherd.

I told the concierge that I would pay her $5,000 in cash right on the spot.

"No way. You're crazy," she said in German.

We went back and forth, and as she started to leave, I said, "I'll give you $75,000."

And just like that I owned a real, genuine German shepherd, and collected my $100 from the stunned concierge.

◆

Back in the U.S., I was still feeling like a goodwill ambassador. New York City, once foreign to me, was now home. The fact is, there's really no place like the City. More important, there are

no people like New Yorkers, and I loved them for the way they treated me and took me in.

Guys like Trump would invite me to be a guest at the U.S. Open. I watched the matches from his suite with Lenny Kravitz and Puff Daddy, both of whom were cool as shit and super smart. I especially enjoyed talking about business with Puff Daddy. He makes more money by being dialed in with Cîroc vodka than he does from all his other businesses combined.

Another guy who was tight with Trump, whom I eventually became good friends with, was Joseph Cinque, president and CEO of the American Academy of Hospitality Sciences. Cinque would fly around the world and give their Star Diamond Award to the premier hotels and restaurants. He knew everybody who was anybody. I never met a guy as dialed in as Joe. He was good friends at the time with New York City's police commissioner, Bernie Kerik, as well as the longtime New York City fire commissioner. One time Joe Cinque was driving to the Carlyle Hotel with the police commissioner and fire commissioner in Bernie's badass SUV to pick me up to go to dinner in Manhattan.

The Carlyle Hotel was where a lot of the big hitters stayed, and also happened to be John F. Kennedy's secret hideout. There was a secret tunnel built for him to access the hotel when he would meet Marilyn Monroe. As I was coming out of the lobby, Cinque turned on the siren and got on the horn with those fucking blasting speakers, and with his New York accent—the greatest accent in the world—he said, *"Lenny Dykstra, come out with your hands up. We have you surrounded."*

For three blocks the whole city froze.

Everyone—I mean *everyone*—was staring at me. Joe had made it seem so real. He nearly shut down traffic on the Upper East Side.

Today, Joseph Cinque is in his seventies and still going strong. When everything went bad for me, I called him and told him, "Joe, I want you to know that I understand that you and I can't hang out anymore, but I'm not mad at you. You have always treated me great, and you and I had some great times. No matter what ever happens, I will always love you, Joe." Joe got real emotional and said how much my phone call meant to him. Business is business, and I didn't want Joe to feel like he did anything wrong, because he didn't. Joe was a funny motherfucker—he was one of the few dudes who could make me laugh at any moment, and he will always be my friend. We had one last laugh over that prank with the police commissioner before we hung up.

Who would have ever imagined that later on in my life, I really would have to come out with my hands up?

Many people don't have the ability to be rich, because they're too lazy or they don't have the desire or the stick-to-itiveness. It's a talent. Some people have a talent for piano. Some people have a talent for raising a family. Some people have a talent for golf. I just happen to have a talent for making money.

—DONALD TRUMP

18

CAR WASH KING

Unfortunately, professional baseball careers are relatively short-lived. In my case, I was able to play twelve years, which is a little more than double the average—5.6 years. Being a forward thinker, I realized midway through my career that I would need to do something that would sustain me after my playing days came to an end. Ideally, I would be involved with a business that would provide me with consistent cash flow.

Needless to say, with baseball consuming most of my life since I was a little kid, I had little, if any, business experience or training. Nonetheless, I knew I had to figure out a way to protect myself and my family in the future. Therefore, I began building my financial empire in 1993, when Lindsay Jones, my good friend at the time, convinced me to start a business with him.

Lindsay was always smart in school, and he became a CPA working for the firm of Coopers & Lybrand. He asked me what I was doing with my money. At the time, even though I was making millions, I didn't have a financial adviser. I had money, but no idea how to take care of it or make it grow so it would last my entire life. Lindsay was able to teach me a tremendous amount

about business. I'll give him that. He won me over with what he knew, and we decided to start a business together.

I am from Southern California, and if there's one thing I know, it's that we like our cars to look shiny and new. As a result, I knew that the car wash business would be recession-proof in California. No matter what the economy looks like, most Californians are still going to get their cars washed. Moreover, it's a business that won't be replaced by new technology.

I knew that if we could locate a prime spot for the business, we'd make money, because Southern California was a car wash haven. The first location I bought was in North Corona. Corona, once called the lemon capital of the world, is a major suburb of Los Angeles and happened to be the second-fastest-growing city in California at the time.

The property we found was across the street from a Costco and in the same parking lot as a Walmart, with people coming and going constantly. *Bam.* I couldn't have found a better location. I paid a million for the land and started to develop my business plan.

It was baseball-themed. The cheapest wash we called a "single," a step up from that was called a "double," then a "triple," and finally, the "home run" was the most expensive. The average cost for a wash was fifteen dollars. By the end of our first year, sales at the North Corona Car Wash exceeded $1 million. Of all the car washes I built, North Corona was always my biggest producer.

My second car wash, in Simi Valley, was the fucking Taj Mahal of car washes. Simi Valley is an upscale LA suburb, about fifty miles to the northwest of LA and home to the Ronald Reagan Presidential Library.

The Simi Valley car wash facility was a sprawling space. I

installed a large shark tank in the store. Watching those sharks swim around was something my customers really enjoyed. I also showcased more than $100,000 of the finest sports memorabilia in beveled glass display cabinets.

I purchased the land from Shell for $800,000, which in actuality was easily worth $1.5 million, ultimately resulting in the firing of the guy who sold it to me because the price was so low. However, it took me five years to get the city of Simi Valley to give me the permits needed to build. It got so fucking bad that I showed up at a city council meeting. City council meetings are complete power plays for the council members who get off on telling people what they can or can't do. It's a fucking joke. Finally, I stood up at that meeting and said, "Just so we are clear, I promise you that I am not building a whorehouse. It's actually going to be the nicest car wash in the world. But you already know that since you have been looking at the plans for five years."

Majestic is what it was.

I then bought a third property at the other end of Corona from a classic little old lady who had been sitting on the lot forever. The property wasn't even listed. Large shopping centers were being developed all around her, and she was one of the last holdouts in an area that had once been only orange groves. It didn't take a rocket scientist to figure out she would sell if I could *somehow* win her over.

So I chartered a helicopter and created one of those enormous checks like you see in those Publishers Clearing House commercials. I landed on her property. After getting out of the helicopter, I presented her with the *big* check for a million dollars.

It took her less than ten minutes to say yes. Stroke of genius, if I may say so.

On the five acres that made up the South Corona property, I not only built a car wash but also a ConocoPhillips 76 fueling center with a world-class convenience store. It was way too nice to call it just a gas station. The fueling center was beautiful, with marble floors and countertops. Simply put, it was stunning. It put the ARCO and Sam's Club stations across the street to shame.

In the third phase of development, I built a twenty-thousand-square-foot multi-tenant triple-net retail center that would be leased out. There is nothing better than a little passive income to add some consistency to your bottom line in order to see you though a seasonal business. After all, car washes in Southern California are here to stay, but it still rains on occasion.

They were the best car washes in the world. The income they produced should have set me up for the rest of my life. The operative words here are *should have*.

Because things began to go south fast.

I came to realize that Lindsay Jones, my business partner, put self-interest in front of the partnership. Although I suspected he was stealing from me, I didn't possess proof. Furthermore, there was a part of me that didn't want to face that my so-called friend was capable of such backstabbing.

Lindsay was scheming and conniving, and because I was playing for the Phillies and wintering at the Bayou Club in Tampa, Florida, I wasn't able to oversee the car washes, and wouldn't have known what to even look for. Lindsay was the working partner. I gave him 25 percent of the partnership to run the show while I was away playing.

In fact, after everything was revealed, I had to go to court to legally remove him as a partner before I could fire him. I hired Dan Petrocelli as my attorney and paid him a small fortune to

get rid of Lindsay. If you remember, Dan represented the parents of the murdered Ron Goldman in the O. J. Simpson civil case. Petrocelli hired the forensic accounting firm of Freeman & Mills, and they did an audit that revealed all of Lindsay's wrongdoing. And let me tell you, it wasn't a small number.

Based on the audit, we filed a suit claiming embezzlement, fraud, breach of contract, and other claims. Lindsay in turn had the balls to sue me, demanding ownership of 25 percent of the car wash business. Well, we went to binding arbitration and the arbitrator buried his ass. He ruled that my so-called friend and business partner took more than $2 million from our business partnership without authority, owed more than $300,000 in unpaid loans, and falsified partnership books and records to enhance his own position. I was awarded $2.4 million in actual damages and another half a million in punitive damages.

The arbitrator also threw Jones out of the business.

I never saw a dime of the award.

Like I told Lindsay the day I fired him, borrowing the line from Mickey Rourke's character in the movie *Body Heat*, "Any time you try a decent crime, you got fifty ways you can fuck up. If you can think of twenty-five of them, then you're a genius . . . and you ain't no genius."

That was the end of Lindsay Jones.

Being with a woman all night never hurt no professional baseball player. It's staying up all night looking for a woman that does him in.

—CASEY STENGEL

19

ROBES & ROOM SERVICE

One of the many benefits of playing in Philadelphia was that it was close to Atlantic City, which meant it was close to the casinos. In gambling terms, I was considered a *whale,* meaning, someone who tees it up for big numbers at the tables. For example, when I was donating, or gambling (they're the same thing in my case), I would bet $10,000 a hand in baccarat. The house knows if they can keep someone like me at the table long enough, I'll lose much more than I win. How do you think they built all of those beautiful casinos? Enough said.

With a single phone call, the casinos would often charter a private jet for me, put me up in their best suites, and even supply me with high-grade blow. *Why?* Because they knew that I was getting paid more than $500,000 a month, every month without fail, and at the end of the day they knew I would have a bad run, go on tilt, and drop a big fucking number. To help matters, I would always draw a big crowd to watch me play.

Once, one of those watching was a well-known writer by the name of Bruce Buschel. Buschel went on to write a story about me that was originally published as "Lips Get Smacked" in the

January 1993 issue of *Philadelphia* magazine (later included in *The Best American Sports Writing 1994*).

I was pissed at the time, but in all honesty, I couldn't have written it better myself. The only thing I found confusing was this guy's infatuation with my lips. He was completely obsessed. Here's what Buschel wrote:

It's Lenny F-ing Dykstra. What a mouth on this guy—not just the utterances that pass through it, but the actual physical mouth. Never closed, even when its owner is ruminative or silent, it is the control center for heavy traffic. Things go in (filtered tips of cigarettes and clear liquids and fingers, one or two at a time) and things come out (a stream of profanity and filtered tips and gusts of smoke and fingers and a tongue) . . .

The croupier collects Dykstra's three orange chips and passes the shoe—the card dispenser—to the far end of the table to the only other gambler, a bald, mild-mannered fellow . . .

Lenny the Lips locates his rolling chair, extinguishes his cigarette, watches a brunette exchange his soiled ashtray for a fresh one, lights another Salem with a thin gold lighter and counts his orange wafers: twenty-one. He decides to slide three more onto the space marked banker and offers encouragement to his hairless compadre. "Let's go, dude. You're the fucking man. Show me something." His voice carries like a high fly caught in a swift wind. As the cards skim along the baize, Dykstra releases his face to a series of ticks and twitches, freezing his gaping yap as if to address an endodontist.

It remains stretched wide until he sees his cards. He likes what he sees. He takes a deep drag. He expels abruptly.

"I love you, dude," he says to the bald gambler, who nods meekly in acknowledgment. Dykstra compulsively smooths out his slender spire of chips; he keeps adding to the stack like a child testing how high his building blocks will climb before gravity intrudes . . .

"We're on a fucking roll, dude."

And so are we . . .

Watching Lenny Dykstra gamble is like having an orchestra seat at a one-character David Mamet tragicomic psychodrama. You are appalled and delighted by the language and the largesse, the exposed and tortured soul. You enjoy the ride. You know it will end badly.

Gambling is all about ego and the three *p*'s: power, partying, and pussy. But not necessarily in that order.

If you think about gambling, and you are honest with yourself, nothing about it makes sense. When you win, you kind of say to yourself, *Cool, just throw that in with the rest.* Meaning, you don't appreciate it, because if you have that kind of ammo to burn, what's the fucking difference? On the other hand, when you lose, it's the fucking worst. Furthermore, the stress I used to put myself through has probably taken years off my life, and for what? To donate? To torture myself?

With that said, at the time I was making so much fucking money, it didn't fucking matter . . . *So I thought.*

One thing I will admit: when it comes to gambling, I have found that high rollers make for some really interesting friends.

One particular example of this was Roger King, owner of

King World. Roger discovered Oprah Winfrey, put Dr. Phil on the map, and entertained millions and millions of Americans with *Jeopardy!* and *Wheel of Fortune*.

The first time I met Roger was in Las Vegas. I was partying at Caesar's Palace when I decided to go sit down at the high-roller baccarat tables. Flanking me on my left and right were some friends who, let's just say, were easy on the eyes. I called the pit boss over and told him to give me a quarter million dollars' worth of chips.

Minutes after I told the pit boss how much I wanted in chips, Roger stood up and demanded $1 million in cash.

See, Roger didn't like it when *he* wasn't the center of attention. While the casino was in the process of putting together his money, Roger turned to me.

"Who the fuck are you?"

When I answered politely, "Lenny Dykstra," he replied with an entirely new tone of respect, "I can't believe I am sitting at a baccarat table with Nails."

I stood up to shake his hand, and he almost crushed my fucking fingers. A former boxer, Roger stood six foot four and had a commanding presence, to say the very least.

Even though I had no idea who he was at the time, we ended up in his suite drinking later that night. Roger was rude, obnoxious, and loud—he was my kind of guy.

In addition to gambling, Roger loved the powder. He also loved pussy. *And* he was a fucking billionaire. Hanging out with him came easy. If we weren't partying at a casino, he'd often show up at my parties at the Peninsula hotel in Beverly Hills when we were in LA playing the Dodgers.

On one particular Saturday night, my teammates and I were hitting it hard, even though we had a one o'clock game the fol-

lowing day. Roger was a degenerate gambler, so when he saw all of us partying and still going strong at four A.M., he got an idea.

We all suited up and played the game the next day, and we won after I laced a double down the right field line in the top of the ninth to drive in what would be the winning run.

After the game, my cell phone rang. It was Roger.

"You motherfucker!" he shouted.

I was completely caught off guard. "What? What did I do?"

"I'll tell you what you did," he said. "You cost me five hundred thousand fucking dollars."

"What do you mean?" I said, thoroughly confused.

"You and your teammates were partying until four in the fucking morning, and I figured there was no way you guys could fucking win. So I bet $500,000 on the Dodgers. And you had to be the motherfucker that got the game-winning hit?"

"You should know better than to bet against me, bro," I said. "Who do you think you are dealing with?" I continued, rubbing it in, "Never bet against Nails."

We both laughed, as he didn't give a shit about the money. Roger King was the man.

Roger suffered a stroke on December 7, 2007, and died the next day. He was only sixty-three years old. Too damn young to die. I loved the guy and truly miss him.

◆

When I was with the Mets in spring training in 1989, I met Mike Croswell. Croz, as I called him, became my personal

assistant and handled all my travel. I will give him credit for being organized and on time. If a person wanted to hang with me and experience life at the highest level, there were a few simple rules: you must be on time and prepared, but the fastest way to get eliminated from living life like a rock star was if there was any body odor or bad breath. That called for an immediate execution (meaning, they were no longer on the team).

Croz didn't have a life. He pretty much failed at everything he did, and that's why he lived for my phone calls. When I would say, *Croz, pick a country, any country. I need to get the fuck out of here,* I could feel the excitement on the other end of the phone. I have to admit, when it came to traveling and hotels, Croz knew his shit.

During the season, for road games, Croz would fly into the city we would be playing in and book suites at the best hotel. Croz helped me discover how to live a life of luxury, like the top 1 percent. I picked up one of my favorite sayings from Croz: "Robes and room service." There are few things better than checking into a swanky suite, putting on a plush bathrobe, and calling down to room service.

On one road trip when we were playing the Expos, I was staying at the Ritz-Carlton in Montreal, a very European, big-league hotel. At eight in the morning of a day game, as I walked by the restaurant, Fregosi and the coaches were having breakfast, and they could tell that I was just getting in after pulling another all-nighter. I could see by the way Fregosi was staring at me. He always kept a close eye on me to see what I was up to. At that particular time in the season, I was playing really well, and Fregosi was giving me some leash. The fact was, I was performing—*literally*—on and off the field. And as far as management goes, if you produce for them, you can do whatever the fuck you want.

♦

Like I said, every time we played in Los Angeles, I would take out pretty much the whole fucking floor at the Peninsula, sometimes the Four Seasons, both in Beverly Hills. I needed space for my entourage, and I needed three or four rooms for the prizewinners at the end of the night, when the party would wind down.

When I say I threw a party at the Peninsula hotel, I'm talking about a real party. I would pay about $50,000 to a party organizer by the name of Gary Walters, and he would line up the best guests. Gary could line up more pussy than God. He had access to celebrities, too, like Jack Nicholson, Mickey Rourke, and Johnny Depp, to name just a few. Gary is also the son of Norby Walters, who was accused of signing college football players to an agency contract and paying them money while they were still in college.

I remember at one particular party, Wilt Chamberlain was in attendance. This was about the time when the story came out about Wilt hitting pay dirt with twenty thousand women. Twenty thousand . . . that's the size of a small city. Wilt was sitting at a table, and his knees—I swear to God—were up to his chin.

I said, "Wilt, man, I don't care about all the women, I just want to know one thing: how in the fuck did you score one hundred points in a game?"

"I was the best" was Wilt's simple answer.

Wilt was cool. And I'm sure the guy had to be hung like a swamp mule, but there's no way he fucked twenty thousand women. There are people in the world who actually know how to do math, and I'm one of them. Average it out—it's not humanly possible.

I also had the opportunity to experience a night of excess with Michael Jordan. The catch was that Michael didn't even know we had hung out together until the next morning.

There was a famous golf tournament every year in Reno, Nevada, and it was nationally televised by one of the major networks. It was a serious fucking tournament in which the winner pocketed a cool $100,000. *Better than a sharp stick in the eye, right?* This tournament was for the world's elite entertainers, whether they were an actor, a football player, a Major League Baseball player, or an NBA star. I was invited to play every year, but I felt my game wasn't good enough so I never participated. But one year I worked really hard on my golf game and was playing well enough, so I decided that I would go tee it up with the big boys.

The night before the first round of the tournament was set to start, I wanted to be sharp. I had an early tee time and wanted to be rested. I went to bed, and in the room next to me, I could hear a dude and his girl fucking like I have never heard any two people fuck before. If I had to hear her scream one more time, "Oh my God, I'm going to come! Oh my God, I'm going to come," I was going to hang myself. She took the term *screamer* to a whole new level. The closer she got, the louder this bitch would get. She was fucking killing me. Then, finally, I think the human factor kicked in, and I heard no more noise. Just as I was about to fall asleep, these two start going at it again. It was like they got their second wind or something, because this bitch got louder and louder to the point where I remember lying in bed asking myself, *How is it humanly possible to fuck for that long?*

At this point, the sun was beginning to come up, which gave me hope that those two were finally done. I was convinced that

the chick next door would not be able to physically walk out of there after the pounding she endured.

I took a shower, put on my best golf outfit, and got ready to go down to the restaurant and eat breakfast. So as I'm walking out of my room, at the same time the door to the room beside me opens up and out strolls Michael Jordan with a big fucking grin plastered on his face. We shared a look and I got him to bust a gut when I said, "And I thought you were my idol on the basketball court!"

◆

Jack Nicholson is one of those people who happens to be cool without trying to be cool. He came to quite a few of my parties over the years and he would always ask, "Where is old Nails?" Classic, fucking classic! One time, he even brought me the jacket that he actually wore on the set when he was filming *A Few Good Men*.

I would bring him on the field at Dodger Stadium for batting practice, and Jack would often bring his son, who at the time was about eight years old. Jack would always point to second base and say, "Son, you see out there? That's the position your old man used to play."

When I was trying to close the deal with a chick, sometimes I would pull out my cell phone and call Jack to help me close. Hey, a dog has to eat, so I was willing to pull out all the stops.

My boy Jack would get on the speakerphone, and in that fucking classic gravelly voice of his, he would ask, "How is old Nails?"

No chick said no after a call from Jack. Best. Wingman. Ever.

The big lesson in life, baby, is never be scared
of anyone or anything.

—FRANK SINATRA

20

1994 MLB STRIKE: NO MORE KOOL-AID FOR ME

In 1993, I was playing for a contract. I was on a mission to get paid real money. I played almost every day, 161 out of 162 games. I had a phenomenal year, posting numbers that led the league in several categories. Moreover, I helped lead the Phillies to the World Series that year. That season, I led the entire National League with 194 hits, 637 at-bats, 143 runs scored, 129 bases on balls, and 325 times on base. In any other year, I am the National League MVP.

However, 1993 was a good year for Barry Bonds as well. He hit .336 with 129 runs scored, 46 homers, 38 doubles, 4 triples, 123 RBI, 29 stolen bases, a .458 on-base percentage, and a 1.136 OPS. Although Barry's team didn't win anything that year, he garnered his third National League MVP title in four years. I was second with 267 total votes (including 4 first-place votes).

I had a monster season in 1993 due to the coalescence of several factors: I was of the perfect age, I was playing to get paid, and I had my good "vitamins."

The 1993 season was a hell of a ride. I needed to produce, and I did, in a huge way, which translated into a $30 million contract. I was finally going to make real money.

In 1994, I played in only 84 games in a season cut short when the owners locked out the players. The owners tried to break the union, and they were so hell-bent on doing it, there was no World Series that year.

During the strike of 1994, I was losing $34,000 each and every day—not every month or every week, but *every single day*. The lockout progressed to the point where it was negatively impacting large numbers of people, players who had families to support, myself included. Despite the financial pain the union was inflicting upon us, their intention was that we had to think long-term. That was great for the future players but completely sucked for those in the here and now. The current players at that time were expected to take a bullet for those who would come after us with no questions asked. Obviously, what they failed to take into consideration was that the window to earn for a professional baseball player is smaller than in virtually any other profession. Therefore, when you go months and months without being paid, it creates a significant reduction in your lifetime earnings. Understandably, the public has difficulty relating to professional athletes who comparatively make large sums of money. However, when you are on the receiving end of getting *zero* every day, it has a negative impact on you and your family, regardless of what your income is.

Another way to look at it is to consider the amount of time you can be proficient at your job. Undeniably, the skills of professional baseball players dwindle rather quickly, with most players only able to play until their early to mid-thirties. And those are the lucky ones! On the other hand, doctors, lawyers, accountants,

businessmen, salesmen, and most other professionals do not have the dramatic erosion of skills that curtail their careers. In fact, it is customary for most people to maintain their skills so they can continue to work into their sixties, seventies, or even eighties!

It got to the point where I sat down my wife and I literally told her the following: "Terri, I'm going to show you what happened to us today."

I got some paper and scissors and made up $34,000 in fake money, and *boom*, I threw the pile of fake money into the fireplace and watched the flames consume it.

"This is what we lost yesterday, this is what we lost the day before, what we're going to lose tomorrow, and keep losing every single day," I told her. "We have to get the union together and let them know what the hell is going on."

I called Don Fehr, executive director of the Major League Baseball Players Association, and I made it crystal clear to him: "Listen, I want you to organize a meeting immediately with every single fucking major league player and agent, and anybody else who has anything to do with this fucking strike. I want to voice some concerns I have about what's going on, and, to be clear, I've talked to numerous players, and they have the same concerns."

Almost every big-league player was there for the next union meeting. Fehr knew I wanted the lockout to end. A whole lot of other players wanted it to end, too, but they just didn't have the balls to stand up and say something.

Fehr was afraid of what I was going to say. "I don't know," he said.

"What do you mean, 'I don't know'? How about this? You work for me, motherfucker. I'm your fucking boss."

Meaning, I pay you, so organize the meeting and let me speak.

I showed up in Orlando, the site he picked for everyone to meet. There were perhaps as many as five hundred players and agents in attendance.

Fehr called me up to the podium and addressed the audience, "Lenny Dykstra wants to say a few words."

I looked out toward my fellow players and spoke my mind. "Let me be clear: first and foremost, I am not here to try to talk any of you into crossing the picket line. I would never cross the picket line. It's about staying unified, but the whole reason I called this meeting was to drive home the point that we can't continue down this path. We have to get this settled."

Some of the players started yelling shit at me, others were talking among themselves. All in all, they were making it difficult for me to be heard. My boy and best friend, Dave Hollins, was in the front row wearing a muscle shirt. He stood up, with that extremely prominent head of his, and screamed, "Shut the fuck up and let the man speak!"

Like E. F. Hutton, when Head talks, people listen! You could have heard a pin drop. No one wanted to have anything to do with Hollins. He put the fear of God in people.

After Hollins silenced the crowd, they actually started listening.

"Fuck this," I said. "I'm losing $34,000 a day. I don't know about you, but how many of you motherfuckers enjoy waking up every morning knowing you're going to take it in the fucking ass?" I explained that most of us have a small earning window and that none of us could really afford to make that window even smaller.

"Remember," I said, "that money's gone. It will never come back. The reason I'm speaking is not to break the union, not to

cut and burn. We need to tell our union heads they work for *us*—we pay their salaries—and the bottom line is this: it's time to get this thing settled."

After I was done speaking, there must have been a hundred players who came up to me and expressed their appreciation, their relief, and the fact that they were worried, too.

The 1994 Major League Baseball season came to an abrupt halt on August 12, 1994, causing the cancellation of the remainder of the regular season, as well as the postseason. For the first time since 1904, the season did not conclude with a World Series winner. Ultimately, the strike didn't end until 232 days later, on April 2, 1995, after 948 games had been cancelled. In addition to limiting most clubs to 113 games in 1994, every team's season was reduced to 144 games in 1995. It was a disaster: the longest work stoppage in baseball history, one that would do irreparable damage to the national pastime.

If we could sniff or swallow something that would, for five or six hours each day, abolish our solitude as individuals, atone us with our fellows in a glowing exaltation of affection and make life in all its aspects seem not only worth living, but divinely beautiful and significant, and if this heavenly, world-transfiguring drug were of such a kind that we could wake up next morning with a clear head and an undamaged constitution—then, it seems to me, all our problems . . . would be wholly solved and earth would become paradise.

—ALDOUS HUXLEY

21

PROMISED LAND

When I walked away from the game it wasn't as difficult as you might think, considering that I could no longer play the game of baseball the *right* way. In my world, you either do it right or you don't do it. I was no longer physically capable of competing with the best baseball players in the world. I couldn't perform at the same level for the fans who paid money to watch me play. The fans deserved more than that. It was my time. If you play long enough, there comes a point when your shit just doesn't work as good as it once did. It's called reality.

When you have to take a combination of drugs just to get on the field every day, that's a problem, *a big fucking problem.*

My own time came a bit sooner than it should have for a couple reasons. I played the second half of my career in Philadelphia's Veterans Stadium, which had AstroTurf. It was like playing on concrete on the street. This took a toll on my knees and my back. Factor in my lifestyle off the field: I partied like I was the lead singer of some rock 'n' roll band. Nobody could burn the candle at both ends like me. Like everything else I do in life, I go big or I go home! So when it came to having fun

after the games on the road, nobody did it better than me, *or as often.*

To put this in perspective: a full MLB season consists of 162 games, of which 81 are played on the road. It was like living two separate lives. The only difference with me was that living two separate lives wasn't good enough, so I lived three or four.

When we would play on the road, I started working smarter instead of harder. Meaning, instead of going out to a bar and dealing with all the noise, all the people dressed up in those bad costumes, and all the other bullshit that goes along with the bar scene, I took it to the next level. I would have one of my people on my payroll check in to the presidential suite at the best hotel in whatever city we happened to be playing in at that particular time. I was always ahead of the curve, so I came up with my own game plan, and it had nothing to do with baseball, if you know what I mean.

I paid my guys to make things easier so I wouldn't waste any time. Their job was to line up the talent, so that when I would arrive in town, everything would be in place. What would follow was an immediate beeline over to the other hotel, where the talent was waiting. What you might find mind-boggling was that during the last five years of my career I never once stayed at the team hotel. Basically, I had my people on payroll bring the bar to my presidential suite, taking room service to a whole different level.

The bottom line: it didn't take me long to figure out how the top 1 percent live.

♦

In 1998, my baseball career was over; what wasn't over was my addiction to Vicodin. It had gotten to the point where I just couldn't get off the pain pills. I never felt good. I was sick all the time and always faced with the problem of having to get more pills.

Anyone who has experienced opiate withdrawal knows what I am talking about. Unless you have been there, it's impossible to explain the pain. It's *indescribable*. It's almost like there is a fire inside of you that you will do anything to put out. It was a vicious cycle and a complete nightmare that began in 1991 after I wrapped my brand-new Mercedes SL around a tree and almost killed myself and my teammate Darren Daulton.

This was when I was introduced to opiates for the first time.

With that being said, I didn't become physically dependent on pain pills until midway through the 1993 season. I was on a fucking mission to win games and get paid, and I didn't give a fuck what I had to do or take to get on the field. I was playing every fucking night, no matter what! The results? During the 1993 season, nobody got on base more than Lenny Dykstra, and I set the record for most plate appearances in a season by a left-hander (773), a mark that still stands.

If you think about what you just read, taking into consideration that MLB began in 1871 with the founding of the National Association, that's a pretty tall statement, even if I have to say so myself. This means I went to the plate more times that season than Babe Ruth; Lou Gehrig; Pete Rose, the all-time hit leader; and every other fucking player who had ever put on a baseball uniform in any season prior to 1993.

If that were a trivia question, what would be the odds on someone answering it correctly? How about zero! Nobody on the

planet would know the answer. Similar to my life, nobody knows what really happened.

♦

There would be days when I would wake up (more like come out of my coma) and be hurting so bad, I didn't know how in the world I was going to tee it up that night at seven p.m.

There was only one way to get on the field on nights when I felt that bad. It was real simple: *Out fucking drug it!*

We all know that the human body is an amazing piece of equipment, but even it has limits. I don't care who you are, or how smart you are, or how much money you make—at some point, and it's different for everyone, if you are swallowing handfuls of pain pills every night there will be consequences.

I remember when it first started happening, I would wake up in the middle of the night sweating, and the next day I would feel what I described earlier: the fire was beginning to burn inside. My only option to put the fire out was to go back to the well. It got to the point where I actually became a walking pharmacy. *I became my own chemist.* I was taking so much shit, it's amazing that I was able to perform at the highest level. What's even more amazing is that I'm still aboveground. I'm serious, especially playing in places like Florida against the expansion Marlins, who joined the National League East in 1993. When you combine the South Florida fucking humidity with thirty Vicodin pills, there were times I really thought I was going to die on the field. I would say to myself, *Breathe, Lenny, just*

breathe . . . don't die on second base after hitting a double. Just calm down and breathe.

My whole life growing up, when I wanted something bad enough, I would find a way to get it or make it happen. That was until I became dependent on opiates. It was almost like I made a deal with the devil. I wanted to stop taking them in the worst way. I was just trying not to suffer, to stay out of withdrawal. I hated the fact that my life was being controlled by fucking pills.

Every time I tried to get off the opiates, I would feel so miserable that I could barely function. At least when you go north, with amphetamines or blow, yes, you still feel like shit and have no energy and feel depressed, but it wasn't that unexplainable fire inside that made me want to crawl out of my own fucking skin like it was with opiates. For me, the pain was so excruciating, it was too much to overcome.

It got so bad, I knew that I couldn't stop on my own. I desperately needed help. So I went on a mission to hunt down the best doctor in Philadelphia. This was a very delicate situation, not to mention scary, for the simple reason that I was afraid that if the Phillies found out I was swallowing thirty Vicodin pills a day, they might refuse to pay me. I was so scared, and so paranoid, that when I went to interview the four best doctors who specialized in addiction, I actually put on a disguise: a mustache, a wig, and an old man's hat, and I told them my name was Todd Wilson.

The first three doctors I interviewed were not qualified for what I needed. I knew they didn't get it. They didn't understand baseball, and I needed a doctor who did. I was losing hope. Then the Vicodin gods intervened and brought me to the doctor who would literally save my life, Dr. Jim Berman.

Dr. Berman treated me on a regular basis beginning in 1994, and I continued seeing him until December 1999, when I moved to California. Dr. Berman is triple smart, and the best communicator I have ever met. He truly has a special gift. Considering the people he treats could virtually form their own think tank or run countries, he's also extremely humble. He doesn't seek attention; in fact, he prefers being a ghost. This allows him to protect the anonymity of his patients, which is of the utmost importance to him. The bottom line is that everyone in his treatment groups are members of the team and are treated as such. He would take a bullet for any of them. And they would not hesitate to take a bullet for him.

He knew how to explain things to me in a way I could understand and relate to without putting the fear of God in me. He would use baseball analogies, or examples of things that happen in everyday life, to teach me about opiates. Most important, he always treated me like a human being: he never passed judgment. Unlike most doctors who use language that makes you feel stupid, Dr. Berman allowed me to arrive at my own conclusions, based on information he provided, that made me feel smart.

I knew I had to trust someone when I was down and out. I trusted Dr. Berman, and he continually proved that he was worthy of my trust. We developed a relationship that was far beyond the usual doctor-patient one. Although I was not the most compliant patient, Dr. Berman was like my Mr. Wolfe from *Pulp Fiction;* he was a master at cleaning up my messes. Furthermore, he clearly appreciated and understood my need for total confidentiality. He told me at our first meeting, "Nobody will ever know you were here, unless you tell them." That statement has proved true to this day. He would even meet me at my house or other locations so I

didn't have to go to his office. I just wish I would have followed his advice sooner.

Dr. Berman explained to me why I felt so bad from a physical standpoint in the most basic terms: "Vicodin, or any opiate for that matter, can be the best drug in the world if used correctly, but at the same time, it can be the worst drug in the world when abused." He explained how our endorphins work, that they are the feel-good chemicals naturally manufactured in our brain when our body experiences pain or stress. He basically defined them as the natural opiates of the body. He went on to say that when you take opiates, it creates artificial endorphins in the brain. That's why, when I first started taking them, I would feel invincible: they would boost my energy, take away my pain, give me an amazing high, and make me feel like everything was going to be all right, even if I had a bad night on the baseball field.

Playing professional baseball is a grueling, rigorous schedule. We played almost every night for six months straight. The game of baseball is also much more physical than it appears, especially the way I played. By the end of the 1993 season, the best season of my career, I played in every game except one, which was the night after we clinched the National League East division title in Pittsburgh. I went five for five on that memorable night.

Unfortunately, my body was beginning to break down. I was always in pain. I would watch my teammates drink fifteen beers to take away their pain after a game, but I just couldn't drink like that. Especially being a leadoff hitter: the team needed me on top of my game every night. I needed a solution, and I needed it fast, as it was getting worse and worse every night. I remember saying to myself, *There has got to be an easier way to take away the pain than drinking fifteen beers after each game.*

It finally hit me. All I had to do was take one of those pills the nurses would give me for pain when I was in the hospital after I was in that horrible car wreck. I would take one Vicodin, have one drink, and feel great. I remember saying to myself, *I re-invented the wheel. I found the secret recipe to take away my pain,* and I would show up at the ballpark the next day ready to rock! No hangover, no nothing. I really thought that I was invincible; the drugs worked that good.

I learned from Dr. Berman that over time, opiates trick the brain into stopping the production of your natural endorphins. This is when the drug, which you thought was your best friend, turns on you and leaves you with no other option but to take more and more pills.

It just becomes a matter of time until you cross that imaginary line, and then you're fucked. You try to capture that euphoric feeling you received when you first started taking the pills. You try again and again, but to no avail. I knew this, but I continued chasing that feeling, or that high, over and over and over.

The only difference between Vicodin and heroin is that if you want to go five miles an hour, you take Vicodin. If you want to go a hundred miles an hour, you take heroin. It's just a matter of how fast you want to get there. No matter what, at some point anyone who abuses opiates realizes that they are in the same car, going down the same road, with the same destination: a dead fucking end! There are no exits on this road; you can't just turn around because you don't like the way you feel.

Remember, what goes up must come down.

◆

I tried so many times to get off the pain pills, but whatever I did, it never worked. Dr. Berman tried everything, including treating my pain with methadone, which worked well for the pain. I didn't like how it made me feel, though, so I wanted off. Dr. Berman explained to me that I would have to taper the methadone slowly. This proved to be nearly impossible. This was before the FDA approved Suboxone, which contains buprenorphine, in the United States, in late 2002. As hard as I tried, I couldn't get off. Dr. Berman tried everything, but when I would get to the end of the detox by tapering down, the pain was too much. I hate opiates!

In 1998, I finally said to Dr. Berman, "Listen, man, I can't take this anymore. I can't let this fucking pill control my life anymore. There's got to be something else, and I don't give a fuck what it is."

"There is something else, but I don't believe it is readily available in the United States. In fact, the procedure is quite new, so we don't have a whole lot of data yet," he said.

I responded by asking, "Are people living afterward?" I immediately followed up that question with another: "Does it work?"

Dr. Berman took a deep breath and said, "People are not dying as a result of the procedure. However, I think it's too early to tell if it works long-term." He went on to explain, "The procedure is called Rapid Opiate Detox. It is a process where you are under anesthesia for six to ten hours and they administer opiate-blocking medications. In essence, you go through intense withdrawal during that time, but you are under anesthesia; therefore, you are unaware of what your body is going through. You wake up opiate-free, but it's very risky. It places tremendous stress on the body."

"Where's this doctor?" I asked.

"That's the problem. He's not in this country; he's in Israel."

"Israel?" I fired back, hoping I misheard.

Even I knew what was going on in Israel at that time. I went on to say, "Isn't that where people are getting blown up and dying from these crazy suicide bombers?" Before he could answer, I fired another question at him: "How much does he want for the procedure?"

"Lenny, it's going to be very expensive. When it's all said and done, with travel, hotel, and the procedure, you are probably looking at six figures. Also, don't forget that if you choose to do this, you will be part of an ongoing experiment by having this procedure performed on you."

"Let me think about this for a minute." Then I said to Dr. Berman, "First, I would have to fly to Israel, where innocent people are getting blown up and killed. Second, I would have to pay some doctor I know nothing about six figures to put me asleep for ten hours, in a country that's on the other side of the world. And third, to top it off, you're saying that I would be part of an experiment this doctor is conducting. Is this correct?"

Dr. Berman nodded, confirming that I was indeed correct. He then said, "I wouldn't do it. It's too risky."

"Fuck it, I'm going. I want off these fucking pills. I am doing this thing, and I want to do it immediately! I can't live like this any longer. I can't let a pill continue to control my life anymore."

I appreciated Dr. Berman's caution, but I had to take the chance.

My mind was made up. *Israel, here I come.*

If I was going to fly to Israel by myself, I knew I had to hire two twenty-four-hour armed security guards who would be waiting for me at the airport to drive me around and protect me

while I was there. When I landed in Tel Aviv, there were two very serious-looking men waiting for me. I had been drinking on the plane the whole flight; I was hammered, completely annihilated. I remember when they approached me, we shook hands and I looked into their eyes and I saw something different. It was a look I didn't recognize, and it didn't matter how much I'd had to drink. These two men, who were both trained in the Israeli Special Forces, were not fucking around; they were trained killers. They helped me get through customs at Ben Gurion Airport. They took me to what I could only assume was the VIP area, as they obviously were friends with the big swinging dicks who were in charge of security at the airport. Still hammered, I stumbled into the bulletproof van my two hired guns had waiting for me.

"Take me to the doctor, man," I told them.

For the first time in my life, I was really scared. It's hard to explain because it wasn't anything I'd ever experienced before. I was alone. I wasn't going to be in an American hospital, and I didn't understand what anyone was saying. On top of that, I was in a foreign country where innocent people were getting killed, and I was submitting myself to a new, very risky procedure with a doctor I knew nothing about. Essentially, my fear was at an all-time high. I can honestly say that I didn't know if I was going to live or die.

They drove me to the doctor's office, which was in a very simple one-story building, nothing like the medical complexes we have here in America. When I walked into the office, there was no receptionist, no staff, no patients, only a dark-haired man sitting behind a desk, smoking a cigarette, staring out the window. As I got closer, I noticed his face was scarred. It was as if he had been severely burned and had also incurred gunshot wounds. His arms

and hands were torn up as well. There were scars that looked like he had been in a war, or tortured, or worse. I thought to myself, *Holy shit, this is my doctor? What in the fuck happened to him?*

I found out later from the two Israeli hit squad members I had hired for private security that the doctor was very famous and considered a hero by all of the Jewish people. It turns out that he was a real legend in the Israeli army. He would work on wounded soldiers who had been injured on the front line. He put his life on the line by doing whatever he had to in order to save them. My doctor was not only a genius—he was the fucking man.

"You're scared, aren't you?" he asked.

"Yeah, I'm scared," I managed to say. I became emotional; it was beginning to hit me. I broke down and started to cry; I couldn't stop, it was a feeling I had never experienced before. I was hours away from an extremely risky, unknown medical procedure that I didn't know if I would ever wake up from.

The only time before this that I can remember crying was when I was playing Little League baseball and had a high fever, and my mom wouldn't let me play. I might have been about eight. Now as an adult, in a situation where I felt I might be on the brink of death, yeah, I cried.

I was embarrassed, as I never had cried in front of a grown man before.

Cigarette in hand, the Israeli doctor got up from behind his desk, pulled me up by my collar, pinned me up against the wall, looked me in the eye, and said, "Listen to me, I'm not going to let you die!"

I'll never forget the way he said it or the look he had in his eyes. There was something special about this man. While in his presence, I felt safe. It was almost as if I was with a higher power.

I nicknamed him Dr. God.

The next thing I remember, I was in an operating room. I could hear the nurses and doctors talking, but I didn't understand Hebrew. It seemed like everything and everybody in that operating room were all moving in fast-forward. Then one of the nurses stuck a needle in my arm, attaching an IV, and everything went dark.

When I woke up, I didn't know where I was, but I could see Dr. God hovering over me. "Everything went fine," he said.

To me, it felt like I had just gone ten rounds with Mike Tyson. I have never felt so bad in my life. It was like my body didn't know what was going on. There was a feeling of emptiness, a lot of body aches. But I remember I didn't crave the drug like I did when I'd attempted to get off the pills before. I was so weak and depleted, I did not have the strength to even sit up. I still experienced all the side effects as before: insomnia, muscular pain and achiness, watery eyes, and a runny nose, but I didn't want to take a Vicodin. I just remember saying to myself, *I need to remember what I am feeling now—the agony, the pain, the suffering—so I don't ever have to feel this way again.*

There is now evidence that proves that while Rapid Detox decreases symptoms, it doesn't necessarily affect the amount of time spent in withdrawal. The reality of the situation is simple: there are no shortcuts in life, no free rides, and everything comes with a price.

With that said, as bad as I felt physically, I was proud of myself. I wasn't a slave to a pill anymore. For the first time in years, I was opiate-free.

My two security guards drove me from the hospital back to my hotel in Tel Aviv. The place was tits and ass, completely renovated

from top to bottom. Everything was state-of-the-art. I remember saying to myself, *If I am going to suffer, at least it will be in style.*

After a long, torturous, sleepless night, the next morning I told my security to take me outside. I needed some air; I needed to see and hear people living life.

After a few more days of recovering by the pool, I told my security that I wanted to see Jerusalem. The next day they set me up with a tour guide, and we all drove from Tel Aviv to the Old City in Jerusalem. I did the whole deal. It was an amazing place!

I finished off my day in Jerusalem by stopping at the Western Wall, also known as the Wailing Wall. My tour guide told me that it's a centuries-old tradition to write a note with a prayer or request, and then place it in a crack in the wall. So I put a yarmulke on my head and walked up to the Wailing Wall, but instead of just scribbling a quick note on a piece of paper and jamming it in the wall, I stopped and took it all in. I wroted on a piece of paper, *I'm alive, I am still in the game, I can still be a factor,* and then I respectfully placed my note in the wall.

If you're offered a seat on a rocket ship, don't

ask what seat. Just get on.

—SHERYL SANDBERG

22

WHEELS UP

I have always believed that pussy was the most powerful thing in the world; after all, it has taken countries down. That all changed when I bought my own private jet. Not just any jet, a Gulfstream, the *big swinging dick* of private aviation.

With money, one has the ability to have more options, to make more choices, than a person without money. That doesn't mean one person is better than the other if he or she has more money; it just means they have the luxury to experience things most people can't.

I chartered my first private jet in 1990. That was the first year I realized that I was definitely in a different tax bracket. It was the off-season, I had just come off a huge year, and I was in LA partying. There were a couple buddies and a few chicks hanging out in my suite at the Beverly Hills Hotel, when one of the girls said to me, "We should go to Las Vegas. That would be so much fun."

I thought about it and said, "Yeah, but it's too fucking far to drive."

She came back with, "Just charter a private jet. We'll be there in thirty minutes."

I had never even thought about that before; up until that point, it wasn't even an option. Then I fired back, "Yeah, fuck yeah, I will hunt one down for us."

I called the concierge and told him what I wanted. Minutes later, I received a call from some dude who asked me how many people were with me and where we wanted to go. After I answered, he said, "I recommend you charter a Lear 35. It's fast and not as expensive as the other options."

That was it; I had the hotel arrange for a limo to take us to Van Nuys Airport, the busiest private airport in the country. I remember when the limo pulled right up to the jet, I thought to myself, *This is fucking cool as shit.* The pilot, along with a beautiful young flight attendant, with a rig from hell, were waiting by the stairs for us to board the plane, and he said, "Drinks are in the back. We'll be *wheels up* in ten minutes and on the ground in Las Vegas in about thirty. Enjoy the flight."

I would continue to charter private planes for a number of years after that. But I would always stay with the smaller equipment, meaning the Lear Jets and the Citations, all of which are classified as small to midsize private jets. At that time, it wasn't so much about the type of aircraft, it was more about the process, the way I could seamlessly get from point A to point B without going through an airport.

It wasn't until later, as you will read, that I got serious about private aviation. And if you have learned anything about Lenny Dykstra from reading this book, you know when I say, "I got serious," then, I got serious. *Real fucking serious.*

◆

Let's fast-forward to the year 2006. I was spending so much money chartering jets, shitty ones I might add, that I finally called my buddy Pete Maestrales, who owns Airstream Jets based in Boca Raton.

"Bro, it's time to take it to the next level. I'm buying my own fucking jet!"

This guy, who was the best in the business when it came to finding me the best possible equipment for the best price, responded by saying, "Oh, no. I already know what you're going to buy."

He knew me so well, he was confident that if I was buying a jet, it was going to be the big swinging dick of private aviation—a *Gulfstream*.

One of the most frustrating and confusing things to me when I would charter a jet was how outdated the interiors were on these airplanes. To make matters worse, the audiovisual system on these planes was so ancient, it was a fucking joke. I didn't get it. The standard answer I would get from the pilots and people in the private aviation business was that the FAA was too strict and had too many rules. I called bullshit on that. Why would the FAA not want an airplane to have the newest, most up-to-date equipment? Regardless, I had a game plan that I had been masterminding for quite a while.

My plan was to design the interior to look exactly like the car I owned, which was a Maybach. There weren't many on the road, probably a direct result of the price tag, a cool $400K. But that's why I chose to customize my first Gulfstream to look like a Maybach. Fortunately for me, I was dialed in with the person who was in charge of Maybach North America. After I told him my idea, he called the powers that be in Germany and got the green light from Ulrich Maybach. Then it was fucking on!

On December 24, 2007, I bought my first Gulfstream jet. I have to admit it was a very powerful feeling to know that I owned a real fucking jet. It made me feel proud. In fact, it was kind of like a drug, *but way fucking better!* The power and freedom I felt when flying around the world on my own airplane was intoxicating.

Imagine that you're bored one day, and you don't know what to do with yourself. Of course, *boredom* is a relative term. Many people are content to sit around doing nothing. I think they call that relaxing. Well, that's not me; I'm wired for action. So when action was lacking, I would mobilize my jet and make a call to my pilots to get the flight plans for whatever country I decided to drop anchor in on that particular journey. I would simply say, "Let's be *wheels up* in one hour." And in one hour my airplane would be in the air bound for my destination.

I flew all over the world, with some of my favorite stops being Italy, the Caribbean, the Virgin Islands, England, Spain, and Paris. Despite the undeniable magnificence and history of Paris, they treated Americans like shit. In fact, I had to remind them that if it weren't for us those motherfuckers would be speaking German!

In December 2008, I flew to Nice, France, where I met Bernard Vuitton, of the famous Louis Vuitton brand. Bernard and I hit it off from the start. Despite the fact that I had bought some expensive threads back in my time, I was certainly not a fashion mogul, by any means. So imagine how I felt hanging with Bernard, who represented perhaps the most celebrated luxury brand in the world.

To my surprise, this guy was fucking cool and incredibly down to earth. Bernard and I communicated with each other numerous times. Among the invitations I received from Bernard, one was to a charitable affair for the Maybach Foundation, on behalf of himself and Ulrich Maybach. The following is the invitation I received.

Dear Lenny,

Hopefully you are doing well since we met at the Martinez in Cannes.

In case you will [be] around, we both, Ulrich Maybach and myself, take a great pleasure in inviting you and your selected guest to join us for the Private Luncheon of the Maybach Foundation on Monday May 18th, 2009, between 12.30 p.m. and 3.30 p.m. at the Hotel du Cap–Eden Roc, Cap d'Antibes. The date being very close to the Monaco Grand Prix and the Film Festival, I thought, Lenny, that you could be around or not too far. If so, please pass by. Being in the host committee of this Event, it would be also a pleasure for me to welcome you and to see you again. The Foundation will again honor a legend of the entertainment industry whose work demonstrates a commitment to giving back to society through mentoring. In previous years the Maybach Foundation gave this tribute to Quincy Jones and Dennis Hopper.

Enjoy sample culinary delights (open buffet), drinks from the premium open bar, and spend a wonderful afternoon on the water front terrace.

Hoping to see you soon. (If you're not around please give me a call so we can get together either in NY or LA sometime next month as there are interesting projects in the tube.)

Best regards,

Bernard Vuitton Juhen
Vuitton Family & Partners

These are merely a few examples of the places my Gulfstream made accessible to me on a moment's notice. I could go virtually anywhere, whenever I wanted, with whomever I chose, by making a phone call and giving the word: "Fire up the jet."

I should mention, that my two flight attendants, one brunette, one blonde, both *canned heat,* traveled with me wherever I went. I know what you're thinking—*He had to have fucked both of them*—but I never went there. Furthermore, my jet was always stocked with the finest liquor in the world, and I never drank when I was on board my plane. Clearly, the incredible feeling I experienced while in my Gulfstream completely curbed my usually insatiable appetite for other pleasures. I literally experienced what it was like to be *higher* than the clouds.

◆

Later, after prison, long after I lost my Gulfstream among other prized possessions, I learned that there are a few other powerful things in this world that you cannot put a price tag on. Meeting Eric Petersen allowed me to appreciate this concept.

About seven months after I was released from prison, I received a call from Mark Slotkin, a friend of mine whom I had met six years prior. He asked if I wanted to meet him for dinner, so we could catch up, and I accepted. When I arrived at his house, he greeted me at the door, and we shared a courtesy hug. I started walking toward his car when Mark said, "No, this way, I invited one of my friends to join us."

Mark and I had an agreement from the past that he would

never Pearl Harbor me like this, as it was invariably some old rich dude who wanted to know what it was like to play in the World Series and talk baseball with me. Mark knew I'd be fucking pissed, but I hadn't seen him for years so I didn't say anything.

We got into a vintage Mercedes, which I could tell was very well cared for and clearly expensive. The dude driving had glasses on and was a walking advertisement for a tattoo parlor, with tats everywhere. But they were not pedestrian or stereotypical tattoos. I could tell that he paid a lot of money for the artwork and put plenty of thought into them.

Mark introduced him as Eric, and we exchanged greetings. There was minimal conversation, both in the car and at dinner. One thing that struck me was that Eric didn't ask me anything about baseball, probably because he didn't know who the hell I was and didn't care. Eric is definitely not a star-fucker.

After we finished dinner, Eric dropped us off at Mark's house and left. As I was getting ready to leave Mark's, I realized I was missing one of my two cell phones. I always carry two phones: one for business and one for nonbusiness. The second is called the "Bat Phone." I figured out that I left it in the backseat of Eric's car, so I asked Mark for his number.

I called Eric. "Hey, bro. It's Lenny. I think I left my phone in your car."

He checked, and sure enough, it was there. I asked if I could come pick it up, and he said, "Sure." I asked him for his address, put it in my GPS, and the next thing I knew, I was parked in front of this big-ass fucking mansion in the best area of Beverly Hills. I remember thinking that I obviously wrote down the wrong address, so I called Eric again.

"Hey, bro. I'm at the address you gave me, but I think I may

have written it down wrong, because I'm sitting in front of some big-ass mansion."

"You're at the right place," he replied, as he proceeded to walk out and hand me my phone. We began to talk, and it became quite evident after about fifteen minutes that everything isn't always what it appears to be. One of my gifts has always been my ability to get a read on people very swiftly.

We started to hang out more frequently, as I loved his rap and I got the feeling that he appreciated the fact that I knew what he meant when he would tell me something. The reality of the situation is that Eric and I were more alike and had more in common than either of us would have believed initially.

◆

A short time after I met Eric, I was forced to leave Terri's house, where I was living, because her landlord told her if I didn't leave, he wouldn't rent the house to her anymore. When Eric found out, he said, "You can stay in my guesthouse if you need a place to stay."

I took him up on his generous offer, and I've been here ever since.

Another thing Eric and I have in common is the fact that we both came from nothing. That doesn't mean we don't have solid parents, because we both do. There is something to be said about a person who worked his ass off to get to the top of his profession, which is exactly what Eric and I both did. The only difference was that I made approximately $60 million playing baseball and

doing business. Eric, on the other hand, made about $100 million grinding his way to the top of his profession.

He understands my situation, and I will be forever grateful to him for what he and Kelly, his wife, did to help me navigate an extremely difficult time in my life. What they have provided me, and continue to provide for me, has had a major impact on my life. Without them, I cannot conceive that I would have had the necessary time to complete this book.

Eric knows how I'm wired; he knows how I value loyalty. Eric knows that I would take a bullet for him and Kelly. He gets it, and I'm incredibly fortunate that he came into my life. I can't imagine where I might be had I reacted in my usual fashion to being Pearl Harbored by Mark Slotkin.

Luck, or a lesson learned? Probably a combination of both.

I know a man who gave up smoking, drinking, sex, and rich food. He was healthy right up to the day he killed himself.

—JOHNNY CARSON

23

RICHARDS & REHAB

After baseball, I was living in Philly and indulging in one of my greatest weaknesses: women, or *pussy*, the most powerful thing in the world. Obviously, greater men than me—leaders of fucking nations—have been brought down by that shit. I'm just being honest. I have been honest throughout this entire book, and there is no reason to sugarcoat anything now.

But the thing is, when you're married you can only say you're going to a psychiatrist once a week, which I was doing, before your wife starts to get wise to what you're *really* up to. At that time, I was seeing Dr. Richard Kogan, and you had to be a celebrity to get an appointment with him. His office was on the Upper East Side right by the Carlyle Hotel, and all he wanted to do was hear my stories about pussy. And for that I gave him 750 bucks an hour—for only fifty minutes. When that clock hit ten till, if I had said, "I'm going to kill myself," his answer would have been "Hold that thought. We will pick up on this next week."

Ordinarily, going to a shrink located in a city separate from your own buys you one night of partying away from home. But

I was a jet-setter. Literally. I was ready to go wheels up at a moment's notice.

That's when my master plan hit me. Inspired by the free pass that my therapist visits gave me, I told my wife, "Terri, I want to get sober and clean up. I've heard there's a rehab in London that's really awesome."

She was all for it. Even though I was off the pills, I couldn't break the drinking habit, and Terri was probably desperate for me to get clean. As far as she knew, I was set to enter rehab for thirty days, where I would not be permitted to talk to anyone from outside, not even my wife. In fact, no one can find out if you're even really there.

Instead of entering the clinic, after I landed in London, I had thirty days to jet-set all over Europe. A perfect *fucking* plan.

Over the years, I played that card *six* different times and hit six different countries. I spread them out. Six different rehabs, but I never set foot in a single one of them. I paid for them, so if you checked, you'd think I was there. I hit Barcelona, London, Italy, and Geneva (that place has one beautiful lake).

One time I flew to Moscow in the dead of winter. I wanted to see what it was like, but I discovered that life over there was a sea of misery. No wonder they all drink vodka. They put the *m* in *misery*. And worse than that, everyone looked like they wanted to cut your fucking throat—without even thinking twice.

Another one of my stops was Monaco, without a doubt my favorite stop on the circuit. That fucking place seemed almost fake. I'm serious. Like the Emerald City in *The Wizard of Oz*.

Before you get too excited, let me clue you in on something: if you are on a budget, or worried about what things cost, then you need to make an adjustment to your itinerary. Trust me on this.

If you want to tee it up on the French Riviera and play the role with the top 1 percent, just know going in that they are going to bend you over, so ask them to slide it in gently, because you will experience pain, believe that! It's almost like they just make up their own prices, like there is no concept of what the true value of money is.

I was in my early thirties, put together like a Greek god, and could have millions of dollars sent wherever and whenever I wanted simply by making a phone call. My ego was just as big as my bank account. Which leads to this weird infatuation I had with wanting to add some royalty to the list. Basically, I was on a mission to fuck Princess Stephanie, not because she was necessarily that pretty, more because I just wanted to put a "royal notch" in my belt.

When I traveled, I always had to take at least two of my people with me, fake friends who were basically just along for the ride. I was okay with it—after all, I had to have somebody to listen to me spin my yarn and agree with me. Since no one by themselves could keep up, I'd bring two, so they would take shifts.

When we got to Monaco, my assistant, Croz, broke the news about the princess: "Bad news, bro, she's not here."

So I scanned the room, and over my shoulder to the right I saw two blond Swedish girls who looked like they'd stepped right out of a TV tourism commercial.

"Go get the 411 on that right now," I told him.

"They're with their fiancés," he said.

"Listen closely, Croz. Look me in the eyes like a man. I will have their suitcases on the fucking sidewalk tonight!"

The next morning I rented a yacht as long as a football field. It was a yacht with a capital *Y*. It was ten in the morning and

Croz and I were sitting on the bow, or whatever you call the front (I don't know shit about boats). We had Coronas in our hands, cruising down the French Riviera heading to Portofino, and there, on the deck of my yacht, were the two blond Swedes sunbathing nude.

"Croz," I said, grinning, "whatever heaven's like, if there is a heaven, this is as close as it's going to get, because it can't get any better than this."

◆

On another of my thirty-day jaunts—when I was supposed to be in yet another rehab—I ended up in St. Barts. There were two presidential suites in the hotel. My entourage and I had one, and next door was another group that had a big fucking yacht parked out in the bay. I'm talking about a serious fucking yacht.

The word was out that De Niro was there, and one afternoon when I came back from the restaurant, I was on my porch, drinking a banana daiquiri, and there was the *Raging Bull* himself, sitting at the next table.

"What are you drinking?" he asked.

"A banana daiquiri," I said.

One thing led to another, and the next thing I knew we were in the bathroom of his suite and it was powder fucking city. This guy was a pro, dipping his finger in the coke and numbing his gums. I don't think he even knew who the hell I was. I could tell he wasn't a sports guy, but he sure liked hitting the slopes with me.

"How do you like the Richards, man?" I asked.

"Richards?" he said. "What do you mean?"

"That's the code name for blow, bro," I told him. It was something I made up for my teammates so we didn't have to say the word *cocaine* around management. "I named it after Keith Richards of the Rolling Stones. He looks like a line of coke." I cut up another line and we were off and running.

The next thing I knew, De Niro took half my blow.

We went back to the restaurant, and he sent over a thousand-dollar bottle of wine. He did this for three nights in a row. On the third night, I walked over and thanked him, and I could see his wife was wondering, *Who the fuck is this, and why are you sending him thousand-dollar bottles of wine?*

As I was getting ready to take off, my boy De Niro leaned over. "Do you think you can leave me the rest of that Richards? I'll pay you for it." I said, "Come on, bro. *Mi casa su casa,* you feel me? It's on me." If I recall, because I was on a nice little run, I don't think he had even asked who I was until I was leaving the restaurant. I answered, "Nails, just call me Nails."

It was an *eight-ball* of Richards.

Not only that, I gave him the keys to the kingdom when I turned him on to my beans, too, Dexedrine. De Niro ended up loving those beans, because you don't want to do blow all day. You want a slower ride, so you take the Dexedrine to keep you paced out right. De Niro adopted my program for a few days and liked it—a lot. "Better, isn't it?" I asked him. "You don't have to worry who mixed it, who cooked it, who skimmed it around, and who knows where that shit came from? This is FDA regulated, bro. You can feel good about taking this, man."

When I was leaving St. Barts, De Niro practically ran me down.

"Do you have any more of those fucking pills?" he wanted to know.

◆

A couple years later, I ran into De Niro at his restaurant in Tribeca, New York, and went up to him. "Hey, remember me?" I asked.

He gave me a look like I was an ugly redheaded stepchild.

There was no wine for me that fucking night, I'll guarantee you that. Celebrities, man. They are more than happy to take all your blow, then act like you're the hired help when you see them out in public.

◆

Eventually, one of the rehabs I agreed to go to was Promises in Los Angeles, the hottest rehab center on the planet. At the time, the cost of going there was about forty grand a month, and I paid it, but I still had no intention of taking it seriously.

I had been flying back to LA every couple of weeks to check on my car washes, and I always holed up at the Beverly Hills Hotel. I was there so often I literally got my mail there.

I can't remember exactly how we met, but the actor Mickey Rourke and I began hanging out together. Mickey's career was hurting, he was down and out, having a tough time, and we

shared a $3,000-a-night bungalow I rented in the Beverly Hills Hotel. Mickey always wore a stupid scarf and he carried that little fucking dog of his with him everywhere.

Mickey and I went on a ten-day run of partying. Mickey had his crew of Hollywood wannabes, bottom-feeders who clung to him like shit on a shoe, and we were all hitting the Richards nonstop. I was supposed to have checked in at Promises on the first of the month, and I was getting calls from their staff every fucking day.

"Where are you?"

"Don't worry. I'll be there," I told them.

We kept hitting the booze and the Richards hard, and finally on the tenth day or so I looked in the mirror and just about shit myself. I was lit up, and in a moment of clarity, it hit me. I could see that I had Mickey's scarf around my neck, and I was holding that little fucking dog of his, and I thought, *Wow, this is fucking bad. I look like the Crypt Keeper from* Tales from the Crypt. *This is an all-time low.*

"I need to get the fuck out of here," I told Mickey. "I'm done. Roll it up, man. I gotta go check in to Promises."

I checked out of the hotel, and the bill must have been three hundred grand. And it wasn't just my and Rourke's bill. We both had our monkeys and group of chicks who drank and ate like there was no tomorrow, and they put it all on my tab. But I didn't give a flying fuck.

I grabbed my shit, got in my limousine, a long-ass ride, and took my group of freeloaders with me to Promises. There was some shit left, so I parked my limo in front of Promises, right outside the gate, and I told my driver, "I gotta go in there and dry out. But when I go inside, I'm going in in a ball of fucking flames. Let's finish this shit up."

That limo was parked out there for five days. It was me and the driver and a bunch of women, the LA fucking pretenders. After five long nights of nonstop partying, we finished off everything we had.

Finally, after the last line of coke was snorted, I walked up and pounded on the Promises gate. "Open up, motherfuckers, and let me in."

Be fearful when others are greedy and greedy

only when others are fearful.

—WARREN BUFFETT

24

STOCK MARKET GURU

My stockbroker, a Gordon Gekko wannabe who was always dressed in a $5,000 suit, played the role and came across as the real deal, a financial titan who had it all figured out. *Just ask him.* He always knew what to say, and he always told me what he thought I wanted to hear.

I will never forget the feeling I had the last time I walked out of his Newport Beach office, located in one of the most beautiful buildings I have ever seen, with panoramic views of the Pacific Ocean. The people always looked fake to me, almost like Stepford Wives. Plus, I could tell they really believed that they were born with a better pot to piss in. I called it *The Land of the Great Pretenders.*

Of course it was Lindsay Jones, still my financial adviser at that time, who introduced me to my former stockbroker and insisted I needed to diversify.

So I agreed and invested $2 million in what was explained to me as so-called safe mutual funds and blue-chip stocks. I insisted that if I was going to invest money in the stock market, I wanted to be conservative, especially since I knew nothing about the market

at the time. Within two years, the stock market plunged and my $2 million investment was down to $400,000. Eighty percent of my money, *a big fucking number,* was gone.

When I was told that the majority of my money had disappeared, the Gordon Gekko wannabe tried to tell me more of what he thought I wanted to hear. But this was the wrong day to feed me that same bullshit. I mean, come on, really? I got hit by a lot of pitches when I played, but not that many. So I snapped him off: "Shut the fuck up! Change the rap!" I was so pissed off. I went on to say, "I want the $400,000 that's left of the $2 million you fucked off wired back into my personal account first thing tomorrow morning." That was curtains for G.G.

Much of my hard-earned money was gone, and I didn't have a clue as to why. I will never forget that feeling of hopelessness. It was humiliating, and I remember saying to myself, *This will never happen to me again.*

So I decided to make it my mission in life to learn everything humanly possible about the stock market. I immediately subscribed to investment newsletters and websites run by professionals who had the best reputations, as well as all the stock market gurus.

To gain more insight, I spent hours each day watching shows that dealt with stocks on CNBC and Bloomberg, and I tuned in regularly to Jim Cramer's then weekly radio show, *Real Money.*

I learned about moving averages, cash-flow ratios, short ratios, option calls, and price-to-earnings ratios. From all my research, and the intensity I put into the effort, I got a damn good handle on how the market really worked.

This was when I learned how powerful options were if used correctly. I discovered a trading strategy known as deep-in-the-

money (DITM) calls. This was the key to converting my remaining $400,000 into millions. By developing my strategy around this type of investment, I was able to control large blocks of stock at a relatively low cost, and without all the risk associated with conventional trading.

For example, say you want to buy a thousand shares of Microsoft Corporation, a stock I have traded many times. Let's assume it's trading at $50 a share. You'd have to spend $50,000 to buy a thousand shares of the stock outright (plus commission). This approach would instantly eliminate the majority of investors, as there simply are not many people who can afford to just fire $50K into an individual stock. Other great stocks like Johnson & Johnson, Disney, and 3M all trade closer to the $100 mark. Spending $50,000 to $100,000 for a thousand shares of just one quality stock isn't an option unless you are incredibly wealthy. Furthermore, this is a recipe for disaster, as there would undeniably be times when the temptation to trade on margin might get the best of you. Trading on margin is like dancing with the devil; if the market turns on you, turn out the lights, the party is over. Anyone who has had a margin call will swear to you that they are being ripped off, as it seems like they make you either bring in more cash or sell some of your other positions to get your account back in line. The bottom line: There is no reason to even fuck with margin, as it will eventually end badly.

The solution? Using my deep-in-the-money-calls strategy, which allows you to control the stock in much the same way as if you owned the stock. Let's use the same stock we talked about earlier, Microsoft (MSFT), and let's assume it was trading at $50 a share. By using my deep-in-the-money-calls system, you can control the same thousand shares, but you would have to invest

only $8,000 to $10,000 by buying ten contracts, which is equal to a thousand shares. Moreover, you will be in control of the stock for approximately two years, but again, instead of it costing you $50K, you would need to spend only $10K. Remember, the only way you can make a profit in the market is by trading in and out of positions when you realize a profit. My deep-in-the-money-calls system gives you *leverage* and puts you in a position of strength, as opposed to having all of your cash tied up in one or two stocks. Furthermore, using my strategy, because we are buying call options, eliminates any temptation to dance with the devil, in this case, margin; the results are incredible.

If I were to buy those Microsoft calls mentioned earlier, I would have made my choice by comparing stock charts and other technical information, then placing a limit order for ten contracts using a formula I came up with for determining the right price I would be willing to pay for the options. If my purchase was filled at the price I set, I would immediately put in a sell order at a point higher, which would then trigger an automatic $1,000 win when the sales price was reached. It was, and still is, beautiful.

I didn't have to sit there watching the stock to collect a win, and with the option price needing to go up only a buck, the stock itself had to go up only about $1.30 to $1.50 for me to earn an easy grand.

The average hold time of one of my stock options was about three weeks, so I didn't have to worry about each investment sitting around for long periods of time. It didn't take long before I would see I had made a quick $1,000 on my $8,000 to $10,000 investment.

The strategy is simple. Those subscribers who followed through on my recommendations since my system has been in

place would have profited well over $1,000,000. Yes, you are reading the number correctly, over a million fucking dollars in net profit! After reading this, you are probably saying to yourself, *Is this really the truth? It can't be.* It's not only the truth; it's a fact and it's indisputable.

Do you really believe that the feds would allow me to have a website that posts my record each and every day if the numbers, or my win-loss record, were wrong? You don't really believe they would let me defraud each and every person who signs up and pays $1,000 for a one-year subscription to my website, www .nailsinvestments.com, if the numbers were not perfect, do you? I put my record out there for the world to see each and every day. Are you fucking kidding me? If those numbers were wrong, they would throw me back in the cooler so fast it would make your head spin.

So, after discovering that my strategy was immensely profitable, I began to send e-mails with questions and stock recommendations to Jim Cramer. Cramer was very popular with individual investors and would soon parlay his fame and stock market acumen into the TV show *Mad Money*, which still airs on CNBC.

As I write my book today, my win-loss record stands at more than 565 wins and 1 loss. That's not a misprint. The only misprints come from all the haters in the media who are either jealous or too fucking stupid to get their facts straight before saying and printing things that are completely false. All anyone has to do is go online to my website NailsInvestments.com. The numbers don't lie!

I will say it again; the only person who has been right about me is Jim Cramer. He was being interviewed by Bernard Goldberg, on HBO's *Real Sports,* when he hung his balls out there by

telling Goldberg, "Lenny Dykstra is one of the great ones." So let's go to the videotape. My record at the time of that interview was 110 wins and 0 losses. Since Cramer made that call on national TV, my record has soared from 110 wins to more than 565 wins. Which leads me to make the following statement: Cramer was the only one who was right about me, but the media loves to take shots at him. Like I said, the numbers don't fucking lie!

When you combine the fact that I filed a Chapter 11 to reorganize with the media's calling me a fraud, while at the same time making me out to be some type of monster, people instantly get the perception that my record is false. This perception led to the media taking shots at Cramer, who, once again, was the only one who was right with his ballsy call.

Back on point. One day I was sitting at home trading in the market, when I received a call from Mike Figliola, the producer of *Real Money.* He said that Cramer was a big-time Phillies fan, and asked if I would be interested in making a guest appearance on his radio show. I agreed, and that's how our relationship began. We talked about the market and my deep-in-the-money calls, and Cramer saw that even though I was an ex–baseball player with no formal background in the markets, I actually knew what I was talking about.

I began to appear on *Real Money* regularly, and I enjoyed sharing my knowledge. No one paid a cent for my advice at the time, but those who listened in were hooked.

Soon thereafter, Cramer asked me if I wanted to be a celebrity columnist on his website, TheStreet.com. At the very beginning, I did it for fun. I also did it because people told me I couldn't. No one believed that anyone would follow my stock advice. They said there was no way I would be successful with a financial column.

As the poster boy for the stereotypical stupid jock, I was told I wouldn't be taken seriously.

When underestimated, I'm motivated in a way I can't explain, just so I can prove everyone wrong. Especially when I know I am right. A shrink might say I excel and thrive on negative feedback.

So in spite of all the haters, I wrote the columns. I included a stock choice for the day and why it was being recommended, and I explained how to implement my strategy. I also added a section I called the Game of Life, in which I wrote about sports, news, and other nonfinancial subjects. Sometimes I spent more time on the Game of Life section, as it was hard for me. There were nights when it felt like my keyboard had to be bloody, because I abused it so much agonizing over each word.

The more columns I wrote, the more of a following I developed. People were using my strategy and it was working. The readers could follow my advice and make money. *And cash in they did!*

Cramer was impressed, and said to me, "You've found a way to get the little guy involved, using options as a stock replacement system."

My column, Nails on Numbers, generated more business than any other column on Cramer's site. I think it was my notoriety as an athlete that drew people in, but the winning advice was what ultimately kept them coming back.

Soon, other media outlets took notice, and I began appearing on TV talk shows, including *Bulls & Bears* and *Fox & Friends,* on which I'd offer up a stock pick of the day for viewers.

♦

It wasn't long before I came up with a subscription model that I was sure would be very successful for both TheStreet.com and me. I called up Tom Clarke, a cool Irish dude and the CEO of TheStreet.com, and asked him to set up a meeting with Cramer and the rest of the brass. "I have an idea that will make your company a lot of money," I told him.

I showed up at the conference room, and all the top dogs were there.

"Okay, so what's your idea?" Clarke asked.

"I have an idea for a newsletter that we sell by subscription."

"What are you going to charge?" he asked.

"A thousand bucks to join for a year," I said.

Everyone broke up, laughing hysterically. They thought I was out of my mind.

Clarke was blunt. "Hey, Lenny, with all due respect, Cramer only charges $350. Are you serious?"

"No, hear me out on this, Tom. My strategy is for the guys who don't have much cash to get in the game, but want to participate in trading blue-chip, high-quality stocks. This is all about the leverage of options."

Options are power and leverage. Most people use options for quick hits, and they lose because they expire worthless. "But my system is different," I told them.

I explained in detail how I use my deep-in-the-money calls as a stock replacement system. They were skeptical but agreed to give it a go.

Sure enough, even though I charged $1,000 for my stock tips and I was an ex-ballplayer who hadn't gone to some Ivy League school, an army of subscribers signed up as soon as it was launched.

I was earning about $75,000 per month from my share of

the subscriptions generated on TheStreet.com. By mid-2009, my record, which I tracked daily, was at 110 wins and 0 losses, when an attorney working for the Securities and Exchange Commission (SEC), one of the most powerful government agencies in the country, headed up an investigation to negate my win-loss record. He called, saying, "You know who I am? I'm with the SEC, and you know what we do? We put people in jail, that's what we do." He continued with his scare tactics: "And that's exactly where you are going for making up a win-loss record of 110 and 0 to defraud people out of a thousand dollars. Nobody can have that kind of record." This guy was a real prick. He had one goal: to put me in jail.

The SEC investigator followed my site closely for about seven months. He studied every one of my picks in detail. The only thing he came up with was air! I was charging $1,000 for a subscriber to receive my deep-in-the-money calls for a solid year. My subscribers were getting their money back and then some. Everything documented on the website was accurate and true.

For seven months, they tried to bring me down, putting my assistant, Dorothy, through the wringer, attempting to trick her into an admission that would send me to jail. We answered all the phone calls, sent in all the documentation they demanded, and explained over and over how it worked. She never backed down and showed up for every meeting. She took every call and pleasantly showed them the door. After bringing their full arsenal, only to end up with nothing, the SEC went dark, hoping that I would just forget about it.

On the contrary, I discovered that I was entitled to a letter from the SEC. Armed with information, I called and demanded a letter stating the results of their investigation.

Acting on my telephone call, the SEC wrote me a letter stating, "This investigation has been completed as to Lenny K. Dykstra, against whom we do not intend to recommend any enforcement action by the Commission under Securities Act Release No. 5310."

Below is the true and actual letter.

UNITED STATES
SECURITIES AND EXCHANGE COMMISSION
LOS ANGELES REGIONAL OFFICE
11TH FLOOR
5670 WILSHIRE BOULEVARD
LOS ANGELES, CALIFORNIA 90036-3648

DIRECT DIAL: (323)
E-MAIL: ▮▮▮▮▮@SEC.GOV

June 14, 2010

Mr. Lenny K. Dykstra
▮▮▮▮▮▮▮▮▮▮
Los Angeles, CA 90024

Mr. Lenny K. Dykstra
c/o Dorothy Van Kalsbeek
▮▮▮▮▮▮▮▮▮▮
Murietta, CA 92562

Re: In the Matter of Nails Investments, LLC (LA-3736)

Dear Mr. Dykstra:

This investigation has been completed as to Lenny K. Dykstra, against whom we do not intend to recommend any enforcement action by the Commission. We are providing this information under the guidelines in the final paragraph of Securities Act Release No. 5310 (copy attached).

Very truly yours,

Kelly Bowers

Kelly Bowers
Senior Assistant Regional Director
Office of Enforcement

When the majority of people hear the word *bankruptcy*, the first thing they think is "This guy is a loser." They usually follow that up by saying, "How could he lose all that money?" That's not the full picture. The reality is that filing a Chapter 11 bankruptcy is an option for many to put the brakes on, so that they can reorganize and put together a viable plan to pay off their debt.

For example, numerous well-known individuals have experienced bankruptcy. Here are some of the more prominent names you will recognize: Abraham Lincoln, Thomas Jefferson, Ben Franklin, Ulysses S. Grant, Mark Twain, Henry Ford, Walt Disney, Wayne Newton, Larry King, Willie Nelson, Tom Petty, Dorothy Hamill, and Burt Reynolds. Those people I just named have all bounced back. The comeback story is part of the American way of life.

◆

Nonetheless, after I declared bankruptcy, the critics were merciless. They said I never really picked the stocks and claimed my whole system was a sham. They were wrong on both counts.

My investment strategy still flourishes today. My website NailsInvestments.com continues to perform and function uninterrupted since its inception. We still have subscribers who pay us $1,000 a year for my strategy and receive three picks a week. And, yes, they are still profiting handsomely.

In closing, nothing else I have done, or may yet do, can ever invalidate that.

A person who never made a mistake, never tried anything new.

—ALBERT EINSTEIN

25

PLAYERS CLUB

While many dream of becoming professional athletes, only a select few realize that dream. The Players Club was uniquely created and designed to understand and appreciate the dedication and commitment that a professional sports career entails.

Perhaps more important, as a former professional athlete, I knew firsthand the needs and desires of professional athletes *off the field*.

After spending twelve years in the major leagues, I recognized that the majority of players had no idea what to do with their money and hadn't even thought about how they would be able to secure their financial future after retirement from the game. Without information or guidance, professional athletes are notorious for making poor financial decisions. Yet nobody, not our union, not management, not veteran players, was helping anyone with this.

Not surprisingly, professional athletes also become accustomed to, and expect, a certain lifestyle that accompanies their first significant contract. They expect their families to participate and benefit from that lifestyle as well. The Players Club was de-

signed to appreciate and nurture the lifestyle desires of athletes along with a strong educational message for prudent financial safeguards.

Simply put, we had three goals: to help professional athletes prosper long-term, to provide financial education for the professional athlete, and to be a conduit for qualified financial products/ partners to assist the professional athlete.

I launched the *Players Club* magazine on April 1, 2008. It was something the professional sports community had been waiting for, and something it desperately needed.

With the *Players Club,* I had figured out a way to get the kind of information the players wanted and needed directly into the clubhouses and locker rooms of every major professional sport, for both men and women. It was the first lifestyle magazine specifically tailored for top athletes.

It didn't start off as a huge enterprise. My idea was simple, as I wanted a way to educate today's players on the importance of financial planning and to show them a way to create and generate recurring cash flow that would kick in after their playing days, allowing them to live in style all the way to the end of their lives. So I would create an educational newsletter like the sixteen-page newsletters I subscribed to for trading in the stock market and mail it to all the professional sports clubhouses. *And* it was going to be completely free for the athletes.

In January 2007, I started out with a modest presentation, a mock-up of the first newsletter, and presented it to UBS financial services. It was well received, but they decided to pass. I went to the Hartford, MetLife, and just about every other top-ranking insurance company to finance it for me, because if the players wanted recurring cash flow, buying an annuity was the way to

guarantee the income. With a financial partner, I'd have a way of covering the costs and monetizing the concept.

It didn't take all that long before I could see the whole beautiful concept of the *Players Club* laid out before me. Out went the cheesy newsletter, and in came the ultra-high-end glossy magazine where we would not only educate but capitalize on the lifestyle the players lived. I wasn't asking that they save all their money, just a nice healthy portion. With players earning millions each year, it's not hard to see that there is room for both. High living and prudent savings, coexisting in perfect harmony. The concepts are not mutually exclusive if you make enough.

Of course, due to my expanded vision, the *Players Club* became quite the high-end venture. Just as I set out in baseball to be the best at what I do, once I decided on publishing a magazine, I set out to publish the best magazine in the world.

The magazine's articles were written by the country's most respected writers in their particular field. The content was a mix of how the elite top 1 percent live, along with heartfelt and hard-luck stories sharing advice to make sure athletes could avoid ever having their own hard-luck story. I had assembled trusted sports figures like Wayne Gretzky, Willie Mays, and Harold Reynolds to be on my advisory board, and popular athletes like Derek Jeter, Tiger Woods, and Danica Patrick appeared on the covers and were also featured in articles.

The business model was truly beautiful. Ordinarily, the hardest part would be to get the message out, especially to an elite group of athletes. However, I set out to put the magazine into the hands of every single professional athlete in every single professional sport and I am proud to say that I accomplished this. That turned out to be the easy part. We were guaranteed a circulation

of millionaires because it would go straight into the locker rooms of MLB, the NBA, the NFL, the NHL, tennis, and golf. It had the potential to be huge.

With a commitment from AIG, the largest insurance company in the world, to provide us with the necessary financial strategic partner, we were on our way.

What happened next is well chronicled, so I won't go into all the details. AIG disappeared and nearly collapsed with the economic bloodbath, along with many other insurance companies.

The Players Club was designed to provide all professional athletes the opportunity and the tools needed to secure their financial future. In so doing, the result would have been a positive impact not only on the professional athletes; it would have also served to help keep the families of professional athletes intact.

Although my vision for the Players Club did not come to fruition due to unfortunate circumstances beyond my control, the need to provide professional athletes with a vehicle whereby their financial health is safeguarded still remains.

God gets you to the plate, but once you're there,

you're on your own.

—TED WILLIAMS

26

BASEBALL GODS

It's time to put your game face on. This chapter will contain no jokes, no pussy stories, no drug-fueled drama, no private-jet pipe dreams, no gambling/donating escapades, no prison war stories, or any other topic that is not about the business of baseball.

For those of you who don't know, or don't care, let me clue you in on something: don't think for one second that professional baseball is not a business. In fact, it's a very serious business. How serious? In 2015, MLB enjoyed revenues of approximately $10 billion.

What you will be reading is not from some fucking "bean counter" who never played the game. Quite the contrary, you can be confident in the fact that *I walked the talk. I did it on the field.*

I played in the major leagues for twelve years. I led the league in hits in two separate seasons. In 1990, I led the league with 192 hits, and in 1993, I led the league with 194 hits. Moreover, I also led the league the same two years, 1990 and 1993, in a stat that 99 percent of you most likely don't even know exists: "times on base." I was on base 288 times in 1990 and 325 times in 1993.

If you want the blueprint for what it takes to be successful at playing the game of baseball at the highest level, keep reading.

It wasn't because I was the best hitter, not even close. It was because I figured out how the game of baseball works over a 162-game schedule.

I learned at an early age that professional baseball players are in the business of entertainment. A player needs to make people want to pay money to watch him play. I loved making the fans happy, I loved putting on a show. That's why I hung my balls out there every time I put on a uniform. Especially today, it costs a small fortune to take a family of four to a Major League Baseball game. After all, when you think about it, without the fans, there is no baseball.

Now, let's get right to the facts. In Major League Baseball, approximately 90 percent of all players are essentially equal in talent. This is a topic that is rarely, if ever, discussed. The reality is that only about 1 percent of the players in the big leagues are what I define as "elite players." Meaning, they are going to be stars no matter what because of their extraordinary talent.

One of the keys to being successful at the big-league level is learning how to manage failure, but a player must also understand how to deal with success as well. I have seen players get hot and think they have it all figured out, only to find themselves sitting in front of their locker, 0 for their last 15, wondering, *What the fuck happened?*

The majority of the players I played with had more raw talent than me, but precious few of them knew the game like me. They didn't understand how hitting over a 162-game schedule works. The majority of past and present players do not understand that there is only one *right* way to hit in order to be successful in the major leagues.

For a player to fully grasp what I am talking about, so that he

can make the right decision, that player has to have the best information. It comes down to getting the best-quality information possible, which is easier said than done.

I am going to give you that quality information, which took me years to acquire. Nobody ever taught it to me; therefore, I had to figure it out myself. But when I finally did, it was almost like God himself said to me, "Okay, I am now going to make your life so much easier, so less complicated."

Now, don't get confused, players will always fail more than they succeed, as there is no way around that fact, but it's *how* they fail and *how* they succeed that will make the difference in the long run. The reality of the situation is that succeeding is actually very simple. Understanding this was the key to my success. It's when you start questioning yourself, and complicating things, that it becomes hard. So here we go.

There is a reason players get three strikes before they are out. What is that reason? Because the game is fucking hard! First, you have to hit a ball coming at you ninety-plus miles per hour. On top of that, today's pitchers have figured out that the best way to get hitters out is to deceive them, which basically means they throw off their timing, and hitting is all about timing! Once the player hits the ball, they have to hit it where someone isn't standing. Remember, there is a reason that the players over the past hundred-plus years man the same positions each inning. What is that reason? Because it's all about percentages backed up by facts. In other words, since the inception of baseball, percentages show that the ball is going to be hit in those areas more often than not. Simple, right?

So, now let's focus on the at-bat itself. If the rules allow players to get three strikes, why would any hitter not use those

same rules to their advantage? Meaning, as a hitter, you must take control of the at-bat until you get two strikes, and trust me, the pitcher knows this fact and so does the umpire. All of these things come into play; these are the little intangibles that make a huge difference in winning and losing. Approximately 90 percent of the players today have no idea how this works. The reason they are still somewhat successful is because of their talent, but they could be better if they had more discipline and weren't so selfish. For example, when a player is leading off the ninth, down two runs, and swings at the first pitch, that player doesn't have a clue how the game works or is too fucking selfish to care about helping his team win. That might sound harsh to you, but it's really not, and I will tell you why. Playing baseball at the highest level is a serious business. They are playing for real money; it's not just a baseball game. That player is paid an enormous amount of money by his organization to play baseball, which means he has a duty and obligation not just to himself but to his teammates, to the fans, and to the people who sign his paycheck to play the game right.

He can't hit a two-run homer with nobody on base, right? That means that player has one job to do at that particular at-bat, which is to get on base, period. Now let's go to the percentages. We all know that the best hitters in the game are going to fail approximately 70 percent of the time. Knowing that, why wouldn't any player make the pitcher throw a strike before he swings at a pitch? Clearly, he is putting himself before the team. Meaning, he knows he is most likely going to get a fastball, so he is swinging. What does that tell us? It tells us that this particular player either has no clue how the game works, or that he made up his mind to swing at a fastball before he even stepped into the batter's box. I

could continue on just this one subject, with multiple reasons why this player failed his teammates, failed the fans, failed the organization, and ultimately, failed himself. And that's just one at-bat. But I will spare you the pain, because I feel the pain myself. So let's move on.

In the business of professional baseball, it's either all or nothing; there is no in between. You either get on base or you don't. Meaning a player cannot get too high and cannot get too low. It's all about sticking to a game plan, day in and day out, as the professional baseball schedule is unlike anything a player dealt with before turning pro.

That said, it took me years to finally figure out the *right way* to hit over a 162-game season. And I stress, *a 162-game season.* That's approximately six months straight (seven if you add in spring training) of playing baseball. I cannot emphasize enough how important it is for an everyday player to understand that once he starts playing professional baseball, he will have to learn how to deal with the nightly "highs and lows" of the schedule.

There is only one "right way" to hit at the major league level.

How do I know that? What gives me the right to make such a statement? Because when I finally figured it out and trusted that the approach I was going up to the plate with would give me the best possible chance to succeed, I gained the confidence to take it into the batter's box every at-bat—every night. But most important, I finally gained the "confidence" that what I was doing would get me the results.

◆

There are two key bits of information an organization should know before they make a decision to commit millions and millions of dollars to a player. The first is the player's age. The second, which was often overlooked when I played, is what kind of lifestyle he lives off the field. Meaning, does he drink a lot? Does he smoke pot? Does he get his rest? An organization should know everything about a player *before* investing mountains of money, anywhere from $1 million to $200 million, in that player. I make this statement today because times have changed, and in a big way. A team must take into consideration that drugs are out! When I played, we could overcome, or offset, "lifestyle issues" by taking more drugs. As much as I hate to admit it, the drugs worked; not just physically, but mentally as well. That is no longer the case. *So it matters! And it matters a lot!*

◆

The overwhelming majority of professional baseball players do not hit the right way because they were not taught how. Nonetheless, I realize it takes tremendous discipline to develop a strategy and stick to it day in and day out. Unquestionably, it is extremely tempting to change things up, particularly when you're in a slump. Similarly, it's just as tempting to get greedy when you're doing well. With a built-in failure rate of at least 70 percent before you step into the batter's box, you need to tilt the percentages in your favor as best you can.

According to Baseball-Reference.com, since 1984, players between the ages of twenty-six and twenty-eight have the greatest

likelihood of being productive offensive contributors. Meanwhile, after turning thirty, they experience a clear and steady decline.

Understanding the demands and nuances of a 162-game schedule dictates that consistently adhering to a simple strategy translates into the best opportunity for long-term success, regardless of your innate talent. Combined with the information on player productivity versus age, that should make the general manager's job somewhat easier. Furthermore, in this era of analytics with a plethora of tools to evaluate talent, one would think that teaching players to hit the right way could only enhance a team's chances for success. Success translates to more fans, which in turn generates more revenue, culminating in better business. When that happens, everybody is happy and everybody wins.

It is well that the people of the nation do

not understand our banking and monetary

system, for if they did, I believe there would be

a revolution before tomorrow morning.

—HENRY FORD

27

BEGINNING OF THE END

I was living in a beautiful home that I had custom built from the ground up, located in one of the most affluent country clubs in the United States, Sherwood Country Club. I bought the lot in 1998 for $1.8 million. That's not a misprint; you're reading it correctly, and that was just for the dirt, which was a bit shy of an acre. The address was 2672 Ladbrook Way, Thousand Oaks, CA 91361. The beautiful eight-thousand-square-foot custom-built house backed up to the first fairway.

Across the street and up the hill (way up the hill) from me was Wayne Gretzky's incredible mansion. I had always told myself that if it ever were to come up for sale, as long as the terms were right, then I would buy it. Owning it, I knew, was a perfect fit for the *Players Club*.

One day, out of the blue, a real estate agent by the name of Nicole Van Parys knocked on my front door at Ladbrook. I happened to be working in my home office—my favorite room in the house, as I had it custom built with floor-to-ceiling mahogany. It looked like it came straight out of *Architectural Digest*. When I answered the door, she introduced herself and went on to tell me

that she represented Wayne and Janet Gretzky. Everyone knew at that time I was flush with cash, and she knew that I was one of the few people living behind the gates who actually had the ability to perform and could buy the place if I wanted, so she took a shot in the dark and paid me a visit. She was a very classy, elegant woman who spoke with a slight accent; I believe she was from Paris. After we finished with the courtesy rap, the conversation went like this: "I know you and your wife are friends with the Gretzkys, and I know that your kids and their kids play together, so I thought I would let you know that Wayne and Janet have decided to privately sell their estate if the number is right." I responded by saying, "What's the number?" Ms. Van Parys answered me by saying $18 million. I said let me think about it, talk it over with my wife. She handed me her business card—it had great paper stock, I might add—and she was very professional and courteous. In saying good-bye, I told her, "If you don't hear from me, come back and see me in a week and we will sit down and talk."

One week later she showed up. I walked her into my office and said, "Ms. Van Parys, first let me tell you why I would even consider making an offer on the Gretzky estate. I started a new company called the Players Club; it's a lifestyle services company for millionaire professional athletes, their wives, and special VIPs. I would use the estate for Players Club events—I would only live in it for the first year, until the Players Club is up and rolling." I went on to say that I wouldn't be selling my house on Ladbrook, and then I pulled out a piece of paper and my black Montblanc pen and drew a line down the middle of the paper and a line across the top. After finishing, I said, "Ms. Van Parys, I am going to make this real simple. You see this paper? I drew a line down the middle for a reason. On the left side I am going to show you what I am

bringing in a month and what my monthly nut [expenses] is, then we will see what's left over and I will write down on the right side what I am willing to offer with 'my terms.'"

At the time, I was bringing in approximately $200,000 a month and wasn't willing to spend more than $35,000 a month, locked in.

They did come back, and they brought me a deal. Financing was arranged with Washington Mutual based on the deal I had outlined, except the monthly payments would exceed $35,000 with all the expenses. It was more than I wanted to pay, but I figured I could still swing it. Washington Mutual would lend me $17.5 million with a negative amortization loan with interest-only payments. I had been coming up with all kinds of ideas for how I would turn the Gretzky mansion into a profitable venture once I owned it. The agreement was simple, all the money was there, and the rate was reasonable, or so they told me. I actually was surprised when a few weeks later at the closing, they changed the deal. I had believed in these guys.

They told me Washington Mutual could only put up $12 million of the $17.5 million purchase price.

"Bye-bye," I told them. "If all you can do is get me twelve million, I'm out. I gave you the terms. It was real simple: no money down, and if those aren't the terms, the deal is off."

It wasn't long before they came back and sweet-talked me into signing a modified version of the deal anyway. In addition to the $12 million I was getting from Washington Mutual, they had arranged for me to meet with another lender, First Credit Bank, who offered to give me short-term financing for one year of $8.5 million at 12 percent. Part of the deal was that my car washes (which were currently in escrow) would be cross-collateralized in

the deal along with my current home. Under this new deal my monthly nut was going to be $150,000 a month—way more than I could afford. So Washington Mutual was selling me a deal in which everything I owned was put up as collateral, I was saddled with a hard-money loan that I had to replace in one year, and every month I was going to run a deficit of $25,000.

The truth was, I really wanted that house, and the financing was supposed to be temporary, very temporary. "In thirty to sixty days," the guy said, "I promise you will get your original deal. We will repackage the two loans into a consolidated loan on the original terms. Don't worry."

I still wasn't going to do it. I'm not an idiot. I knew I couldn't afford it long-term.

"Do the math," I said to him. "I won't be able to make the payments if there is a delay in refinancing."

He laughed, as if to suggest my fears were irrational. I figured he was right. Why would Washington Mutual set me up with a loan they knew I couldn't afford? Of course they were going to refinance the deal right away. Why would they create a scenario that would fail?

The suits at Washington Mutual promised me, swore on a stack of Bibles, that within a month Washington Mutual would come up with the rest of the money and we would go back to the original loan deal.

In the end I trusted that it would work out. I really wanted it to.

I risked everything I owned by signing that deal.

Remember, this was 2007, and lenders all over the country were getting rich by talking homeowners into loans they could never really repay. The practice at the time was to finance a ri-

diculous amount with super-low initial rates and affordable payments, and then buyers would refinance or sell for a fat profit before the real terms and adjustable rates kicked in and could bite them in the ass. If the homeowner couldn't manage the payments when the terms got ugly, then what the fuck did the bank care? It would be just another house on the market for them to earn another commission from. Besides, they must have known the writing was on the wall by then, and so were just jamming through as many bad loans as possible before it would all be over.

There was a plague of unconscionable loan deals by lenders across the land, and WaMu was one of the biggest offenders. According to a U.S. Senate permanent subcommittee investigation, WaMu paid high commissions to employees and outside mortgage brokers for the loans they brought in, and allowed borrowers to qualify for the loan by evaluating whether they could pay a low or even the minimum amount available under the loan. As long as home prices were appreciating, borrowers were able to refinance. Once housing prices stopped rising and then started falling, borrowers couldn't refinance. Many people became stuck in homes they could not afford and began defaulting in record numbers.

I really like the way Senator Carl Levin put it in his "Opening Statement Before the U.S. Senate Permanent Subcommittee on Investigations on Wall Street and the Financial Crisis":

On September 25, 2008, Washington Mutual Bank, a $300 billion thrift, then the sixth largest depository institution in America, was seized and sold to JPMorgan Chase. It was the largest bank failure in U.S. history.

By then, hundreds of billions of dollars in toxic mortgages had been dumped into the financial system like polluters

dumping poison into a river. The toxic mortgages polluted the river of commerce upstream. Downstream, Wall Street bottled the polluted water, and ratings agencies slapped an attractive label on each bottle promising safe drinking water. Wall Street sold the bottles to investors. Regulators observed the whole sordid process but did little to stop it, while profits poured into the participating banks and securities firms. Investors the world over—pension funds, universities, municipalities, and more—not to mention millions of homeowners, small businesses, and U.S. taxpayers—are still paying the price and footing the cleanup bill.

At the time, we couldn't anticipate the hell these idiots would put us through. Who would have thought that bankers would be out to bankrupt their own customers? Who knew they were willing to bankrupt themselves and the country in the process?

Looking back, I can say with honesty that I never should have agreed to do this deal. All the warning signs were there. Even the owner of First Credit Bank told me as much. To his credit, and I give credit where credit is due, he did try to warn me.

"Listen to me," he said. He was serious and I respected him. "I like you. But I want you to know, this is business. When you sign those papers in front of you, I'm going to loan you this money, but it's a bad loan."

He wanted to make sure I knew I was risking everything by taking the deal.

But I wanted the Gretzky house badly enough, and, ever the optimist, I signed the papers.

I became insolvent the instant I signed that deal all on a promise from a Washington Mutual broker who knew he was going to

make some big numbers for the month. All my life I wanted to come in first. Well, I now had the number one most predatory residential home loan in the country, but I didn't feel the bite yet.

♦

After the loan closed, for the next couple of weeks I called the loan broker to get an update on my new loan and find out when it would be papered. Each time I called, he assured me it was in the works. And then one day he didn't return my calls. He also stopped responding to e-mail.

And the next day. And the next.

Escrow had closed on August 31, 2007, and before a month was up, my friendly loan broker had disappeared without a trace.

At this point I knew I would have to scramble to keep my head above water. One of the first things I did was put the Gretzky house on the market. There were no takers.

I made the Washington Mutual payments for a year and the First Credit payments for ten months as the world slowly collapsed in on me.

It was the beginning of the perfect storm from hell. I had no choice, given the monthly payment, but to liquidate my nest egg, the $38 million note from the sale of my car washes at a fraction of their value. This transaction, in turn, caused a cascade of financial cataclysms when the buyers of the note failed to perform as agreed.

There was no one to fix the nightmare I was in.

The bottom line: the loan on the Gretzky house was the end of me.

Government's first duty is to protect the people,

not run their lives.

—RONALD REAGAN

28

I FOUGHT THE LAW AND THE LAW WON

On July 7, 2009, I was forced to file an emergency Chapter 11 bankruptcy petition to stop the trustee sale of my $17.5 million "Gretzky mansion" that was scheduled to be sold at auction the following morning.

According to *In Plain English* by attorney Salene Kraemer, "Chapter 11 bankruptcy is a worthwhile option and a financially prudent decision for certain businesses or individuals wishing to reorganize, restructure their debts, reject undesirable contracts, and/or orderly liquidate certain assets under the jurisdiction and protection of the bankruptcy court."

Unfortunately, the very nature of the bankruptcy system places people in situations where seduction abounds. Unequivocally, lawyers, like doctors, are and should be held to a higher standard than the rest of us. After all, lawyers are "agents of the court." Therefore, ethics should always trump financial gain for lawyers. The two do not need to be mutually exclusive.

However, there are times that unethical behavior can have a

dramatic effect on financial gain. As we all know, money can be a blinding intoxicant that can cause even those held to a higher standard to compromise their ethical obligations. Ultimately, when this occurs, the entire system fails, and we all suffer as a result.

In an effort to minimize systemic failures, a trustee must sign an affidavit under penalty of perjury that discloses their relationships, past and present, with any of the parties that have an interest in the outcome of the bankruptcy proceedings. The expectation is this will be an honest disclosure so that ethics prevail and the result is fair and just. In legal terms, the ethical obligation of the court, and by extension the "agents of the court" (trustees and lawyers), is to eliminate "conflicts of interest." What follows are the professional and ethical obligations of an appointed trustee, as defined by the United States Bankruptcy Code.

TRUSTEE PROFESSIONALISM AND ETHICS
CONFLICTS OF INTEREST

A trustee must be knowledgeable of sections 701(a)(1), 101(14), and 101(31), as well as any other applicable law or rules, and must decline any appointment in which the trustee has a conflict of interest or lacks disinterestedness. The trustee must have in place a procedure to screen new cases for possible conflicts of interest or lack of disinterestedness upon being appointed. 28 U.S.C. § 586.

If a trustee discovers a conflict of interest or a lack of disinterestedness after accepting the appointment, the trustee shall immediately resign from the case. Conflict waivers by either the debtor or creditor do not obviate the trustee's duty to resign.

The trustee must advise the United States Trustee upon the discovery of any potential conflict or lack of disinterestedness so that a determination can be made as to whether the appointment of a successor trustee is necessary. In addition, the trustee must disclose any potential conflicts on the court record or at the meeting of creditors, or both. The trustee also must advise the United States Trustee upon discovery of any circumstances which might give rise to the appearance of impropriety. 28 U.S.C. § 586.

♦

The following is a copy of the verified Statement of Disinterestedness, executed on September 4, 2009, by the trustee, Arturo Cisneros, Esq., in my Chapter 11 bankruptcy case, signed under penalty of perjury, as an "agent of the court."

Item 4(B) states that Mr. Cisneros's law corporation

. . . has represented certain secured lenders, including Countrywide Bank, Bank of America, Washington Mutual Bank, and Wachovia Mortgage in unrelated matters. However, Malcolm Cisneros (Mr. Cisneros's law corporation) does not and will not in the future represent said lenders with regard to the within matter.

Of note, Countrywide Bank had a first-priority mortgage on my Ladbrook residence in the approximate amount of $4 million;

Case 1:09-bk-18409-GM   Doc 71   Filed 09/04/09   Entered 09/04/09 14:36:09   Desc
Main Document   Page 1 of 4

1 | A. CISNEROS

2 | Riverside, CA 92501
   | Telephone: (949) ███
3 | Telecopier: (949) ███

4 | Chapter 11 Trustee

5

6

7

8 | UNITED STATES BANKRUPTCY COURT

9 | CENTRAL DISTRICT OF CALIFORNIA

10 | SAN FERNANDEO VALLEY DIVISION

11 | In re: Case No. 1:09-18409 GM

12 | LENNY KYLE DYKSTRA,   Chapter 7

13 | Debtor.   STATEMENT OF DISINTERESTEDNESS

14 | (No Hearing Required)

15

16 | I, A. Cisneros, declare and state as follows:

17 | 1.   I am a Panel Trustee appointed by the Office of the

18 | United States Trustee.

19 | 2.   I have been nominated as Chapter 11 Trustee for the

20 | case of LENNY KYLE DYKSTRA ("Debtor"), Case No. 1:09-18409 GM.

21 | My appointment is subject to proof of disinterestedness.

22 | 3.   I have briefly reviewed the schedules and statement of

23 | financial affairs for the Debtor. I have spoken with respect to

24 | this case to an attorney employed by the Office of the United

25 | States Trustee responsible for this appointment in this case.

26 | 4.   To the best of my knowledge, information and belief,

27 | neither I, nor any employee thereof, now hold any interest

28 | adverse to the Debtor, the creditors of any party-in-interest,
   | T'sdmt of disinterestedness.doc

1 except:

2   (A)   that I am nominated Chapter 11 Trustee; and

3   (B)   that Malcolm & Cisneros, A Law Corporation ("MC"), to

4 which I am a shareholder, has represented certain secured

5 lenders, including Countrywide Bank, Bank of America, Washington

6 Mutual Bank and Wachovia Morgtage in unrelated matters.

7 However, MC does not, and will not in the future represent said

8 lenders with regard to the within matter.

9   5.   All of the foregoing facts are within my personal

10 knowledge, and if called upon as a witness I could and would

11 competently testify there.

12   I declare under penalty of perjury that the foregoing is

13 true and correct and that this declaration was executed on this

14 4th day of September, 2009 at Riverside, California.

15

16

17 _____
                A. CISNEROS, Trustee

18

19

20

21

22

23

24

25

26

27

28

2

Wachovia Bank had a second-priority lien in the approximate amount of $750,000.

Moreover, astoundingly, there is absolutely no mention by Mr. Cisneros that he was representing JPMorgan Chase in fifty-two cases prior to becoming trustee in my case, all of which were in the U.S. Bankruptcy Court for the Central District of California, the very same court where my case was being heard.

On the very same day he signed his Statement of Disinterestedness in my case, he also filed appearances as counsel for JPMorgan Chase in three other cases in that very same court.

What's more, JPMorgan Chase—the largest creditor of my estate, with a claim of more than $13 million—hired Arturo Cisneros in more than two hundred new cases subsequent to the court's approval of Mr. Cisneros's appointment as trustee for my bankruptcy proceeding on September 8, 2009. This new surge of business from JPMorgan Chase likely took Cisneros's law firm to levels it had never experienced before.

Armed with this overwhelming information *and* the documentation to support our claim, we challenged Mr. Cisneros's ability to act as the trustee in my bankruptcy case by filing a motion with the court. Mr. Cisneros's attorneys, Shulman and Huttenhoff, opposed our motion, insisting that Cisneros did not have any conflicts of interest. Furthermore, Judge Geraldine Mund allowed Cisneros to continue as the trustee.

After legal wrangling back and forth, we arrived at Judge Mund's courtroom on the morning of the hearing, August 3, 2010. My attorney Moshe Mortner said to me as we were walking into the courtroom, "Isn't it a good feeling knowing that you're going to win one for a change?" Imagine our surprise when Judge Mund promptly announced that by request of the Office of the

United States Trustee, Mr. Cisneros was asked to resign, and he had complied.

"The trustee overseeing Dykstra's estate abruptly resigned last night," CNBC reported. "The trustee's office says that 'the appearance of impropriety rose to a level' that they requested his resignation. The impropriety was not revealed, but Dykstra's attorneys claim the trustee, Art Cisneros, was colluding with JPMorgan Chase, which holds the first mortgage on Dykstra's former mansion."

"Trust me, he didn't resign because he wanted a vacation," I was quoted in the *Wall Street Journal.*

After this debacle in the bankruptcy court, I called my attorney Moshe Mortner and I told him I wanted to sue Mr. Cisneros. I refused to let that guy walk away without being held accountable. I wanted to believe the system would correct itself, but I couldn't let it go. Ultimately, after several discussions with Moshe, we agreed that he would write a letter to Mr. Cisneros, outlining his egregious misconduct and offering to resolve the matter out of court. Indeed, the law takes misconduct by trustees so seriously that if a trustee acts improperly, he can be personally liable for damages and the plaintiff doesn't even have to prove he was damaged. That worked for me, so I said, "Moshe, make it happen now!"

Moshe sent a beautifully crafted letter to Mr. Cisneros. It clearly and methodically detailed his egregious misconduct, citing case law to back up my claims. Furthermore, the potential legal consequences of his actions were delineated. The appointee of the United States Trustee, Mr. Arturo M. Cisneros, was in my crosshairs, and I had him *dead to rights.* Or so I thought.

Less than twenty-four hours after Mr. Cisneros received that

letter, the seemingly limitless resources of the federal government were mobilized in the blink of an eye, and federal agents handcuffed me, arrested me, and ultimately transported me to where I would be detained. Why would the feds need to act so quickly? What threat did I pose? Regardless of the answers to those questions, I was scooped up in a massive display of force and escorted into oblivion. In essence, I was forced to go dark.

That was a fastball I couldn't catch up to!

Everyone wants to ride with you in the limo, but what you want is someone who will take the bus with you when the limo breaks down.

—OPRAH WINFREY

29

DETAINED

The United States Constitution guarantees every American certain rights when accused of a crime. That was not the case when it came to my particular situation. I was thrown in a jail cell and locked up for six straight days. In California, they must bring you before a judge "without unnecessary delay" within forty-eight hours of being arrested. Failure to do that is a violation of your rights. This is the law, or was *supposed to be the law*.

♦

On April 14, 2010, I walked out my front door and was Pearl Harbored by what seemed to be an army of undercover cops. It was almost like a movie; they came out of nowhere. I was stunned and completely at a loss as to why I was being handcuffed and treated like a criminal. But it didn't take me long to realize *it wasn't a movie,* it was as real as real gets. You would have thought that they'd just captured Osama bin Laden. I'm serious.

After they handcuffed me, they threw me in the back of an unmarked police car. I kept asking them, "Why are you doing this to me? What is going on? What did I do? Where are we going?" They wouldn't answer, so I snapped and shouted, *"What the fuck is going on! Where are you people taking me?"*

Finally, one of the wannabe tough guys said, "You are going to see the big man."

"Who the fuck is that?" I was losing it. I kept shouting, "What is this? Who in the fuck are you? Are you arresting me for something?"

They would not answer me, only telling me that I was being taken to see "the big man" and that "the big man" would explain what was going on.

They then took me to some underground location and stuck me in what I could only guess was an interrogation room. It looked like it was right out of *Law & Order*. I still had no fucking clue why I was in this dark, dirty room being treated like a fucking murderer. I was losing my mind, as nobody would tell me anything.

Then two people wearing suits walked in and said they were with the FBI as they showed me their badges.

I was going fucking crazy at this point and started screaming at them, "Why am I being treated like a murderer?" One of the FBI agents responded by saying very calmly, "We are here to talk to you about your bankruptcy." I immediately fired back, screaming, "What in the fuck do you want to know about my bankruptcy that's not on the docket? You mean to tell me that you treat me like a fucking murderer and drag me down to this hellhole to talk to me about my fucking bankruptcy?"

The FBI agent then said, "We can't talk to you until you sign

this." I started reading the piece of paper and got to the last line, which said, *You have the right to an attorney.*

I looked up and said, "Well, since I am being held hostage in a fucking interrogation room with two FBI agents and being asked to sign my rights away, and still have not been told *what the fuck is going on,* I think I will choose *that* option—the right to an attorney."

They immediately put away the papers they brought in with them and started to head toward the door. I once again started screaming at them, "What the fuck is going on? Why are you doing this to me?" They didn't even look back, and then they were gone.

After the FBI agents left, I was waiting for someone to come in and tell me what the hell was going on, but nobody showed up. I then looked around the room and could see that I was indeed in an interrogation room. I started yelling at the cameras, "Why are you doing this to me? What did I do?" I was close to losing it when finally a man walked in and I immediately screamed at the top of my lungs, "Listen, motherfucker, either take me home or put me in jail!" His response was "Okay, come on, follow me." I noticed he was walking me toward what looked like a big jail when I said, "Where are you taking me? What is this place?"

I will never forget the smirk that little cocksucker had on his face. The next thing I knew, I was being manhandled by two deputies, telling me that they were booking me. I was so spent, so exhausted, and so confused as to why this was all happening, I just went numb. The next thing I remember, the cops were taking my mug shot.

I was then thrown into a jail cell. At that point it didn't matter where I was. I passed out cold.

The night they let me out, I was free for less than a minute,

as the same two FBI agents were waiting for me. I saw them and said, "You two again?" I asked them what was going on. They told me that I was being indicted in the morning. I responded by saying, "What's that mean?" They answered, "Your attorney will explain." They then took me to the Metropolitan Detention Center (MDC), also in downtown LA.

On April 20, I went in front of the federal magistrate, where I was charged with bankruptcy fraud. The US attorney was dead set on me not getting bail. This guy wanted me locked up in the worst way; it was obvious there was a whole lot more to my situation than met the eye. He was given orders by somebody way up the food chain to do whatever he could to keep me locked up.

In the courtroom, Dorothy signed a $75,000 signature bond against her home to bail me out. You can't put a price on loyalty, and Dorothy's loyalty has been unwavering since I hired her in 2006.

That which does not kill us, makes us stronger.

—FRIEDRICH NIETZSCHE

30

IN CUSTODY

When I appeared in court on June 6, 2011, I was taken away in handcuffs before I knew what hit me. I had been informed by my attorney Mark Wersksmen that a few days before, Deputy District Attorney Alex Karkanen, a very senior and experienced DDA who is normally assigned to a Special Auto Theft and Auto Fraud unit, was going to file felony charges against me for car leases from Galpin Ford. Mr. Wersksmen stated that Mr. Karkanen's charges were based on me presenting false documentation about the new company my attorney had formed for me, Home-Free Systems. Mr. Karkanen told my attorney that Home-Free Systems was just a "shell company."

I was incarcerated at the Los Angeles County Men's Central Jail for almost five months. Due to my celebrity status, I was placed in the so-called high power unit, where extremely dangerous inmates were held. I was placed there supposedly for my own protection, as they felt I would be at significant risk if I commingled with the general population. They told me they didn't want me to get killed under their watch. Nonetheless, I was placed in solitary confinement for leasing a car.

To make matters worse, visitation protocols were so arduous that most people were not willing to go through everything that was involved in order to visit their loved one in the high-power unit. However, Dorothy, as she always does, persevered, doing everything necessary to be allowed to communicate with me. I was able to call Dorothy once or twice a month. While I was incarcerated at LA County Men's Central Jail, Dorothy was essentially my only contact to the outside world and my only visitor other than my lawyers.

During my stay, I was informed that my mother was seriously ill and death was imminent. I was devastated that I was incapable of visiting her due to my inability to post bail. Dorothy was able to reach the prison chaplain, who at least arranged for me to talk to my mom by phone. She died the day I talked to her. Because I was unable to post bail, I wasn't even permitted to attend her funeral. Needless to say, that will haunt me for the rest of my days.

As for the charge of grand theft auto that landed me in prison, the basis of the charge was that I formed a shell company that was not properly registered. I pleaded with those who were detaining me to speak with my attorney Moshe Mortner in New York, who had properly registered the alleged shell company nearly a year prior to my indictment. Ignoring my pleas, they never contacted Moshe. What follows is the declaration written by Moshe, under penalty of perjury, where he affirms the proper registration of the entity Home-Free Systems, LLC.

Lines 16 and 17 of the document that appears on pages 289–290 state, "I declare under penalty of perjury, under the laws of the United States of America that the foregoing is true and correct."

Numbers 4 and 5 in the document clearly delineate that $300,000 was raised from an investor, who received a promissory

DECLARATION OF MOSHE MORTNER

I, Moshe Mortner, declare as follows:

1. I am an attorney admitted to the practice of law in the State of New York and before the United States District Court for the Southern District of New York. In, 2010 I applied for admission before the US Bankruptcy Court for the Central District of California, San Fernando Valley Division, to be admitted *pro hac vice* for the limited purpose of representing the Defendant Lenny K. Dykstra in connection with the aspect of his bankruptcy proceedings that concerned the secured claim of JP Morgan Chase.

2. Additionally, I was engaged by Defendant to set up the company Home-Free Systems LLC.

3. Accordingly, I arranged for the formation of the entity Home-Free Systems LLC on July 12, 2010, which I caused to be registered with the New York Department of State, Division of Corporations and Records.

4. Home-Free Systems LLC, and the Defendant raised $300,000 from an investor who was given equity in the start-up company and a promissory note. As Mr. Dykstra's attorney, I was responsible for preparing the promissory note in the amount of $300,000 for the investor.

5. The $300,000 investment for Home-Free Systems LLC was wired directly to my **Client Trust Account**, and I immediately distributed those funds per the instructions of my client, Defendant.

6. HOME-FREE-SYSTEMS, LLC, received all of the legal documentation required under the law to become a legal and active limited liability company in the State of New York.

7. In addition, pursuant to Defendant's instructions, I applied to the IRS on behalf of Home-Free Systems LLC for an EIN, and the number was issued on August 3, 2010.

8. Upon information and belief, defendant created Home-Free Systems LLC to do business under the name Predatory Lending Recovery, which Defendant later changed to StoptheGreedyBanks.com.

1

9. At various times I was asked by Defendant to provide consulting services for Home-Free Systems LLC in matters pertaining to residential foreclosure defense and related services. In fact, I spent two full days in Los Angeles consulting with Defendant and his associates as to the development of the company's business model.

10. Residing and practicing law in the State of New somewhat limits my availability for the Defendant from time to time.

11. When the Defendant was taken into custody, I was out of the office and unavailable to produce needed documents for the Defendant's case. Additionally, I was not aware they were needed at the time.

12. At no time prior to or subsequent to Defendant's arrest was I contacted by law enforcement officials or investigators asking for any information with regard to the Defendant or Home-Free Systems LLC.

13. It was not intentional that the information in my possession concerning Home-Free Systems LLC was not made available to the defense in this case in a timely manner. I am a commercial attorney and I had no involvement in Defendant's criminal defense.

I declare under penalty of perjury under the laws of the United States of America that the foregoing is true and correct.

DATED: February 28, 2012

Moshe Mortner, Esq.

By: _Moshe Mortner_ 3'02

Moshe Mortner, Esq.

2

note, prepared by my attorney, as well as equity in the start-up company. Moreover, said $300,000 was wired directly to my attorneys Client Trust Account, whereupon he immediately distributed the funds as per my instructions.

From the declaration, number 12 states the following: "At no time prior to or subsequent to Defendant's arrest was I contacted by law enforcement officials or investigators asking for any information with regard to the Defendant or Home-Free Systems LLC."

Therefore, Moshe Mortner, my attorney, substantiates that I told Detective Contreras the truth. Please note that Moshe's letter is dated February 28, 2012, prepared for my sentencing hearing approximately eight months after I was incarcerated for Grand Theft Auto in June 2011.

For the normal person, this must sound like I am crazy. The fact of the matter is, *I am far from crazy*. The only thing that was crazy was that I was getting locked up no matter what. Let's think about this for a minute. Follow me through the actual sequence of events.

If the detective was doing his job, which was to investigate the case and find out the real truth—*We are talking about a man's freedom here, this was not just another day at the ballpark*—he would have called my attorney Moshe Mortner to ask him if what I claimed was true regarding Home-Free Systems. I had begged Contreras to call my attorney, as Mortner would clear this whole mess up. Their allegation of a so-called shell company would have been proven wrong. They would have had no case. The facts were all supported by my attorney who formed the company, and the Grand Theft Auto charge would have been dismissed.

During my arraignment hearing, my criminal defense attorney, Andrew Flier, asked Detective Contreras, a twenty-four-year LAPD veteran, a series of questions. Specifically, Detective Contreras, the investigator who handled my entire case, was asked under oath if he had ever bothered to check if I was telling the truth when I explained that Home-Free Systems, LLC, was indeed a real company, not a shell company as they alleged. In fact, Detective Contreras stated under oath that Home-Free Systems, LLC, was a shell company with no money. Flier had even read from the interrogation transcript that I was begging, and then screaming at, Detective Contreras to call my attorney, Moshe Mortner. Mr. Flier went on to say, "I'm reading from the transcripts that Mr. Dykstra was pleading with you, 'Please, call my attorney, he can verify everything, all you have to do is call him and he will tell you that Home-Free Systems is not only real, but, in fact, it was my attorney, Moshe Mortner, who formed the company.'" Initially, Detective Contreras would not answer the question of whether he contacted Mortner to find out the real truth. When the judge told him he had to answer the question, Detective Contreras, in a very low voice, replied, "No."

Therefore, under oath, the investigator in my case admitted that he had never attempted to follow up on my request to contact my lawyer to prove that Home-Free Systems, LLC, *was not a shell company.* He didn't want to know the truth, that's why he didn't call. So, instead, this man, who stated under oath that he would "support and defend the Constitution of the United States," failed miserably.

Unfortunately for me, Moshe's letter was never entered into evidence or even considered until we produced it at my sentencing hearing. I was incarcerated for approximately six months without

an investigation. After sentencing, I was incarcerated once again, and entered into a world for which there is no adequate primer. Little did I know that what I was about to embark upon would alter my perspective on life forever.

Again, I ask the question "Does this represent justice?"

The rights of every man are diminished when the rights of one man are threatened.

—JOHN F. KENNEDY

31

IN THE HOLE

When the prison cell door slams shut for the first time, your mind is flooded by a plethora of emotions. First and foremost, that sound becomes indelibly etched into your brain. Regardless of what other thoughts you might have racing through your mind, one thought predominates and is constantly reinforced: *I am no longer free.* You can't prepare for that feeling, because we take freedom as a given. So when that door shuts, and you hear that sound, you are transported to a place that is incomprehensible.

Darkness engulfs you, invades you, and establishes a parasitic relationship with you. You see the same four walls and hear the same sounds every single day. The nights are particularly challenging, because it's difficult to turn your brain off. Moreover, there's virtually nothing to do to distract you from your thoughts. In essence, it's pure fucking monotony.

A few days into my sentence, I laid on my cot fully expecting another night of unending boredom. I was learning how to allow my mind to just drift way out there until I became, as the song says, *comfortably numb*.

Just before I checked out for the night, a voice startled me from the adjacent cell. "Hey, man, you all right over there?"

"Yeah, ah, I guess," I replied, not sure who it was.

"You read?" the low, rough voice asked.

"No, not really."

"Man, you got to learn to read in here, or you're gonna do some hard time," the voice cautioned.

Then I heard a noise outside my cell, and there before my door was a book that he had tossed to me from his cell. I opened the food slot in my door and snagged it. It was *The King of Torts* by John Grisham.

Literally, in the blink of an eye, I was awakened to the unchanging misery of my circumstances.

What a great fucking read. For a few days I became Clay Carter, the main character in the book. I even dreamt I was him. Never having read before, I got sucked into the world of well-written fiction, hard and fast. And any Grisham narrative sure beat the shit out of nightly oblivion.

Lenny Dykstra and reading? Undeniably, they were mutually exclusive until I was incarcerated. Prison changes a man, and it made me a bibliophile. I devoured as many books as I could get, transporting myself into the stories to help forget where I was and what I faced.

Meanwhile, the dude next to me, *the voice,* would have bags and bags of shit delivered to him on commissary days. Other inmates paid tribute to him, and there was respect for his position. Being a new kid on the block, I wasn't sure how it all worked, but it was abundantly clear that this dude was wired and dialed in. I'm not sure how he did it, but on commissary days, you might have thought he went on a shopping spree at the mall.

The voice from the cell next to me turned out to be Lalo Martinez, the head of the Mexican Mafia, who ran the whole fucking jail from his cell down in the hole. Lalo kind of took me under his wing. He would throw me soups and other shit I didn't have from his stockpile of goods. We talked about books, pussy, religion, just about everything. For a major league crime boss, in the hole for nearly thirty years, he was kind of surprising. He was very intelligent, which I credit somewhat to all the books he read.

Lalo taught me something early on about the accommodations. There were video monitors looking into each of the seven cells along G-Row, each one of them filming everything 24/7, including when I took a shit.

Lalo told me, "Man, you hang up the towel to block the camera, or your ass will be sold to TMZ. It happens all the time." He didn't have to tell me twice.

I'm relatively certain that his sway there at Men's Central was why I was never bothered by any of the other inmates. Unfortunately, other inmates turned out to be the least of my worries.

◆

Lalo and all his influence could not help me on one particular night. Close to lights-out, I was relaxing in bed, preparing for that nightly journey to nowhere, when I heard a commotion coming down the cellblock toward my cell. This huge motherfucker—the deputy who always egged on the other deputies to commit their petty bullshit—was taunting me, laughing and singing "Take Me Out to the Ball Game."

"Not tonight, man," I said. "I don't want to hear it."

The next thing I knew, at least three guards came crashing into my cell and proceeded to beat the holy fuck out of me. They slammed my head against the wall as they pounded on me, knocking out at least one of my teeth and doing major damage to the rest. As I faded in and out of consciousness, I vaguely remember being dragged down the cellblock like an animal.

I was cleaned up and my injuries were cataloged and videotaped, based on what they were told to record. All of this occurred before I was fully conscious. When I finally came to, I was in the hospital. To this day, I have absolutely no recollection whatsoever as to how I got to the hospital, or where I stayed for three days.

After being released from the hospital, I regained my senses and became lucid, which prompted an internal investigation into what really happened to me. I was emphatically told that if I did not corroborate their version of what transpired to their satisfaction, the next time, I would not be waking up. Fearful for my life, I heeded their advice and told no one what really happened . . . until I was released from prison.

That savage beating eventually led to the removal of all my teeth. Furthermore, the repeated severe blows to my head may have resulted in some brain damage.

This brutal attack came from out of nowhere, with absolutely no provocation from me. I realize that I am lucky that I did not die from the beating. Nonetheless, I had to serve the remainder of my time there, saying nothing about the incident, or risk death if I did. Needless to say, I lived in constant fear that they would come back and finish me off.

Many of your rights are taken away when you enter prison. Some believe that this is a just penalty for breaking the law. How-

ever, there are certain rights that are unalienable. The vicious and reckless assault of an individual by these men, without provocation, regardless of the setting, cannot be construed as right. Moreover, the perpetrators of such an act should be punished to the highest degree that the law allows. When you find out that this type of behavior is not an aberration but rather a microcosm of a systemic culture, this can only be reviewed as egregious.

I wish I could say my situation was a rare occurrence. But in light of the indictments and sentences of Los Angeles prison authorities and guards, it obviously is not. In case you aren't on their e-mail list, here are some headlines from the FBI litigation newsletter:

- "Current and Former Deputies Charged with Federal Crimes, Including Illegal Beatings of Jail Inmates and Obstruction of Justice"
- "New Indictment Stemming from Civil Rights Investigation into Los Angeles County Sheriff's Department Alleges Two Deputies Abused Inmate"
- "Six Current and Former Los Angeles Sheriff's Deputies Sentenced to Federal Prison for Obstructing Federal Civil Rights Investigation"
- "Ex–LA County Sheriff Lee Baca Pleads Guilty in Jail Scandal"

◆

It was dark in the hole. It was even darker when you contemplated your existence there. Nonetheless, I was adapting, fol-

lowing the rules, doing what I was supposed to do. When they turned my lights out, that was a shade of darkness I could not possibly fathom.

The epic Simon and Garfunkel song "The Sounds of Silence" begins with: "Hello, darkness, my old friend. I've come to talk with you again . . ."

Well, with all deference to Paul and Art, I would change the lyrics, based on my experience, to: "Good-bye, darkness, you never were my friend. I hope to never see you again."

Don't give up on your dreams, or your dreams
will give up on you.

—JOHN WOODEN

32

LEGACY

Although incarceration was difficult at best, I am forever grateful that I was released just prior to the start of my youngest son Luke's senior year in high school. Having the ability to be present in Luke's life throughout his senior year was a tremendous gift for both of us. Of course, I helped him with his studies, emphasizing, "If you don't get the grades, you don't get to play baseball." More important, I was able to guide him in making difficult life choices that could drastically affect his future. We all remember what we did when we were high school seniors, which, in all honesty, makes it somewhat difficult to counsel your kids fairly. Regardless, I cautioned Luke about hanging out with the wrong crowd and encouraged him to always consider the consequences of anything he was about to do.

Luke has the uncanny knack of knowing exactly what to say to appease his mother. After all, he is my son. But I'm the King Operator; nothing gets past the master, who has seen and done it all. Luke knew that I loved him, but he realized that appropriate discipline is a responsibility that comes with being a father.

Admittedly, I was somewhat limited in my ability to help Luke

304 HOUSE OF NAILS

with his studies (all this new shit!). However, I could and will continue to provide him with my extensive knowledge about my expertise—playing the game of baseball, the right way. I spent countless hours every day with Luke, discussing the nuances of the game. I was preparing Luke for pro ball, as I knew from talking to the scouts that he was going to be a high draft pick. Luke made it abundantly clear to me that he wanted to become a professional baseball player rather than go to college. Therefore, it was incumbent upon me to prepare him the best I could.

In 2015, Luke, who is the perfect size for baseball at six foot one, 195 pounds, was drafted in the seventh round by the Atlanta Braves. He signed, and his dream of becoming a professional baseball player has been realized. He is on his way.

In Luke's first full season, he was promoted to the Braves' mid-level Class A team, the Rome Braves. Luke put up All-Star-caliber stats, hitting .348 with an on-base percentage of .378.

My son Cutter, Luke's older brother, was drafted by the Milwaukee Brewers in the second round of the 2008 draft. He was then traded to the Washington Nationals, where he was the organizational player of the year in 2013 and 2014, which earned him an invitation to his first major league spring training in 2015. I see the big leagues in Cutter's future. He's a winning player and I know he can help a team win.

While it took a while for my stepson, Gavin, to find himself, he has grown into a fine young man, and I am proud of him. He is a great father to his son, Marshall, works hard to provide for him, and is a constant presence in his life.

And as proud as I am of Cutter's baseball achievements, I am even more impressed with Cutter the father and husband. In many ways, he is a better father and husband than I have ever

been. On January 16, 2016, in a beautiful ceremony held at the Parker in Palm Springs, California, Cutter married Jamie-Lynn Sigler, a wonderful young woman. Many of you know Jamie-Lynn as Meadow Soprano, the daughter of Tony Soprano, on the long-running HBO series *The Sopranos*.

Jamie and Cutter have an awesome, beautiful little boy, Beau. Beau is nearly three years old now and completely obsessed with baseball. The countdown to a third-generation Dykstra in professional baseball has officially begun. It's hard to believe that Lenny "Nails" Dykstra is a grandfather, but I wouldn't have it any other way.

Undeniably, I have made some monumental mistakes in my life, some of which, inadvertently, have had a negative impact on my family. Despite my indiscretions, my love for my boys cannot be questioned. Incarceration deprived me of valuable time with my sons. While I can't get the time back, I can make sure that I do everything in my power to maintain a constant physical and emotional presence in my sons' lives now and going forward. Circumstances have hammered home to Nails what is truly important in life. I look forward to watching my sons grow and contributing to that growth by providing the wisdom I have gained throughout the years. Perhaps, more important, I am looking forward to my sons providing me with insight to aid in my own personal growth. Never lacking confidence, I assure you, I fully expect my relationship with my sons to continually grow and strengthen until the day I die.

I am not sure who said it, but this quote describes how I feel about my sons: "A truly rich man is one whose children run into his arms when his hands are empty."

In the end, we will remember not the words of

our enemies but the silence of our friends.

—MARTIN LUTHER KING JR.

33

TO BE OR NOT TO BE LENNY

Although that outbound Greyhound bus ride from prison is a mere speck in my rearview mirror, I have a far better understanding of its meaning now. On the one hand, that Greyhound bus was my conduit to the freedom I desperately craved. Yet I realize now that it is also a reminder of where I have been and all that I have lost. Perhaps, more important, it is the recognition that objects in the rearview mirror are larger than they appear.

Sitting on a dirty bus going thirty-five miles per hour at the command of someone else was a stark contrast to lounging in my Gulfstream at an altitude of thirty-five thousand feet going six hundred miles per hour. Incredible highs and unbearable lows, the story of my life! Nonetheless, I have had a great deal of time to reflect and better understand what is truly important in life.

I would be lying if I said that prison didn't break my spirit to a certain degree. But I didn't let it break me completely. I found a way to survive. Prior to the nightmare of prison, fear was an emotion I rarely experienced or chose to acknowledge. Now fear creeps into my thoughts more than I prefer.

I have fulfilled my court-ordered five hundred hours of com-

munity service and completed the three years of probation that my sentence dictated. So the penalty phase is over, but the penalties persist. Undoubtedly, the greatest penalty of all has to be living with what I did to my family. Realistically, I will never be able to completely atone for the damage I have inflicted. I can, however, step up to the plate for my family by becoming a productive member of society again.

Obviously, money is an integral component when it comes to helping us live and provide for our families. The more money we have, the more we can provide for them. Sometimes we get intoxicated with money and it becomes just another drug. We are seduced by the high it provides, and it convinces us that we must generate more in order to maintain what we have. When the love of money becomes the driving force in your life, you compromise yourself and those around you with the misconception that "you were doing it for them."

The reality is that you are doing it for the money, usually unknowingly. Regardless, when you have been where I just came from, you realize you did a lot of things that you now regret.

◆

I would like to believe I am taking ownership of my misdeeds and I'm in the process of changing for the better. When Luke turned eighteen, I received a call from the MLB players' pension guy, who asked, "Where do you want your money sent?"

"What do you mean?" I responded. "It goes to my ex-wife every month."

He replied, "Yeah, but the divorce agreement states that when your youngest son, Luke, turns eighteen, it reverts back to you. By law, it is yours for the rest of your life. We will need you to fill out our paperwork so we know where you want us to have your money sent by direct deposit on the last day of every month. We're talking about six thousand dollars a month, free and clear, for the rest of your life."

I thought about it, then told him, "Give me fifteen minutes and I will call you back."

Since pieces of my body are splattered all over the National League, I did earn the money, and I sure could use $6,000 a month, every month, without fail, for the rest of my life.

After some serious soul-searching, I called back the man who handled our MLB pension and said, "Send me over the agreement with the papers that say that I want my money to continue to go to Terri Dykstra for the rest of her life."

Why should she be penalized for my transgressions? She did not contribute to my downfall. On the contrary, she probably stood by me too long. She's a wonderful person who certainly did not deserve the fallout caused by my actions. So I gave it all to her. It was the right thing to do.

◆

Most of my life, up until the last decade, I got whatever I wanted, whenever I wanted. Not that it was always easy. I was often told I couldn't, but I did anyway.

I was living the dream with all the trimmings, soaring above

it all in my bird, looking down upon all that was mine. Unfortunately, your view gets distorted up there, and you literally can't see the little things. I completely lost sight of what was important and made decisions that I hope my kids will never make.

Eventually the bird must come down. For most, that means a smooth landing, followed by periods of normalcy. Even I realize that traveling in your own Gulfstream is way beyond the realm of normalcy. Undeniably, my jet did not have a smooth landing. It "crashed," nearly killing me and injuring everyone dear to me in the process. Living the dream culminated in a horrific nightmare. Fortunately for me, I have survived to live another day.

◆

One could argue that the title for this book could have been *All or Nothing*. After all, that essentially is the story of my life. It has been full of triumphs and tragedies, most of which are attributable to my performance, but some have been completely out of my control. I've come to realize that baseball has actually prepared me for what I need to do moving forward.

As a leadoff hitter, one of my many responsibilities was to give my teammates an opportunity to see what the opposing pitcher had that day. Often that meant taking some pitches, particularly at the start of the game. As you know, I prided myself on working the count to give me the best chance to succeed. Unquestionably, I was good at what I did. My brash, arrogant style, although distasteful to some, made me the baseball player that I was. While at times that brash, arrogant style served me

well in the game of life, it eventually was instrumental in my undoing.

So as I contemplate my life moving forward, I find myself consistently reflecting on the parallels between baseball and life. For some, baseball never ends. They stay in the game in one way or another, until they die. For most, the game ends and you must move on. Life, on the other hand, doesn't end until you die. That line from *The Shawshank Redemption*, shared between Andy Dufrense (Tim Robbins) and Red (Morgan Freeman), kind of says it all: "It comes down to a simple choice: get busy living or get busy dying." I fully intend to "get busy living."

◆

I will conclude with this: the only predictable thing in my entire life has been that every day is unpredictable. If I start telling you that I promise to do this and will never do that, then I would not be true to who I am. I would not be true to the person I've been telling you about. I would not be true to the man you hopefully learned about. I know I have many flaws and have made many mistakes over the years. I know, too, that I will make more mistakes as I continue to work on regaining a life built with happiness and contentment; a life that I can be proud of again.

What will that life look like?

How the fuck do I know!

Will it be interesting? Will it be unlike any other person's journey?

Will it contain the highest of highs or the lowest of lows? Or both?

Possibly.

But as I said, *unpredictable* is an adjective that best describes who I am.

So I think the best way for me to end this book is by saying three words:

"To be continued . . ."

WHALE HUNTING WITH LENNY DYKSTRA

By Tom Borowski

My name is Tom Borowski, and Lenny Dykstra is a dear friend of mine. Shortly after getting to know Lenny, I found out pretty quickly that he approaches life the same way he approached the game of baseball: with tenacity, resilience, and a fearless attitude. For those of us who have had the privilege of knowing Lenny, you know that he's authentic and loyal and has absolutely no filter. These are just a few of the qualities that I admire in the guy. So when Lenny called me up one day and told me that he wanted to ask John Grisham to write the foreword of his book, I knew Lenny wouldn't reach out to Grisham by the traditional means of going through agents—no, he was going to fly from California to Virginia to approach Grisham man-to-man and give him the manuscript personally. Meaning there would be no appointment, no scheduled meeting, no anything. As Lenny would say, *I'm going to Pearl Harbor this guy . . .*

He had called to tell me his plan and to invite me out to help him accomplish it. But as it turned out, there really was no set plan. Lenny was going to find Grisham—one way or another—

and respectfully approach him so that he could tell Grisham how he inspired and influenced him, then ask him to review his book and consider writing the foreword if he found it worthy.

Pretty simple? Nothing with Lenny is simple.

A few days later, Lenny arrived in Charlottesville, Virginia, where my girlfriend, Melissa, and I drove out from New Jersey to pick him up at the airport. How did he know where the reportedly very private John Grisham lived? As with everything in his life, Lenny finds a way, and he had several ideas he was kicking around about how to make this happen.

It was a typical cold February afternoon when we set out to find Grisham's private residence in North Garden. The moment we turned off the main highway, we began a half-hour ride into as rural, desolate, and beautiful a place as you've ever seen. That said, the roads were extremely narrow with crazy hairpin turns, looming trees acting as our guardrails, and steep ditches on both sides of us. We saw plenty of green pastures, cows, horses, and small bodies of water . . . everything except people.

We were in the middle of unimproved parklike property for as far as you can see.

Lenny looked at me and said, "This looks exactly like where a writer would want to live, bro."

We kept driving for what felt like hours, but in reality it was only a few minutes, when Lenny announced that Grisham's house should be coming up pretty quickly. We soon approached a large black iron gate at the bottom of a hill, the gate conveniently open. I glanced at Lenny and asked, "Are you ready to do this?"

Lenny's crooked smile was his only answer.

I'd been through this before with Lenny—he's not afraid to go

anywhere. Just a month earlier, when he was visiting me in Jersey, I wanted to show him a potential development site that the real estate company I own is in the planning stages of. Lenny has a good eye for property and design and wanted to see the existing on-site building, currently a catering hall.

Lenny took one look and said, "The building is great, bro, you can incorporate this into your design—let's take a closer look."

Before I could stop him, he had already headed into the building to check the place out. A guy working there asked if he could help us, and Lenny said he was looking for one of the bigger rooms. The guy asks, "Susan's birthday party?"

Lenny responds, "Yeah, Susan." Before I can even try to stop him, he takes the direction to that room and we wander into this elderly lady's birthday party. Lenny checks out the room quietly, casually says happy birthday to the obvious birthday girl—who thanked him—and we exit out the patio doors on the side. To this day, Susan has no idea who she met among her guests at her birthday party.

While that was fun, this felt unnerving and intense. I'd had too much time to think about what we were doing, driving up to John Grisham's estate out in the middle of nowhere.

So I drove onto the private property, where we went over some railroad tracks, shortly followed by a second gate, which was also open. Without hesitation, I drove on through and saw a sign that said, CAUTION HORSES.

As soon as we pulled past this gate, a woman in a car approached us in the opposite direction. In hindsight, it makes sense why the gates were open—Lenny and I had some lucky timing. The woman slowed down and unrolled her window. "Can I help you?" she asked.

"I'm here to see Mr. Grisham."

After she asked if we had an appointment, Lenny held up his manuscript and waved it as his response, and she directed us to speak to the men up ahead.

We knew he was there and that was that. One hurdle down.

I slowly pulled forward and we were on the driveway to the main house. A gravel driveway led to a beautiful but modest yellow plantation-style home. Then, seeming to come out of nowhere, a pickup truck pulled up nose-to-nose with our car, completely blocking us from driving any farther.

At this point, I was getting a little nervous . . . all right, *a lot* nervous.

The driver of the truck didn't come out or speak to us, but instead the passenger, a thirtysomething man wearing overalls, got out and approached us cautiously.

It was show time.

Lenny quickly introduced himself and explained why he wanted to meet Mr. Grisham. In his typical, somewhat rambling style, Lenny apologized for intruding and explained how he had flown all the way across the country from LA just to personally give his manuscript to Mr. Grisham. Lenny told the overall-wearing man that if Mr. Grisham liked what he read and found it worthy, he would be honored if the author would consider writing a foreword for the book.

The man in overalls said that Mr. Grisham wasn't there, and in fact was out of town. It was pretty clear that he wanted to send us on our way.

But Lenny hadn't come all this way for nothing. "Are you sure? I'm pretty sure he's home. I don't want to take much of his time or intrude, but if you could please tell Mr. Grisham that Lenny

Dykstra is outside, and that I would be honored if he could spare a few minutes to discuss this."

Although Lenny had introduced himself and stated who he was and the reason for his appearance on the property, I don't think the man quite processed everything. I decided to interject and asked for his name. He told us his name was Curtis.

"Curtis, are you a baseball fan?" I asked.

He responded affirmatively, and I decided to elaborate a little about Lenny's career and accomplishments. I wanted to make sure Curtis clearly understood that there was a legendary All-Star, World Series–winning center fielder standing right before him. I told Curtis that Lenny's book was being published by HarperCollins, one of the world's largest publishing companies, and that Lenny wasn't asking for anything but a few moments of Mr. Grisham's time.

As Curtis and Lenny talked baseball for a bit, and a little about the book, I could see that his guard was starting to slip and that he was really enjoying meeting Lenny—Lenny tends to have that effect on people.

Curtis finally agreed to go inside and try to locate Grisham. About ten minutes later, Curtis reappeared and told us that Grisham *was* in town, but he was currently getting ready for a dinner party. He also informed us that Grisham would be attending a Little League tryout the next morning before leaving town for a few days. But he said that Grisham agreed to accept the manuscript and instructed Curtis to leave it on his desk.

While Lenny wrote a personal note to Grisham, humbly apologizing for showing up unannounced and saying how much of an inspiration he was to him, I pulled up YouTube on my phone and started showing Curtis some of Lenny's career highlights: his

walkoff homer in the NLCS in '86, his World Series homers in '86 and '93.

With it fully sinking in that he was in the presence of a legend, Curtis quietly said that he wished he had a ball or something so he could get an autograph from Lenny. Lenny said he had a couple of his cards and would be happy to sign them for him, and for Grisham as well.

Curious, I asked Curtis if anyone had come to the house before. Curtis told us that he'd worked for Grisham for twelve years and we were only the *second* unannounced visitor. The first was a fan who wanted a bunch of books signed.

Lenny felt satisfied that the mission to get the book into Grisham's hands was accomplished. It would have been a little more satisfying to meet with Grisham personally, but the letter, cards, and manuscript would have to do. After Curtis had mentioned the Little League event the next day, Lenny said that we would be in town a few more days, and if Grisham's schedule opened up, he would love to meet with him briefly. Lenny even offered to meet the kids at the Little League, talk to them about baseball, and even take a few swings, if Grisham could spare a few minutes for Lenny afterward. Curtis took Lenny's number, we shook hands, and he said he would ask Grisham to call him.

Curtis, who had probably just had his most interesting and bizarre experience in more than a decade of working there, signaled to the truck in front of us to back up. I pulled forward and made a U-turn in Grisham's front driveway, then headed off the property. On the way out, all the closed gates were remotely opened as we approached.

We both felt good about this exchange and confident that we'd left the book in the personal clutches of Grisham.

◆

We never did hear back from Grisham.

As much as I believe Lenny would have really liked to have at least heard back from Grisham, by the time we left Virginia Lenny had accomplished what he set out to do, which was to gain some experience in preparing to bag the biggest whale in the sea, Stephen King. That doesn't mean Lenny is not a huge fan of John Grisham, because he is, and we were both treated with the utmost respect by Mr. Grisham's people. But Lenny had his sights set on Stephen King, whom Lenny calls a genius, so he was mentally preparing for his big move from Los Angeles to Florida—to bag the biggest whale. Stephen King is a devoted Boston Red Sox fan, and I don't believe it's a coincidence that he bought his Florida spread in close proximity to where his beloved Red Sox have spring training.

Stephen King was in our near future.

ACKNOWLEDGMENTS

Terri, you have been the rock and the foundation. You have always put everyone else first. You are an amazing mother to our boys. And I hope you know in your heart that you are the only woman I have ever loved.

Cutter, Luke, and **Gavin,** while all of you are different, each of you holds a special place in my heart. I have watched you grow from babies, to boys, to men, and now to fathers (Gavin and Cutter). I realize that my fame and infamy have certainly complicated your lives at times. Although I was physically removed from you for a couple of years, our unbreakable father-son bonds sustained me and were the driving force that allowed me to persevere when I was incarcerated. As a parent, I can only hope that you have inherited whatever is good about me and been spared the rest. At the very least, I hope you learn from my mistakes. You are the ones who will carry the Dykstra name forward in a positive fashion. I could not be prouder of the men you have become and will continue to be. I am incredibly fortunate to be your dad.

Beau Dykstra, you truly reinforce what is really important in life. By the time you can comprehend this, I fully anticipate that you will be dominating Little League. More important, because of your wonderful parents, you will be well on your way to establishing yourself as a quality human being. I treasure the opportunity to witness and aid in your evolution. Take advantage

of what life affords you. I eagerly await celebrating your triumphs with you and helping you when you fall. What a blessing you are and will continue to be.

Marshall, I've watched you grow from a fine young boy and know that you'll be a fine young man. Your spirit and your attitude make you a pleasure to be around, and I wish only the best for you.

To **Mom, Marilyn,** I will never forget you. Everyone knows the real truth, but what matters most is that I love you. You were the best mom in the world.

To **Dennis Dykstra,** my only dad: I am so grateful that you came into my life.

To **Grandpa Pete** and **Grandma Rose,** I always looked forward to the Sundays when I knew I would be with you. To my aunts, **Carol, Bonnie,** and **Penny,** and your beautiful families—all of you have been there for me, even when you had to make tough decisions to do so. The fact that you know the truth and stayed loyal means more to me than you know.

To **Eric** and **Kelly**—Eric, you are one of the smartest guys I have ever met. I am proud to call you my friend. I love the rap. I learn from you every day! I have to say, I have never seen so many sleds—you've got every country and emblem covered, bro! Kelly, Eric is lucky to have you. You are the best! You and Eric made this book a possibility, and for that I will be forever grateful. I am honored by your trust and loyalty.

To **Kelly Hutchinson,** thank you for helping shape my boys into the men they are today. You will always be family.

Tom Borowski, your intelligence and discipline have allowed you to become extremely successful. However, it is your work ethic that separates you from the rest; you are the hardest-working man

I know. I was told by other pro athletes that your company Striker Realty was the go-to brokerage for real estate in New Jersey, and I would agree after experiencing the vast knowledge and resources that you possess. Most important, you have treated me with respect, as you do everybody, from the first day we met. I greatly appreciate your generosity; you truly have a heart of gold. I am so fortunate that you came into my life. I value your friendship, and look forward to strengthening it in the years to come. Although our initial road trip did not land the whale, we were able to see where he swims. Fortunately, our ensuing road trip bagged us an even bigger whale on the beach. Those memories will last forever. I thoroughly enjoyed the rides with you, and assure you they will not be our last. Thanks for being there. Melissa, thanks for your gracious company and friendship and including me in yours and Tom's lives.

To **Bert Brodsky** . . . what can I say? Not only were you the best man at my wedding, you also arranged the ceremony at a moment's notice. Through thick and thin, you have always been there for Terri, the boys, and me for the past thirty years. You could have easily and understandably bailed when things went south, but you decided to stay the course. I will be forever grateful for your loyalty, guidance, and support throughout the past three decades. I look forward to sharing the good times with you again. You are a special person, and I consider myself extremely fortunate that you came into my life. You are my hero!

Noah Scheinmann, I would like to express my gratitude to you for helping me navigate my way through this book. Thank you for all your help with the media and launch. You are a true genius, bro! But most important, thank you for having the balls to tell me the truth, even if it wasn't what I wanted to hear.

Joe Longo, my friend, there's so much to thank you for that I'll never get it all in. *Honesty* and *integrity* are two words that will always define you.

To my good friend **Eytan Sugarman** from New York. Is there anybody you don't know? Honestly, you are the most dialed-in dude I know. When I really need to talk to God, I am going to ask you for an intro. Seriously, though, I am sincerely thankful for our friendship. Moreover, hanging in there with me regardless of the circumstances has not gone unnoticed. I look forward to enjoying many good meals with you in the future.

Dr. Howard Samuels, thank you for taking me in and providing much-needed clarity . . . or something like that. I don't know where I would be today if it weren't for you. You are the real deal. You walk the talk.

Larry Winokur, your humility aside, you are truly a giant among giants. Having you as a part of my team in this endeavor is invaluable. While your professional accomplishments speak loudly, particularly the incredible cachet of your client list, your humanity to me speaks much louder. Thank you for being there.

To the quiet but intimidating **Dave Hollins** (Head). The ultimate gamer! Best base runner I ever played with, especially first to third. Undoubtedly, the best teammate I could ever have. You put the fear of God in every opponent. Having you in my foxhole, in which you have always been, made me even more surly and pugnacious. It's a wonderful feeling knowing someone always has your back. That aside, you are my best friend in baseball. Now that our careers are over, we are left with a lasting relationship, which was forged on the diamond but is even greater now. I look forward to our evolution. Regardless of how it turns out, you will always be a "Head" above the rest.

Dr. Jim Berman, it's hard to put into words what you have meant to me. You are not only a great doctor who is triple smart, you also use your gifts to change people's lives. Most important, you always treat people with respect and dignity even though they may be disrespectful and undignified at times. Simply put, *You get it!* Knowing that your patients know that is enough for you, and that is a remarkable quality.

To **Leo Giovagnoli,** a great friend and a great man and father. You are a man of your word. I have the utmost respect for you, especially when it comes to the relationship you have with your son, Tony, who has also become a dear friend of mine as well. Your resourcefulness and undying support and encouragement are very much appreciated.

John Bolaris, Michael Butler, Larry DiSipio, Marc Falcone, and **Mark Vajcovic,** a shout-out to each of you for being there for me when no one else was, and going the extra mile when no one else would.

Thanks to my agent, **J. L. Stermer**—you are a true professional.

To my editor, **Peter Hubbard,** for believing and trusting in me and for your unimaginable patience. HarperCollins should double your salary for enduring this long and tumultuous journey with me. On a serious note, it's been an honor to work with somebody as brilliant as you. You're a stud.

Special thanks to **Ayn Carrillo Gailey** and **Samuel W. Gailey** for helping me find my writer's voice, for being team players throughout the transformation of the final manuscript, and for the great homemade meals during our late-night writing sessions. Your talent and dedication (even at two A.M.) will always be appreciated.

To **Peter Golenbock,** thanks for your time and wisdom. You're a good man. To **Scott Bernberg,** thank you for being part of this process. Your intelligence and input were invaluable.

To all my **NailsInvestments.com subscribers.** Thank you for sticking with the strategy when everyone else lost faith in me. Your continued success using my strategy is proof that the system works.

A big thank-you from the heart to all **the fans of New York and Philadelphia.** It was an honor and a privilege to play the game of baseball for the best sports fans in the world. Not only are you passionate, you're also extremely knowledgeable about the game. As a player, I always appreciated that you, the fans, paid your hard-earned cash to watch my teammates and me perform. I felt obligated, not only to myself but also to you, to give the best performance possible on a daily or nightly basis. I was keenly aware that the entire mood of the city could be predicated upon our win-loss record. Hopefully, I played with a style that allowed you to know that I gave it everything I had, and then some, each and every time I put that uniform on my back. In a way, you became like extended family. It pained me to let you down, and it was awesome to celebrate successes with you. Unequivocally, the energy and emotion you brought to the park pushed me to play at the highest level possible. I will always be grateful for the love and support you provided me with throughout my career. I tried my absolute best to represent you well. I hope I accomplished that.

To **Barbara McIntyre,** thank you for going out of your way to help me get my manuscript to the legendary Stephen King. You are truly a special person.

And, lastly, to **Dorothy,** assistant, sounding board, and most

important, my best friend. You never quit on me, you never turned on me, and you know I would take a bullet for you. You said I was your mentor, but at this point, I'm not sure who mentors whom. Thank you for being you. And a special thanks to your husband, **Ken Van Kalsbeek,** and daughters, **Sarah, Megan,** and **Elaine,** for all the understanding and support they provide in helping you do what you do.

Follow Lenny Dykstra:

LennyDykstra.com

facebook.com/LennyDykstraOfficial

twitter.com/LennyDykstra

instagram.com/ldykstra

NailsInvestments.com

INDEX

Philadelphia (magazine), 186
Philadelphia Phillies
  1989 season, 94, 97–98
  1990 season, 101–2, 126–28
  1991 season, 118, 119–20
  1992 season, 120, 149
  1993 season, 149–64, 195, 207.
      See also National League
      Championship Series (1993);
      World Series (1993)
    bench players, 151–52
    Dodgers game, 131
    Marlins game, 204–5
    pitchers, 149–50
    player lineup, 150–51
    regular-season record, 152
    statistics, 106, 195, 203
  1994 season, 196, 199
  Fred Lynn incident, 25
  handing out baseballs to fans, 19–20
  Mets trade, 94, 97–98
Piazza, Mike, 91
Pines, Myron, 24, 29–30
Pitch count, 123–24
Pitchers, 100–101, 257
  strike zone, 123–25
Platoon players, 93, 97
Players Association. *See* Major League
      Baseball Players Association
Players Club, 249–50, 252, 264–65
Players Club (magazine), 250–52
Poker games, 115–18
Pratt, Todd, 151
Prison. *See* Victorville Federal Prison
Pro baseball mold, 27–28, 29
Probation, 308
Promises Treatment Center (Malibu),
      134–35, 232, 233–34
Protection players, 38–39
Pulp Fiction (movie), 206
Pussy. *See* Sex

Radomski, Kirk, 110
Rapid City, South Dakota, 32–33
Rapid Opiate Detox, 209–14

Reading, in prison, 296
Reagan, Ronald, 270
Real Money (radio show), 238, 242–43
Rehab
  lies to wife Terri about, 227, 228
  at Promises (Malibu), 134–35, 232,
      233–34
Rennert, Dutch, 61
Reno-Tahoe Open, 192–93
Reynolds, Harold, 251
Rice, Jim, 77
Richard, Maurice "Rocket," 13
Richards, Keith, 231
Ritz-Carlton Montreal, 190
Rivera, Ben, 150
Robbins, Tim, 311
"Robes and room service," 190
Rockefeller, John D., 92
Rockne, Knute, 68
Rodriguez, Alex, 108
Rolling Stones, 231
Rome Braves, 304
Ronald Reagan Presidential Library,
      180
Rose, Pete, 116, 203
Rossi, Scottine, 136–38
Rourke, Mickey, 183, 191, 232–33
Rudi, Joe, 19
Rule 5 draft, 38–39
Ruth, Babe, 111, 203
Ryan, Nolan, 60, 63

Saberhagen, Bret, 90
Sabermetrics, 261
St. Barts, 230–31
Sambito, Joe, 77
San Bernardino Greyhound Station, 10
Sandberg, Sheryl, 216
San Diego Padres, 25, 81
Sandomir, Richard, 80
Santana, Rafael, 77
Schaefer, Bob, 45–47
Schilling, Curt, 1993 season, 149–50
  NLCS, 153–54
  World Series, 158, 161